Praise for
KILLERS OF ROE

"Amy Littlefield is one of the best journalists reporting on abortion, and her sleuthing shines in *Killers of Roe*. Littlefield's curiosity and gumshoe reporting unfold an interesting cast of characters as she uncovers the complicated questions surrounding the fall of *Roe*. *Killers of Roe* is a perfect read for true-crime readers, cozy-mystery aficionados, and reproductive-freedom activists alike."
—Renee Bracey Sherman, coauthor of *Liberating Abortion*

"*Killers of Roe* is *the* true-crime story of our political moment. Amy Littlefield traces the hidden architects and quiet enablers behind the end of *Roe v. Wade*, revealing how power rearranges itself in plain sight. It's gripping, furious, and deeply human—a story about what was stolen from us and who's still fighting to get it back."
—Samantha Leach, author of *The Elissas*

"Amy Littlefield connects history, politics, and humanity, showing how power, faith, and control collided to end a fundamental right. Deeply timely and a blueprint for how more rights could dissolve, this is a must read for the moment."
—Clay Cane, *New York Times* bestselling author of *The Grift*

"Littlefield has written a gripping, must-read investigation into the secret architects and unlikely characters behind America's greatest rollback of rights. *Killers of Roe* reads like a political thriller, but one with real material harms and life-and-death consequences."
—Soraya Chemaly, author of *Rage Becomes Her* and *All We Want Is Everything*

"*Killers of Roe* is not just a compelling whodunit; it's a searing call to arms. With curiosity and compassion, Amy Littlefield takes readers inside the movement that brought down *Roe*. She brings moments of humor and levity to this serious task and reminds us not to forget the suffering the antiabortion movement's success has produced."

—Mary Ziegler, author of *Personhood*

KILLERS OF ROE

KILLERS OF ROE

My Investigation into the Mysterious
DEATH OF ABORTION RIGHTS

AMY LITTLEFIELD

LEGACY
LIT

New York Boston

Copyright © 2026 by Amy Littlefield
Cover design by Kayla Areglado
Cover image © Ute Klaphake / Trevillion Images
Cover copyright © 2026 by Hachette Book Group, Inc.

Hachette Book Group supports the right to free expression and the value of copyright. The purpose of copyright is to encourage writers and artists to produce the creative works that enrich our culture.

The scanning, uploading, and distribution of this book without permission is a theft of the author's intellectual property. If you would like permission to use material from the book (other than for review purposes), please contact permissions@hbgusa.com. Thank you for your support of the author's rights.

Legacy Lit
Hachette Book Group
1290 Avenue of the Americas
New York, NY 10104
HachetteBookGroup.com
@LegacyLitBooks
First edition: March 2026

Legacy Lit is an imprint of Grand Central Publishing. The Legacy Lit name and logo are registered trademarks of Hachette Book Group, Inc.

The publisher is not responsible for websites (or their content) that are not owned by the publisher.

The Hachette Speakers Bureau provides a wide range of authors for speaking events. To find out more, go to hachettespeakersbureau.com or email HachetteSpeakers@hbgusa.com.

Legacy Lit books may be purchased in bulk for business, educational, or promotional use. For information, please contact your local bookseller or the Hachette Book Group Special Markets Department at special.markets@hbgusa.com.

Library of Congress Cataloging-in-Publication Data has been applied for.

ISBNs: 9781538769041 (hardcover), 9781538769065 (ebook)

Printed in Canada

MRQ-T

10 9 8 7 6 5 4 3 2 1

For those who have died from abortion restrictions—the few whose names we know and the rest whose names we do not.

CONTENTS

Introduction   *1*

PART 1: THE FIRST DEATH OF ROSIE JIMENEZ

Chapter 1: The Believer   7
Chapter 2: The Man Who Wasn't Named   33
Chapter 3: The Serial Kisser   49

PART 2: THE SECOND DEATH OF ROSIE JIMENEZ

Chapter 4: The Listener   73
Chapter 5: The Accomplices   93

PART 3: THE DEATH OF BECKY BELL

Chapter 6: The Salesman   115
Chapter 7: The Actor   131
Chapter 8: The Polite Killer and the Perfect Victim   147

PART 4: DEATHS IN THE NAME OF LIFE

Chapter 9: The Ringmaster   161
Chapter 10: The Fetus Keeper and the Felons   179

PART 5: DEATHS BY ABORTION BAN

Chapter 11: The Renegades   201
Chapter 12: The Goofy Bastard   221
Chapter 13: All the Killers Who Were Never Caught   245
Chapter 14: The First Victim   255

Acknowledgments   *265*
Notes   *267*

INTRODUCTION

> The great thing in these cases is to keep an absolutely open mind. Most crimes, you see, are so absurdly simple.
>
> —Miss Marple in *The Moving Finger* by Agatha Christie

On September 18, 2020, I was a new mom with a five-month-old, living in pandemic isolation, when Supreme Court Justice Ruth Bader Ginsburg died.

"NO," I texted back when a friend sent me the news.

I knew it was the end of the right to abortion. President Trump would appoint a third Supreme Court justice, marking the final stage in a plot I'd watched the antiabortion movement assemble for years. For a decade I had reported on incremental cuts to the right to abortion. I knew from this reporting that people were going to die.

They are going to kill people, I thought, gritting my teeth as I nursed my baby at 3:00 a.m. How had the antiabortion movement managed to *kill* a constitutional right supported by the majority of Americans?[1] I didn't have the answers then. I was a love-drunk slug with an anxiety disorder. Motherhood, I learned, changes your brain as dramatically as adolescence, which is one of those details no one tells you ahead of time.[2] I could see the parallels. I was using the same strategy to escape the anxieties of pandemic parenthood that I had used to cope with adolescence. I was reading murder mysteries, putting in my AirPods during feedings, disappearing into Agatha Christie's chintzy drawing rooms and lush country estates.

The difference was that now, I was filled with rage at the idea that states would soon force people into this world of aching love and every-three-hours feedings. In early adolescence, I was antiabortion. I don't know where it came from, because it was not the norm in my Boston suburb, but I remember how comforting it felt in the tumult of puberty to anchor myself to an absolute belief. When my dad tried to tell me that wealthy women got abortions, even when it was illegal, while poor women died, I batted him away. Abortion was murder. End of story.

In high school, I discovered feminism, and my neat world exploded. A beloved teacher clearing out her basement gave me a battered paperback of Susan Brownmiller's second-wave feminist classic, *Against Our Will*, a book about how rape enforces male control of society. Lying on the hammock in my yard, horrified by scenes of violent domination, I realized how wrong it was to force a rape victim to carry a rapist's child. My antiabortion phase was over. I became a rapid convert to radical seventies feminism, three decades too late, in the less-than-ideal environment of high school. To my peers, I was insufferable. I accused an indignant male friend of having a *rape instinct*. I burst into tears in the passenger seat of my boyfriend's Jeep because I couldn't get him to see that porn was like *rape*.

I had seen the light. I understood how gender oppression controlled our lives—and I could never go back.

I needed an outlet, badly, and when I got to Brown University, I found it in clinic escorting and journalism. I had always liked listening to people's stories. My favorite detective, Agatha Christie's sweet old-lady sleuth, Miss Marple, had taught me that listening could be subversive. It could be a way to expose evil.

So I studied journalism, and one day each week, I made my way down the hill to the Planned Parenthood clinic to shield abortion patients from Joe Manning.

Manning was an older, bearded white man with stooped shoulders, who showed up at 4:00 a.m. to set up a block-long display of bloody fetuses.[3]

With his clipboard and pamphlets, he was a fixture on that street corner, just outside downtown, between the bakery and the highway. I would throw on a pink canvas vest and walk with patients from the chain-link-enclosed parking lot to the clinic, forming a human barrier between them and Manning. He would lean in as close as he could to the patients' ears, and hiss, "There's another way, a better way."

I wanted to shove Manning away in these moments, but the clinic had asked the escorts not to engage with the handful of regular protesters. So we ignored them, except occasionally when their signs blew over in the wind, or they shrieked that we were the devil, and then we laughed at them openly.

To the escorts, the protesters were religious freaks. Relics of a bygone era.

They believed they were saving babies, although I never saw them succeed in changing a patient's mind.

We believed people should be able to walk into a health-care appointment without getting a lecture from a stranger.

They believed in hellfire.

We believed in our own futures.

Back then, we felt like we were winning. Now I wonder if we did feel their victory coming, even then?

There's a grainy photo of my friend Lily and me standing beside the clinic parking lot in our pink vests, the chain-link fence behind us. It's the thirty-third anniversary of *Roe v. Wade*, the Supreme Court decision that established a national right to abortion. We're holding a sign that reads "Save *Roe*. Act Now."

In sixteen years, a span of time almost as old as we were then, the Supreme Court would reverse *Roe*.

By then, I was a journalist covering abortion, married, and living in Boston. I had channeled my feminist rage into reporting on the little-known antiabortion laws and policies that put people's lives at risk, even before *Roe*'s demise. One woman I interviewed, Alison, sought emergency care for a miscarriage at the only hospital in her town in the Pacific Northwest, which happened to be Catholic. The hospital sent her home three times. She almost died, she told me, recalling how the pain from her infected uterus made her arch off the bed like the demon-possessed girl in *The Exorcist*.

They are going to kill people, I thought, at 3:00 a.m., all those years later, breastfeeding in the dark. Soon my baby was in daycare, and I was back on the beat. And while my feminist thinking had matured since my teen years, I still held on to the comfort of my mysteries.

There are certain rules in murder mysteries that applied to the story I needed to tell after the Supreme Court finally reversed *Roe* in the summer of 2022. Or maybe I just needed the comfort of this familiar paradigm to tell the story. In a murder mystery, you get an account from all the witnesses, because one of them might have seen something important. You consider not just the means the killer used, but the motive. And always, the person you least suspect turns out to be the culprit. In the case of who killed *Roe*, I knew the obvious offenders: the Supreme Court justices and Republican presidents and the Christian Right legal organizations like Alliance Defending Freedom.[4] But what about the lesser-known, more behind-the-scenes suspects, the people like Joe Manning that I had been inclined to laugh at or dismiss rather than understand? Weren't they guilty, too?

I knew what the suspects had done. They had killed the constitutional right to abortion. Plus, they were linked to other crimes: the deaths of women not just in the United States but around the world, the rise of white supremacy and Donald Trump, the crumbling of our democracy, attacks on transgender people, and climate change. They had relied on unexpected accomplices: Democratic politicians and even pro-choice activists, some of whom had seriously underestimated their opposition, just like I did on that sidewalk outside the clinic.

The crime was simple. But understanding who did it, and why, would be more complicated. To do it, I would channel Miss Marple. I would listen to the murderers.

PART 1

THE FIRST DEATH OF ROSIE JIMENEZ

CHAPTER 1

THE BELIEVER

Every murderer is probably somebody's old friend.
—*The Mysterious Affair at Styles* by Agatha Christie

I AM ON MY WAY TO MEET A MAN BECAUSE I'VE GIVEN HIM THE IMPRESSION that he has a chance to save my soul from eternal damnation.

Paul Haring, an eighty-six-year-old retired IRS attorney and devout Catholic, has reserved two hours in a conference room at the public library in Annandale, Virginia, to save me.

I'm not out to be saved—although for the sake of my investigation, I'm willing to keep an open mind. I'm out to hear Haring's confession. This former bureaucrat and grandfather living in suburban Virginia is an unacknowledged father of one of America's most diabolical antiabortion policies.[1] He wrote a first draft of the Hyde Amendment,[2] which has banned federal funding of most abortions under Medicaid for fifty years. The ban has forced many of the poorest people in this country to pay out of pocket for abortion or stay pregnant if they couldn't. According to one estimate, by 2010 the Hyde Amendment had caused more than a million people who couldn't afford an abortion to give birth instead.[3] Plus, it shaped the abortion rights movement into a mutual aid operation, forcing many of its most dedicated activists to spend their days raising money to plug the gap left by federal funds.

And it killed at least one person.

As a journalist reporting on abortion, I sometimes felt like my real beat was Dead Women or, far more commonly, women who had *almost* died from antiabortion policies. After the fall of *Roe*, I began digging into the suspects behind these preventable tragedies.

To escape from the grim reality of this mission, I imagined myself as a detective from the Agatha Christie novels I read for escapism. My favorite was Miss Marple. Admittedly, the parallel wasn't perfect. She was a fluffy white-haired old lady with Victorian manners, a lap full of knitting, and a quiet devotion to a God I don't believe in.[4] I'm a foulmouthed mom in her late thirties with wild curls who can't knit to save her life. Still, Miss Marple and I got to the truth the same way. We were white women who were seen as unassuming, so bad people talked to us.

For my reporting, I spent a lot of time attending conservative gatherings where, if I could manage not to snarl, I blended in as well as Miss Marple knitting by the fire at Bertram's Hotel. All it took was a high-necked dress from a thrift store for this white mom with a wedding band on her finger and a blond child on her phone screen to fit in so well it gave me an identity crisis.

So, I reached conclusions the same way Marple did: by listening to murderers.

And the Hyde Amendment was my smoking gun.

Passed in 1976, the Hyde Amendment was the first major cut of hundreds that would ultimately kill the national right to abortion. Medicaid recipients across many states were among the first to lose this right. In fact, they had begun to lose it even before the federal right to abortion was *won*. New York restricted Medicaid abortions in 1971 through an administrative policy that was later ruled unconstitutional.[5] In Michigan, abortion opponents began strategizing mere weeks after *Roe* about how to capitalize on antiwelfare sentiment to curtail Medicaid funding of abortion.[6] Over a dozen states including Pennsylvania and Connecticut set restrictions on Medicaid coverage of abortion that were ultimately upheld by the Supreme Court in 1977.[7]

At the federal level, Congress has renewed the ban on abortion funding each year, with varying exceptions for a pregnant person's health and for rape and incest. Over time, policymakers have extended Hyde-like bans to Peace Corps volunteers, military service members and their families, people in federal prison and immigrant detention, federal employees, Children's Health Insurance Program enrollees, and Native Americans who rely on the Indian Health Service.[8]

But the Hyde Amendment wasn't just a policy that impacted millions of people. It was the key to decrypting the motives of the killers of *Roe*. The Hyde Amendment encapsulated "in a nutshell" two threads of the wider conservative agenda of which the antiabortion movement would become an integral part. Those two threads were attacking welfare and attacking feminism, the political scientist Rosalind Petchesky wrote.[9] Hyde and the Supreme Court decision that upheld it tapped into an iconic American narrative that motivates conservatives to this day: that being poor is, in and of itself, an individual moral failing, rather than a societal one. By shifting the blame for poverty to poor people, especially poor women of color, conservatives have managed to impose a twisted paradox on the American people: They have made it unaffordable to get an abortion while simultaneously making it unaffordable to have a kid.

Besides motive, the detective looks for two key elements to solve a mystery: means and opportunity. In the case of the death of *Roe*, the means loosely followed the plot of Agatha Christie's novel *Murder on the Orient Express*. (Spoiler alert: In that book, a coalition of people from all walks of life conspire to commit a murder by stabbing the same body, one after the other.) The death of *Roe* was death by a thousand stab wounds, some of them shallow and haphazard, some piercing and fatal. These blows were administered whenever any of the suspects could find an opportunity. As of this writing, states have passed more than 1,500 restrictions on abortion since *Roe*, according to the Guttmacher Institute.[10] The Supreme Court has twisted the knife, upholding many of these state restrictions, including parental involvement requirements for minors and restrictions on public funding.

And each time the antiabortion movement cut away at abortion rights, people died.

At least some of these deaths were recorded in detail.

We learned the dead women's names: Rosie and Becky and Porsha. We learned how they loved their children or loved horses or hung posters of Marilyn Monroe on their bedroom wall and how they dreamed of a better life and how their youngest child chased after women who looked like them on the street shouting "Mommy" after they were gone.

Yet the cuts kept coming.

And when a particular opportunity seemed to demand it, the antiabortion movement would, like any savvy murder suspect, obscure their motives. Sometimes they would claim it wasn't about abortion or women at all. They would claim it was about parental rights or *taxes*.

"We are told there are only two things certain in life," Henry Hyde would declare in defense of his amendment in 1978, "death and taxes, and that is what we are really talking about here, death and taxes."[11] As far as motives went, protecting "taxpayers" sounded much better than picking on the poor, the very people Jesus loved best.

The taxpayer argument was a red herring that would appear over and over in my investigation. It wasn't hard to decrypt. When the word "taxpayer" appeared it was often code, "a way of talking about white people—and especially white male heads of households, homeowners, and business owners—and the imagined Black underclass that's coming for their money," as scholar Camille Walsh wrote.[12] Arguments about white men's money ("taxes") were used to justify not only the withdrawal of abortion funding but the coercive sterilization of Black women. Both these cuts to bodily autonomy centered on that most fundamental American right: the right of white Christian men not to pay for things they might find undesirable, like Black babies or abortion.

In the early 1900s, states began passing laws that targeted the fertility of disabled, mentally ill, and incarcerated people. In 1927 the Supreme Court validated these laws, allowing the forcible sterilization of people deemed "imbeciles." One goal of these programs was to eliminate future generations of people considered "unfit" to reproduce who might end up on the dole, costing taxpayers money. Almost 70,000 people were sterilized across 32 states before these official programs ended in the early 1980s.[13] Women of color were also frequent targets of forced sterilization. In Puerto Rico, an estimated one-third of mothers of reproductive age were sterilized by 1965.[14] The sterilizations of Black women in the South became so ubiquitous that they were known as "Mississippi appendectomies."[15] In 1973, the same year *Roe* was decided, a lawsuit filed on behalf of two Black sisters helped reveal more than 100,000 mostly Black, Latina, and Indigenous women had been sterilized under US government programs.[16]

The sociologist Dorothy Roberts captured a conversation between a white ob-gyn and a Black mother in South Carolina that showed how "taxes" could be code for white men's control over Black women.

"Listen here, young lady, this is my tax money paying for this baby and I'm tired of paying for illegitimate children," the doctor warned. "If you don't want this sterilization, find another doctor."[17]

Not long after *Roe*, the antiabortion movement would throw its weight behind Ronald Reagan, the man who made "I Shouldn't Have to Pay For That" the hallmark of one of history's most successful presidential campaigns. Forty years later, Donald Trump and Elon Musk pushed this logic to its conclusion by destroying swaths of the federal government, all in the name of "taxpayers." Conservatives had fantasized about dismantling programs like USAID and Medicaid for decades; when they couldn't do that right away, they just stabbed where they could, removing abortion funding under these programs.

So when I looked at the inequities of our time, including the fact that abortion, as of this writing, is banned outright in twelve states, I could trace the trail of bloody footprints that got us here right back to the Hyde Amendment.

That's why I was now headed to a public library in Annandale to talk with my first suspect.

After ten years of covering abortion rights, I had never heard of Paul Haring. But in my twenties, I'd worked as a counselor in abortion clinics and seen the impact of the Hyde Amendment. The first clinic where I worked was in Massachusetts.

Thanks to a state court ruling, the public insurance program credited to our human boat shoe of a former governor, Republican Mitt Romney, footed the bill for Medicaid abortions. (Today, Massachusetts is one of nineteen states that pay for Medicaid abortions with their own funds, either voluntarily or because courts have ordered them to.[18]) That meant that for most low-income patients, abortion was free. So I'd spend my days at the clinic supporting women, listening to them cry or vent, handing them tissues, ensuring they were confident in their decision, and holding their hand during the procedure. If they had Medicaid, it took just seconds to deal with the financial part of their visit.

Then I got another job at a clinic just twenty minutes south in Rhode Island. It was completely different—thanks in part to Paul Haring.

Rhode Island, the tiniest state, an oceanside blip with the highest number of Catholics per capita, was like most states at the time; it followed the terms of the Hyde Amendment and banned Medicaid coverage of abortion unless the patient had been raped or the pregnancy threatened her life. (In 2023, Rhode Island passed a law authorizing state funding for Medicaid abortions.)

So at the clinic in Rhode Island, I felt less like a counselor than like a deskbound auctioneer who spent her days shouting various numbers into a phone. It seemed like every day a low-income patient would make it past the gauntlet of protesters to the glass window only to confess that she didn't have enough money. Often patients had already begun calling abortion funds to scramble for money on their own, but sometimes they still showed up for their appointment short of what they needed. I would scribble down their information on a Post-it note, then work my way down a list of volunteer-run abortion funds that raised money for these emergencies, begging for $50 or $100 on the patient's behalf. Then I'd see what discount the clinic could offer, hold my breath, tally it all up, and hope it was enough.

I was part of a crowdsourcing approach to abortion that had sprung up to try to fill the gap left by federal funding. This ad hoc system included billionaire-backed foundations, national organizations like the National Abortion Federation, and abortion funds that were often staffed by volunteers. While it's never been enough to compensate fully for the lack of federal funds, this network has funneled millions into paying for people's abortions and the costs associated with traveling to get them. In the year after the Supreme Court killed *Roe*, after a spike in donations related to the ruling, the hundred funds that make up the National Network of Abortion Funds spent almost $37 million.[19]

A decade earlier, sitting behind the desk at the clinic, I felt like the abortion fund folks and I were on a mission together. We were like the pro-choice version of the Salvation Army Santa standing outside the grocery store furiously ringing a bell to save the vanishing right to bodily autonomy. *Most* Americans don't have $500 to cover the cost of an emergency,[20] which is about what a first-trimester abortion in a clinic costs.[21] You can see the issue. Abortion access was a fragile landscape held together by frantic phone calls, often made by patients themselves, or by workers like me, and by abortion funders like the ones I called, and by tens of millions of dollars that could have been spent on something else—if abortion hadn't been carved out from the rest of health care in 1976.

This was the reality of unwanted pregnancy in most of the United States.

Abortion was legal in every state, but it was out of reach for people who were on Medicaid if they lived in a state that didn't allocate its own funding for it. It was out of reach for teenagers in a majority of states if they couldn't inform their parents about their abortions or didn't want to stand before a judge and plead not to be forced into parenthood. It was out of reach for many people in the South and Midwest who lived hundreds of miles from the nearest clinic.

Finally, in 2022, the Supreme Court issued the fatal blow.

Roe was gone. Democratic politicians and my peers in the media were blaming Trump and the Supreme Court, unpacking the legal strategy and the 2016 election. But I knew from my time in the abortion funding trenches that the crisis had started long before Trump.

It had started, at least in part, with Paul Haring.

PAUL HARING WAS BORN IN 1937 AND GREW UP WITH HIS TWO BROTHERS in the small Texas town of Goliad. He went to a Catholic school where two nuns taught all eight grades. His mother was a devout Catholic who transmitted that devotion to her son. The family attended church twice a week, for her sake. Haring's father worked for Aloe Army Airfield during World War II and later owned a tailor shop and sold farm equipment. He left work to have lunch each day at the home where the family lived with Haring's maternal grandmother. Haring's mom volunteered for the Red Cross and worked as a census taker. When his dad got cancer and couldn't work, his mom went to work at an insurance company that she later owned. The family didn't have much money but, according to Haring, you didn't need much to get by back then.[22]

Each Sunday, the Haring family would file into the pews at Immaculate Conception Church. The male members of the family sat on one side, while his mother sat with the women. This division wasn't the only one that shaped his childhood. The South was racially segregated. When Haring got old enough to work, he ran the projector at the movie theater, watching for the signal to flash on the screen and tell him to swap the reel. Like the iconic image of a carefree child growing up in the 1940s and 1950s, he delivered newspapers. To hear him tell it, he lived a happy life in simpler times to which he would like us to return.

By the 1960s, when he began serving in the Texas state legislature, his mission was to roll the clock back to those earlier times by making it harder to get a divorce. The women's movement was advocating for more lenient divorce laws and championing the rights of abused women to escape violent marriages, but Haring, concerned with the sanctity of marriage, authored legislation to make the process take longer.[23]

In 1964, he graduated from law school at the University of Texas Austin. He couldn't recall hearing the word "abortion" in the legislature or in school, where one of the rare women among his classmates was Sarah Weddington, the lawyer who would go on to win *Roe v. Wade*.

Abortion didn't come up much for Haring until 1971, when his wife's former roommate, who was a nurse, told the young couple that the hospital at Lackland Air Force Base near San Antonio had scheduled fifteen abortions for the following week. A 1970 Department of Defense policy had allowed abortions on military bases for medical and mental health reasons. Haring felt as if the lives of fifteen babies were on the line—and it was up to him to save them. So he used his law degree to act out the teachings of his church.

Those teachings were not as fixed as we assume today. Up until 1869, most Catholic theologians taught that the fetus did not become a human being with a soul until at least forty days after conception for males and eighty days for females.[24] That tracked with the relative permissiveness of English common law in the United States, which allowed abortion up until "quickening," when a woman could first feel the fetus move. In the mid-1800s, male doctors who wanted to professionalize and run midwives out of business sought to ban abortion, and contemporary concerns about immigration and the falling birth rate among white Protestants worked in their favor. Abortion became a crime in every state by 1910.

By the 1960s, when the birth control pill came on the market, there was a push to modernize the Catholic Church; after all, many lay Catholic women were using the pill to avoid the huge families they'd grown up in. A church commission debated the issue for two years, considering letters from Catholic women who detailed the devastating toll on their purses and bodies of multiple pregnancies. In 1966, the commission recommended the church lift its ban on contraception. But at the last minute, a few officials became afraid that easing up on birth control would erode the authority of the church.[25] Instead, Pope Paul VI doubled down on his opposition to birth control and abortion, emphasizing that every time a married couple had sex, they needed to remain "open to the transmission of life."[26]

Driven by his devotion to these teachings, Haring filed a lawsuit to stop the abortions at the air force base. He believed that as a "taxpayer," he had the right to represent "unborn children and husbands" of the women scheduled for abortions. The case framed Haring as akin to a German raising his voice to defend the innocent lives "snuffed out by" Nazis.[27] He managed to convince a judge to stop the abortions at the base for four days—until another judge declared that Haring lacked a sufficient personal stake to have brought the suit.[28] Then he appealed to the Fifth Circuit, which ultimately agreed with the lower court. This failed effort gave him a reputation within the nascent antiabortion movement, which back then was mostly fellow Catholics trying to stop states from liberalizing their nineteenth-century abortion bans. Among these early antiabortion leaders was L. Brent Bozell Jr., a militant anti-Communist and Catholic theocrat who defended racial segregation as a form of states' rights.[29]

Bozell asked Haring if he'd like to direct a new organization called Americans United for Life—an organization that Bozell would eventually wind up leaving because he believed (as Haring did) that they were too soft on birth control.[30]

By the time he took the helm of Americans United for Life, Haring was working for the IRS and living with his wife in a brick apartment complex in Chevy Chase, Maryland. Soon, they would be raising a family of six children under the Catholic Church's recently affirmed rules for married couples.

Today, Americans United for Life is one of the nation's leading antiabortion organizations, credited with introducing model legislation that chipped away at abortion access before the fall of *Roe*.[31] But back then in its early days, Haring worked as a volunteer, while keeping his job at the IRS. So in effect, the man who helped lead the attack on taxpayer-funded abortion was subsidizing his antiabortion activism with taxpayer funds in the form of his government paycheck. And soon, he would find another way to use his government job for the cause. In 1979, he sued the IRS, claiming he had been passed over for a promotion because of his Catholic beliefs. He asked a judge to enjoin the agency from granting tax-exempt status to "abortion clinics and other organizations promoting abortion and homosexuality," which the judge declined to do.[32]

"Not the sharpest knife in the drawer," was how Sean Kelly, a political scientist who first uncovered Haring's role in the Hyde Amendment, described him.[33] It was true that Haring had spent decades as an anonymous bureaucrat, emerging into the public eye periodically to run long shot campaigns for political office focused mainly on the issue of abortion, the most recent of which he had lost by 47 percentage points in 2017.[34]

But I saw something sharp in Haring, something key to understanding how the antiabortion movement won. I saw it in his willingness to meet with me. He was a true believer.

After *Roe* fell, every journalist on the beat was trying to explain how it happened. Understandably, we were looking in high places—at the Supreme Court justices and the Alliance Defending Freedom, which had devised the legal strategy behind *Dobbs v. Jackson Women's Health Organization*, the Supreme Court ruling that killed *Roe*.³⁵ But I was also looking closer to the ground, at the grass roots. I suspected that the reason we lost lay in the complicated and decades-long alliance between politicians and true believers like Haring, who had not only voted these politicians into office but given them their ideas.

The opportunists included most recent American presidents, who tended to show their lack of true belief when they flipped sides as needed. Donald Trump had declared himself "very pro-choice," then appointed the Supreme Court justices who ended *Roe*, then tried to make himself look like a moderate on the issue to win reelection in 2024. President George H. W. Bush was a zealot for family planning—until he became the running mate of Ronald Reagan, who had himself signed an abortion liberalization law when he was governor of California but was widely seen as the first pro-life president. Joe Biden voted against exempting rape and incest victims from the Hyde Amendment in 1977 and 1981 before caving to political pressure and denouncing the ban in 2019. Bill Clinton expressed opposition to taxpayer funding of abortion while he was governor of Arkansas before calling for the repeal of the Hyde Amendment when he ran for president.³⁶

Much of our news coverage centers on the opportunists because they are the ones with power. Yet it is the believers like Haring who keep the faith alive, and who, with their tireless activism and long shot schemes, create the opportunities for people like Henry Hyde to take.

THE HYPOCRITE

Henry Hyde was a friendly guy; even some of his Democratic colleagues thought so.³⁷ A former basketball player, six foot three, round-jowled, paunchy, and with a helmet of white hair, Hyde represented Illinois in

Congress for thirty-two years, until just months before he died in 2007. In the 1990s, Hyde would captivate the nation when he presided over the impeachment trial of President Bill Clinton. As head of the powerful House Judiciary Committee, Hyde made the decision to refer Clinton for trial for lying about his affair with a White House intern. But even as Hyde spearheaded the inquiry into Clinton's misbehavior, it emerged that he himself had carried on an extramarital affair in the 1960s.

The wronged husband of Hyde's lover spoke to *Salon* when he couldn't take the public adoration of Hyde any longer. "These politicians were going on about how he should have been on the Supreme Court, what a great man he is, how we're lucky to have him in Congress in charge of the impeachment case," Fred Snodgrass fumed. "And all I can think of is here is this man, this hypocrite who broke up my family."[38]

But it wasn't hypocrisy that made Hyde famous; it was abortion, and an opportunity that fell into his lap because he was charming—and because Bob Bauman wasn't.

Bauman, a stocky, spectacled congressman from the eastern shore of Maryland, shared Hyde's Catholic faith. He had tried to introduce a version of the Hyde Amendment in the House in 1975,[39] while Senator Dewey Bartlett introduced a version in the Senate. Bartlett's effort generated a stir, largely because of how passionately the Catholic Democratic senator from Massachusetts, Ted Kennedy, spoke against the effort.[40] But Bauman's effort failed swiftly—at least in part because Bauman was a sanctimonious archconservative and by that point, the Democrats who held the House majority would reflexively vote against just about anything that bore his name.

So Bauman decided Henry Hyde should do it instead.

"When he got up and he spoke, everybody listened, because he was so impressive, and so I knew that he had the quality to support the amendment," Bauman later told me. "I don't think either one of us ever thought the Hyde Amendment would go as far as it did."

Hyde was raised Catholic and went to a private parochial school, where he worked as a janitor to afford the tuition. In 1969, he was a young lawyer, serving in the Illinois General Assembly, when a Democratic colleague asked if he would cosponsor a bill to liberalize the state's abortion ban. Bills like these were being introduced all over the country. Women sickened by unsafe, illegal abortions were dying of infections and hemorrhages in hotel rooms and hospital septic wards. A growing movement of doctors, lawyers, feminists, and mainline Protestant and Jewish clergy were demanding the bans be loosened; it was a matter of life and death. Hyde went home and thought it over. Guided by the writing of fellow Catholic Charles E. Rice, a scholar who believed draft evaders and abortion seekers were caught up in a "common refusal to serve others,"[41] Hyde "quickly decided that abortion was something to be resisted strenuously," he later wrote. So he opposed the bill and with his help, it was defeated.[42]

Illinois's abortion ban would instead fall four years later when the Supreme Court issued *Roe*. Two years after that decision, Hyde entered Congress, a rare Republican in a wave of Democrats swept to a resounding House majority by outrage over the Watergate scandal. Hyde was now a firm believer in the antiabortion cause. At the time, the movement's goal was to ban abortion through an amendment to the Constitution. But they didn't have the support they needed to pull it off. So in 1976, at Bauman's urging, Hyde proposed a ban on abortion that would apply specifically to poor people. Then, in a move that would upend the congressional appropriations process, setting the stage for regular battles over what used to be a mostly routine affair, they attached the ban to the appropriations bill as a rider. That meant objecting to it would risk derailing funding for the federal government.[43] The rider enshrined into law what has long been the unspoken rule of abortion access across time and place: Wealthy people would tend to remain beyond the reach of policymakers. Poor people would stay pregnant or die.

"I certainly would like to prevent, if I could legally, anybody having an abortion, a rich woman, a middle-class woman, or a poor woman," Hyde famously said during the congressional floor debate over the ban in 1977. "Unfortunately, the only vehicle available is the... medicaid bill."[44]

Hyde and his allies managed to sell their ban as a compromise, and they pulled it off so well that it remains in effect to this day, renewed as part of the annual appropriations process every year since 1976.

And what has happened to the millions of people who have been denied coverage of abortion because of the ban? One estimate from 2009 found one in four have given birth instead.[45]

Henry Hyde was the household name who had always been held responsible for all this, but according to Paul Haring, it was his idea.

THE MISSIONARY

I called Haring up in February 2023. He was in a nursing home, recovering from a broken hip, projectile-vomiting blood, while trying to convert the Muslim aide who was taking care of him to Catholicism. His wife, Gloria, had responded to my email from their shared address.

"He doesn't care to talk about the Hyde Amendment," she wrote. "But he would be happy to talk to you about abortion."

On the phone, his voice was soft and raspy, with a Southern accent. He told me that reading my articles made him think of Saint Paul, the first-century apostle who persecuted Christ's followers until one day he experienced a vision of Jesus and converted.

So that's why he took my call, I thought.

"Do you believe in God?" Haring asked.

"No," I said, adding, "not really," to soften it. I gave Haring the line my father had given me as a kid, about seeing God as the good in people. I might as well have said I saw God in my avocado toast.

"If you don't think there's any God, there's no real standard," he said.

"Is God really all that keeps you from killing people?" I swallowed the impulse to ask. I was in my home office looking out the window at the darkening winter sky. My toddler was downstairs playing with my husband. Screeches of baby talk echoed through the door.

Haring asked if I had read *The Gospel of Life*, Pope John Paul II's letter about the evils of abortion, published in 1995. I wanted to keep up the conversation so I told him that I would be interested in reading it.

Not long after, a white envelope arrived in my post office box. It came from a Catholic supply store called the Paschal Lamb in Fairfax, Virginia. The slim blue book contained a handwritten note: "Thank you! God Bless."

I let it sit on my desk for months. Much of my career as a journalist up to that point had involved investigating how Catholic teachings put the lives of women and trans people at risk. I'd investigated the impact of the church's antiabortion policies without thinking very hard about *why* people believed them. It was easy to see those who espoused antiabortion beliefs as simply *wrong*—the same way that Haring likely saw me as a nonbeliever.

But I was channeling Miss Marple here. That meant I had to uncover the most important element of any murder investigation: motive. The motive—the question of *why* people like Haring did what they did, was the part I understood the least. To get there, I would have to dive further into their ideology.

So I sat in bed underlining passages, dog-earing pages, muttering to myself, reading parts aloud to my husband. I tried to keep an open mind. There were aspects of the pope's writing on the sacredness of life that I appreciated, like his solidarity with the poor. But the encyclical divided the world into two, in terms that felt stark and almost warlike: There was the "culture of life" and the "culture of death."[46] The biblical scene I couldn't get out of my head involved a meeting between two pregnant women: the Virgin Mary and the mother of John the Baptist. As the two women draw close, Fetus John "leaps" in recognition of Fetus Jesus. The two male fetuses are the protagonists here. Fetus John is filled with the Holy Spirit, which he passes to his mom, who is a passive vessel for his experience of grace. Pregnancy was *not* a passive experience. I had shaken, vomited, screamed, and pushed through a solid wall of pain to deliver my baby, emerging from this tunnel of chaos stunned by the realization that *this* was what it took to get us here.

I pictured the pope in his white robe, waving incense, incanting over pregnant bellies, as if he alone knew the mystery, when *he* had never felt a fetus kick his organs from the inside.

"Plus, the pope straight-up admits that abortion is *never* mentioned in the Bible,"[47] I told my husband. I tossed the book on my nightstand. I was hoping now Haring would answer *my* questions. "Could we meet to talk about *The Gospel of Life*?" I asked.

He said yes.

LIKE ANY DECENT DETECTIVE, I HAD ASSEMBLED MY EVIDENCE, AND I reviewed it as I sat at a coffee shop near the library on a spotless blue-sky day. The scholar who had studied Haring's role in the Hyde Amendment, Sean Kelly, sent me the most important clue: a handwritten memo he discovered in the archives of the Catholic bishops. Titled "Paul Haring's Proposal," it documented a meeting in September 1974 between the bishops' representatives and Haring.[48]

Haring had a plan to ban federal funding of abortion, and he wanted the Catholic Church's blessing.

"Haring admits the unlikelihood of succeeding unless the bishops endorse and support his effort," the memo read. Then, in a flourish that illustrated just how much power the Catholic Church held over abortion politics at the time, the unnamed author crossed out the word "unlikelihood" and wrote "impossibility."

Haring "wants sermons in every parish on a specific Sunday... This is a sine qua non for success, in Haring's mind," the notetaker wrote.

"The political strategists are sure this won't work," the note continued.

Unfortunately, they were wrong.

In the bathroom of the coffee shop, I changed out of my airplane clothes. I had spent an inordinate amount of time deciding what to wear.

"What do I wear to meet a man—"

"Who hates women," my friend Heron said, finishing my sentence the night before while we were having dinner at my house. Heron is a nonbinary lawyer who researches laws that have banned transgender people from using the appropriate bathroom and accessing medical care. These laws are being advanced by the same organizations that took down abortion rights. For Heron and for most people on our side, the motive is crystal clear: They hate us.

That's what I'd been taught to believe while covering abortion, too: Opponents of abortion hate women and want to control them. For Heron, the answer was simple. This guy hated women, or else why would he have spent his life trying to take away their autonomy?

Yet I found myself resisting Heron's explanation. I wanted to keep an open mind that Haring might surprise me. As a college student, wearing my pink vest and escorting patients into Planned Parenthood, I had found it easy to laugh off the antiabortion picketers as women-hating relics. But while we were laughing, the Paul Harings and Joe Mannings of the world had pulled off the biggest political achievement since the civil rights era. I wanted to know *why*.

I wanted to scale what sociologist Arlie Russell Hochschild calls "the empathy wall" that separated red and blue America. After five years of studying Tea Party members in Louisiana, Hochschild had arrived at the understanding that white people in communities ravaged by pollution voted Republican because they believed in a deep story: The evil federal government was helping women and people of color get ahead while the poor white folks she was researching felt left behind. She wrote a hypothetical letter to friends on the Left: "Why not get to know some people outside your political bubble?" she wrote. "Consider the possibility that in their situation, you might end up closer to their perspective."[49]

Heron, on the other hand, suggested I shield my arms to the wrist. "I would want to be so covered," Heron said. "I would feel so uncomfortable."

In the bathroom of the café the outfit I pulled from my duffel bag was not the subtle kind I often wore to conservative gatherings. It was a plum-colored pantsuit.

Perhaps, I texted Heron, I needed a little act of defiance.

Once I got to the library, I browsed the shelves, waiting for Haring to arrive. There was a tap on the glass window that overlooked the lobby. I turned and behind me there was a petite woman with gray hair in a white blouse—Haring's wife, Gloria. Beside her was Haring. He was a pink-skinned white man hunched over a walker, dressed in a blue collared shirt with a crown of white hair surrounding his scalp. With his blue eyes, pink cheeks, and paunch, he reminded me of a frailer version of Bernie Sanders. Gloria stood straight as a soldier, as if guarding him. She greeted me and left to get her husband a sandwich from a nearby Chick-fil-A.

Haring motioned for me to walk ahead of him into a tiny conference room off the lobby, past a display on the US Constitution in a glass case. We sat on either side of a gray laminate conference table where someone had put two miniature plastic water bottles on paper napkins. Haring slid a bottle across to me. He had a boyish grin that showed dark spots between his teeth, watery eyes, thin gold-rimmed glasses, and a tendency to blush.

He seemed nervous.

We started by making small talk, about my husband and child, about his late wife and his current wife, Gloria.

"We met on the web," he told me.

"Really? On one of the dating sites?"

"Yes," he said. "A Catholic website...Ave Maria."

I looked out the window at the sunny parking lot, searching for a bridge between my world and his.

"My grandmother was Catholic," I said, flailing.

"Did she have you baptized or not?" Haring asked.

"No," I said. "Bad news for me."

"There's still time." Haring grinned.

"Have you heard of Dr. Bernard Nathanson?" he asked.

Here we go.

Bernard Nathanson was an ob-gyn who witnessed the bloody toll of abortion bans in the years before *Roe*. He recalled being summoned to the emergency room in the middle of the night as a resident in New York City in the mid-1950s to treat feverish, frightened patients who were desperately ill from botched or self-induced abortions; sometimes these patients would survive, and sometimes they would die terrible, painful deaths as their bodies filled with foul-smelling pus or gangrene. Invariably, he recalled, these patients were Black and Puerto Rican. Private patients and the wives and daughters of doctors could turn to their own gynecologists.[50]

Nathanson was no perfect ally to feminists, whom he would openly scorn, after his shift on abortion, as "harridans" and "squaws."⁵¹ But seeing a need for safe abortions to stop the deaths, he helped found the movement to repeal abortion bans and ran one of the first clinics in New York. Later in his career, he began to have doubts and wrote in the *New England Journal of Medicine* that he had come to feel like he had presided over "60,000 deaths."⁵² In 1996, Nathanson, who had been raised Jewish, was baptized as a Catholic, proving in the minds of believers like Haring that anyone could be saved. Haring asked if I had seen Nathanson's twenty-eight-minute-long film, *The Silent Scream*, in which Nathanson narrates an abortion in graphic detail, slowing down the ultrasound footage to make it appear as if the fetus is screaming.

"I think it's very good," Haring said. "I just watched it yesterday."

"In preparation for meeting with me?" I asked.

Haring blushed. He had queued up the video on his iPhone.

"If he became pro-life, there's a lot of hope for you," he said.

We went on to talk for two hours.

The most important thing I learned about Paul Haring is that his life is structured around the belief that when we die, we go to one of three places: heaven, hell, or purgatory. In hell everyone hates each other and is stuck burning for eternity, which, compared to our lives here, is a long time.

I don't believe this because I wasn't raised to believe it. And I suspected I wasn't alone. After my meeting with Haring I collapsed on my hotel bed and googled how people come to believe what they do about God. Sure enough, I found a study from 2023 of more than 1,800 teenagers that proved my theory.⁵³ In the study, just over 80 percent of Protestant and Catholic parents produced teenagers who shared their religious affiliation. Atheist parents like mine had even more success; 86 percent of religiously unaffiliated parents produced religionless teens. When it came to politics, 81 percent of Republican or Republican-leaning parents had teens who leaned Republican, while 89 percent of Democrat or Democrat-leaning parents had teens who leaned the same way. I was raised in a house where, one night when she was first learning to read, my younger sister had looked over at the bookshelf behind our dining table and asked, innocent as a baby lamb, "Mom, what's the Holly Bibble?"

I may have opposed abortion in my early adolescence, but by the time I left for college, I was a lost cause.

Haring, it turned out, was more unusual than I was; according to a 2016 Pew Research Center study, for Americans who grew up in homes with a Catholic parent and a non-Catholic parent, there was a less than fifty-fifty chance that they considered themselves Catholic as an adult.[54] As teens grow older and leave home, they are more likely to shed religion than find it, and Catholicism has the highest attrition rate of all. But as Pew religion demographer Alan Cooperman told me, each generation has become *less* religious than the last, which means Haring's generation was far more devout than mine.[55]

I channeled Arlie Russell Hochschild and tried to put myself in Haring's shoes. I imagined myself attending church twice a week with a devoted mother who taught me to believe she would hold me again in heaven. I imagined myself as a little boy, sitting on the men's side of the church, running across a wide lawn in a small town, gazing up at the big blue bowl of the sky, picturing heaven.

I could almost see it.

Haring and I were discussing his belief that life begins at fertilization, which he views as a scientific fact, when Gloria came back into the room with his chicken sandwich. I watched her unwrap the sandwich and apply ketchup to it from a plastic package.

Have you ever watched someone you disagree with eat a chicken sandwich?

The thing is, there is no neat way to eat a chicken sandwich, or if there is, Paul Haring had yet to discover it. He tried his best not to make a mess. He folded a paper napkin over the bottom of the sandwich to prevent the chicken patty and lettuce from slipping out. He unfolded a second napkin and tucked it into his shirt collar so that it covered his entire front. He took a bite. A piece of chicken fell onto the napkin covering his chest and stuck there, where it remained for most of the rest of our conversation.

At some point, watching him eat, I climbed the empathy wall.

I began to see Haring not as a cartoon villain but as a human being.

THE MARTYR

In 1961, an Italian pediatrician named Gianna Molla received a devastating medical diagnosis. Like Haring, Molla was a devout Catholic who believed what her church taught her to believe: that life began at fertilization. She had three children and was pregnant with a fourth. So when she learned that she had cancer, she refused a hysterectomy to treat it, believing God would have wanted her to save the life she was growing. Just days after her child was born, Molla died at the age of thirty-nine. She is an icon in the antiabortion movement, someone who had fascinated me ever since I watched her daughter speak at the annual March for Life in Washington, DC, a tiny lady in a fur-lined parka declaring before a cheering crowd: "I would not be here now with all of you if I had not been loved so much!"[56]

Pope John Paul II, author of *The Gospel of Life*, canonized Gianna Molla as a saint. One day I fell down a Gianna Molla rabbit hole on the internet and discovered a cottage industry of Molla swag peddled by religious suppliers, including a board book filled with anime-eyed characters that described how Molla's parents taught her to "give of herself for the sake of others." "Because of her courageous love," the book concluded, Molla "went to Heaven to be with Jesus."[57]

"Do *not* let our kid find that," my husband chided when he saw it, making me hide it on my bookshelf.

"It's a heroic act," Haring told me of Molla's sacrifice. "It's one she freely chose to do."

"Do you think, though, that all women in that position should do that?" I asked.

"No, I don't think so," Haring replied. "But, certainly, I think she should be recognized as being very heroic."

It didn't sound like Haring hated women. Rather, it sounded like he reserved a special reverence for women like Molla, who followed the teachings of his beloved church.

"I have to say," I confessed, "there's parts of Catholic Church teaching that for me, being a woman, are hard to connect to."

Like I said, I didn't read the Bible as a kid. Instead, I got a degree in comparative literature, so this literary analysis was the best I could manage. The Bible was *full* of unrelatable characters—like the Virgin Mary.

"The way it talks about her being this passive recipient of life is hard for me to relate to. For me, pregnancy was such a grueling experience. You have to eat a certain way; you have to take care of your body. And if I hadn't been fully accepting of it, I think it would have been very difficult."

Well, the *Virgin Mary* didn't feel that way.

"She accepted it very easily," Haring said. "When she had the child and she wasn't married, she could have been put to death. So she's risking her life, you know, and she freely accepted that—happy to do it."

Happy to do it.

There's another dead woman I need to talk to Haring about—one who wasn't so willing.

Her name was Rosie Jimenez. She was a twenty-seven-year-old Mexican American woman raising a four-year-old daughter in the border town of McAllen, Texas. Three years after Paul Haring pitched his idea for the Hyde Amendment, she would find herself pregnant by a man who wasn't her fiancé. Her fiancé was in jail, and Rosie Jimenez needed to keep the pregnancy from him. But she learned that Texas Medicaid no longer paid for abortions. Rosie wanted to stay in school. She wanted a better life for her daughter. She needed to get rid of the pregnancy. So she went to a midwife, who charged Rosie $100 to insert a piece of plastic tubing into her cervix. I thought about getting as graphic as Bernard Nathanson in *The Silent Scream*. I thought about mentioning how the blood leaked out of her eyes, how her skin turned greenish brown. That as she lay dying, a doctor hounded her to confess that she'd had an abortion. That even after she had lost her capacity to speak, and began to smell of death, she scribbled out her dying wish: to be left alone, to die in peace.[58]

"She had a scholarship check in her purse that she could have used to pay for a legal abortion, but she was saving that money for her education," I told Haring. "On the abortion rights side of things, they talk about her as being the first victim of the Hyde Amendment. I don't know if that's a story you've ever heard."

"No," Haring said. There was a pause that held everything or maybe nothing.

"You can't kill somebody because you want to get a better education," he said, and we sat, like two walls, facing each other, listening to the ticking of the clock.

Agatha Christie always delivers a neat ending and after my day with Haring, I looked for one. In her books, the detective gathers everyone together and confronts the culprit with the evidence. The killer confesses. Sometimes he begs for forgiveness.

Haring didn't do any of that. He didn't take responsibility for Rosie's death, because Rosie was the one who did something wrong—she killed her baby.

But he did do something that surprised me.

He told me a story about the civil rights movement.

"At that time, everybody was a Democrat," he said, and in his Southern drawl the word was like "Err-e-body."

The Democrats had been the party of slavery. Known as the "Dixiecrats," Southern Democrats included segregationists like George Wallace and Senator Jesse Helms—who left the party in 1970 because it was getting too liberal. When Haring joined the Texas state legislature in 1961, every single member of the body was a Democrat.[59]

"Most of 'em, they were racists," he went on, describing a bill introduced by his colleagues to allow the prosecution of anyone who entered a business and refused to leave if it so much as appeared that their presence was unwelcome to management.

Haring waited a beat.

"I voted against it," he said. "Told 'em how wrong it was."

"What gave you that conviction?" I asked, surprised.

"Well, it *was* wrong," he said.

What surprised me about this story was that it went against my understanding of the relationship between the civil rights and antiabortion movements.

As the civil rights movement forced the nation to confront white supremacy in the 1960s and 1970s, the antiabortion movement offered white conservatives an escape valve, Jennifer Holland wrote in *Tiny You: A Western History of the Antiabortion Movement*. Instead of thinking too hard about the moral implications of whiteness, white conservatives could join their own version of the civil rights movement—"a civil rights movement for fetuses."[60]

This version of the civil rights movement co-opted the language of social justice that animated the Black civil rights movement, inviting white people "to think of themselves as abolitionists and the nation's saviors," Holland wrote.[61] But their cause was the purest of all, for they were saving the fetus, who was wholly innocent, and in the plastic dolls and imagery used to humanize it, almost always white.

So it was that white conservatives worried about the changes brought by feminism and civil rights anointed themselves civil rights champions as they worked to dismantle the rights of women and people of color.

It was a theme that would keep recurring as I investigated the killers of *Roe*, from Ronald Reagan to the leaders of the "rescue" movement to the true believers of today.

"This was a conservative 'civil rights movement' that had a single solution for the nation's many problems of discrimination and disenfranchisement," Holland wrote, "and one of its primary effects has been to undermine most efforts to do anything about them."[62]

Sitting across from Haring, watching him pack up his empty chicken sandwich box, I tried to reconcile my understanding of this history with the fact that he had taken an early stand against discrimination in the segregated South. It was the tiny wrinkle of complexity I'd been looking for, and a sign that none of my suspects would be a straight villain or hero.

When I dug into the history later, I learned that Haring wasn't alone. There were other early antiabortion leaders who fought against the segregation of public schools and housing, like Joseph P. Witherspoon, with whom Haring collaborated on his lawsuit over abortions at the air force base.[63] But figures like these were a minority within a movement that would ultimately use the civil rights playbook to sabotage the gains of the movement that drafted it.

And like a classic murder mystery, this story offered yet *another* plot twist.

Because today Paul Haring, the man who had taken a stand against segregation in the South, was a supporter of Donald Trump. And while it was clear as the water bottle on the table in front of me that Trump's disparagement of Mexicans and war on "DEI" was an effort to roll back the advancement of Black and brown people, Haring did not see Trump as a racist.[64]

I would think back to Haring's trajectory later in my investigation when I interviewed one of the architects of the conservative movement—a man who spoke openly about how abortion was a "door" through which many people entered conservative politics.

There was no nuance at all in Haring's final pitch.

"I hope you become another Dr. Nathanson, and I hope you become a Catholic, too," he said. "The most important thing is we go to heaven."

Outside, he leaned on his walker, and told me that most Catholic churches begin their education classes in the fall, and I could be baptized in time for Easter.

I remembered Sean Kelly's words: "not the sharpest knife in the drawer."

Haring's pitch felt more like a blunt object than a sharp knife. But he had cut to the core of the motive.

The most important thing is we go to heaven.

Haring was reluctant to talk about the Hyde Amendment in that first meeting. He told me he didn't want to give people reading this book any ideas that might help them promote abortion. But I kept coming back to him with evidence I'd collected from others, and eventually, he did talk about it. Throughout these conversations, he never stopped trying to convert me. One cold March day, over the phone, he read me passages of *The Gospel of Life* aloud, pausing to ask for my reaction after each one. I told him that as a woman, I still had trouble accepting the Catholic Church's teachings. And he kept trying to save me, like he had saved his father.

When Haring's father was nearing the end of his life, he told his son that he was finally ready to convert. Haring left the hospital room and told the priest, who saved Haring's father before he died.

Over and over Haring repeated his pitch: *The most important thing is we go to heaven*, a place where he believes we will meet our loved ones again.

There was a long pause during one of our phone calls.

"I guess you think I'm a pretty hopeless case," he said.

"No," I said. "I think you're someone whose worldview is very different from mine and I'm trying to understand it."⁶⁵

I was trying to understand what it was like to orient your entire life toward the moment you imagine will happen at the very end.

"I believe that I will one day render an account to God for what I did and failed to do about the issues that have caused such deep distress in our national life," Henry Hyde once wrote.⁶⁶

The most important thing is we go to heaven.

Haring was a true believer. Yet it all sounded so transactional—get the priest, get baptized, get into heaven. I wondered, in the end, if he wasn't an opportunist after all.

CHAPTER 2

THE MAN WHO WASN'T NAMED

> I believe at least in one of the chief tenets of the Christian faith—contentment with a lowly place ... the desire to succeed—to have power—leads to most ills of the human soul.
>
> —*Appointment with Death* by Agatha Christie

THERE WERE FOUR MAIN SUSPECTS IN THE NEXT CHAPTER OF MY INVESTIgation, all of them white male members of Congress who helped turn Paul Haring's idea for a ban on federal funding of abortion into law. They were: a racist from North Carolina who prefigured Donald Trump; the bat-eared brother of a conservative icon; a jovial ass grabber; and a disgraced gay conservative turned tax avoidance expert. All of them are dead except the last one—Bob Bauman, who, for reasons I didn't understand yet, was willing to talk with me.

If it hadn't been for the sex scandal that torpedoed his political career, Bob Bauman might have gone down in history as a run-of-the-mill conservative with an especially pronounced fetish for offshore tax avoidance. He would not have gone down in history as the congressional mastermind of the ban that led to Rosie Jimenez's death, because he had been forced by his own unpopularity to arrange it so the policy would bear Henry Hyde's name instead. It wasn't the only time Bauman would act as the man behind the curtain of Henry Hyde's career; in 1995, he told me, he had ghostwritten a book published under Hyde's name by the Cato Institute titled: *Forfeiting Our Property Rights: Is Your Property Safe from Seizure?*[1]

Once again, every road with these men seemed to lead back to the right to keep their money (and property).

Bauman was the perfect suspect for a murder mystery. The rules of the genre require that the person you least suspect is the killer. Always, there are plenty of people who look guilty—the jealous ex-husband or the conniving heiress. But you can usually eliminate those people *because* they're obvious. The real brains of the operation will turn out to be someone you failed to notice or forgot about—the matronly housekeeper or the parish archivist. Often their unobtrusiveness helps them succeed. Certainly, it makes for a gratifying payoff when they're unmasked. So as I played Miss Marple, calling up all the bad guys I could find, trying to listen my way to an understanding of how we got here, I took a particular delight in finding people whom, even after a decade of reporting on abortion, I'd never heard of. I liked finding people like Paul Haring—the killers who had gotten away with it. These old men were out shuffling around to church and the grocery store without anyone realizing they had blood on their hands. Unmasking them was just as satisfying in real life.

Bauman was hiding in the kind of obscurity brought about only by disgrace. One morning in 1980, the FBI arrived at his congressional office, and Bauman knew the jig was up. He had been cruising the streets of Washington, DC, in a drunken fog behind the wheel of a Lincoln Continental with congressional plates, picking up men and paying them for sex. At least one of the men turned out to be a boy of sixteen. Bauman was far from exceptional as a closeted gay man in Washington, DC, but he *was* exceptional as a closeted gay man who was widely considered one of the most conservative members of Congress.[2] The Bauman scandal, as he wryly called it, had put an end to his political career right as the conservative movement he had helped to launch elected its first president.[3]

Through Internet sleuthing, I discovered that Bauman had moved to Wilton Manors, Florida, known as one of the gayest cities in the United States,[4] and built a second career writing dictionary-length manifestos with titles like *Where to Stash Your Cash Legally* and *Swiss Money Secrets*. It was a perfect coda; the man who had helped cut off taxpayer funding of abortion had gone on to a second career helping corporations and the ultrawealthy avoid paying taxes at all. To reach him with an interview request, I had to fill out a form pretending I was a potential client with an eight-figure fortune. Thankfully, Bauman never asked me about my finances. Once I disclosed I was a journalist he probably understood that I didn't make anywhere near eight figures.

"If we can arrange a mutually agreeable day and time, I will be pleased to be interviewed," he wrote, adding, "A review of your many articles makes clear your view on the right to death."[5]

THE RACIST

There was another suspect who came before Bob Bauman, one I really wanted to ignore because he was *too* obvious. This guy was no quiet housekeeper; he was the archetypal villain twirling his mustache while swinging a pistol. His crimes were right there, as brutal as the death squads he defended in El Salvador. The late Senator Jesse Helms of North Carolina was an unequivocal asshole. He once refused to meet with the mother of a child who had died after contracting HIV from a blood transfusion because he believed HIV was just a gay disease that gay people deserved to die from. He did everything he could to prevent Martin Luther King Jr. Day from becoming a national holiday. He called all Black men "Fred" because he thought it was funny. After the Senate's only Black member, Senator Carol Moseley Braun, succeeded in blocking his effort to renew a patent on a Confederate flag insignia, he sang the Confederate anthem "Dixie" at her in the elevator and vowed to continue until she cried. "Sen. Helms, your singing would make me cry if you sang 'Rock of Ages,'" Moseley Braun coolly replied.[6] He ought to have been fed to a pack of hungry feral hogs. Instead, he spent thirty years in the Senate, retired in 2003, and died, old and comfortable, on the Fourth of July.[7]

Unfortunately, Jesse Helms was essential to understanding this history, and as I examined the crime scene, I started to find his bloody footprints everywhere.

Helms was a devout Baptist from the land of hog farmers and tobacco, a product of the Jim Crow South, who hated Communists and slept only four or five hours a night. There's a story he liked to tell about growing up in Monroe, North Carolina, where he loved the prancing horses and fireworks that punctuated the Fourth of July. His father drove the town's only hook-and-ladder fire truck, and on the Fourth the town's children were encouraged to climb aboard to ride down Main Street. One year, the merchants in town raffled off a car, and Helms's father handed him three tickets.

"Keep them," his father said, "but don't count on getting an automobile for nothing."

Helms nursed a tender throbbing bud of hope in his little-boy heart, examining the ticket stubs "so often that they were almost tattered," he later wrote, and sleeping with them under his pillow. When he didn't win the car, his father sat his brokenhearted eight-year-old down and told him he shouldn't expect to win anything without hard work.

"He told me that in America people who work hard and save can do amazing things," Helms wrote.[8]

Maybe we'd all be better off if Helms had won the damn car. Or maybe it's a story he made up to justify his disdain for anyone who needed government assistance. Or maybe, in the end, the only real conclusion we can draw from this story is that the Fourth of July was Helms's favorite holiday, and it's kind of nice that he died on it.

Regardless, he went on to become a man so Trumpian in his presentation that researching him made me wonder if he had hidden a piece of his soul for Trump to discover, like Tom Riddle's diary at Hogwarts. He had started out as a pundit on talk radio. He disregarded norms. He knew how to harness white male anger through blistering populism.[9] He was even said to have small hands.[10] And he was brash and rude but knew how to channel anxiety over the civil rights movement into a force that would turn white Southern Democrats away from their party. Plus, he opposed sending US aid down what he called "ratholes" in poorer countries of the world, places that decades later Trump would call "shithole[s]."

After he was elected to the US Senate in 1972, Helms set his sights on the main vehicle for humanitarian aid to the "ratholes"—the US Agency for International Development. The head of that agency was Dr. Reimert Ravenholt, a handsome Dane with a shock of hair and a mad scientist vibe who was trying to address the fact that tens of thousands of women around the world were dying horrible deaths from unsafe abortions. Learning about Ravenholt briefly distracted me from my pursuit of *Roe*'s killers. I could not at first wrap my head around the fact that this man was a government agent, because in the early 1970s, Ravenholt had directed USAID to issue a government contract to the Battelle Corporation to reengineer a certain lifesaving device for mass production. It resembled a giant syringe with a thin tube on one end that could be inserted into the cervix. When you pulled a plunger at the other end, it would vacuum out a pregnancy without the need for electricity. Ravenholt was so proud of this device that he always traveled with one in his suitcase so he could whip it out and demonstrate it to anyone who would watch.[11]

I felt like I had just drunk one of Agatha Christie's hallucinogenic poisons when I learned that the US government had funded the development of one of the world's most important abortion technologies. Really, I was just experiencing the United States before Helms got his say on the matter, in an era when many US leaders thought population control abroad might be a good way to limit the number of poor people of color who might become Communists.

Helms soon found a way to plug the "ratholes" while sticking it to the pro-choice movement just months after their victory in *Roe*. He introduced a rider to the Foreign Assistance Act that prohibited USAID funding from being used for abortions. The ban put an end to Ravenholt's plan for using government funds to save lives with his miracle device, the manual vacuum aspirator.

"It appears that we are attempting to deny the women abroad the freedom of choice in family planning that our own Supreme Court has recently granted to women in this country," the legendary New York congresswoman "Battling" Bella Abzug protested on the House floor, trying in vain to stop the Helms Amendment.[12]

But it passed and fifty years later it remains in place, renewed regularly by Congress, and an estimated 17,000 women die each year around the world who could be saved if the ban were repealed.[13]

"Tens of thousands of mothers, aunts, sisters, daughters, and others have died unnecessarily because of the Helms Amendment—because of my grandfather," Helms's granddaughter Ellen Gaddy wrote in an op-ed for *Politico* in 2022. "Congress should repeal the Helms Amendment in its entirety, but Biden already has it within his authority to roll back some of the measure's harshest restrictions. He should act immediately."[14]

The article was Gaddy's public break with the political dynasty she'd been raised in. As a child, she had participated in Helms's political campaigns, appearing in his ads and with him onstage, her unease over his politics growing until she went off to college in California and broke with it for good. She began to commit her life to unspooling Helms's legacy, starting with unpacking her own relationship to it by getting a PhD in liberation psychology, an obscure branch of the discipline started by a Jesuit priest in El Salvador who, Gaddy discovered, was murdered by a death squad created by one of her grandfather's friends, Roberto D'Aubuisson. Later, Gaddy began donating money to a global reproductive health nonprofit called Ipas based out of her native North Carolina, only to discover the organization was founded because of the Helms Amendment; as a private entity, it could continue distributing the manual vacuum aspirator.

Her article was a plea to a man who had brought her comfort at her grandfather's funeral: Joe Biden, who had the single-handed power as president to soften the Helms Amendment by clarifying that it did not apply in cases of rape or when a patient's life was in danger. Biden never responded.

"I'm still waiting on that phone call," Gaddy told me wryly on a video call in 2023, pushing her mane of long blond hair back from her face.[15]

So in the grand alliance of abortion politics, was Helms a true believer or an opportunist? Gaddy's answer surprised me. She said she believed his vociferous position on the issue was at least in part a strategic move to win over Evangelical voters.

"He absolutely needed the Evangelical vote to win," Gaddy wrote to me when I asked. "The Helms Amendment secured the Evangelical vote for the rest of his time in office and has harmed women globally ever since."[16]

THE MISER'S BROTHER

In the midst of my investigation, my family flew to New Mexico to spend a week at my mother-in-law's house. While my kid played with Nana, I sat with my legs folded on a plush red armchair, basking in the bright Southwestern sun, searching the 1973 Congressional Record for the word "abortion" like a stereotypical gumshoe who couldn't leave work at the office. Then I came across a passage that made my heart pound.

Everything I had found up to that point suggested that the Hyde Amendment was Paul Haring's idea, one he came up with in 1974. But the record was clear: A version of the ban had been introduced a year earlier, by someone whose last name sounded strangely familiar.

Heart racing, I googled him.

What I found was a picture of a mid-thirties British sitcom star with a head shaped like an acorn. It turned out that the guy I was really looking for, James Buckley, a man who lived in his more famous brother's shadow, was now, in death, living in the shadow of another James Buckley who was more famous than he was. The James Buckley I was looking for, who appeared halfway down the page, was a bat-eared senator from New York who grew up in Sharon, Connecticut. His brother William F. Buckley Jr. was the founder of *National Review* and the man who made being stingy sound like a sound intellectual principle.

"I will not cede power to the state," William F. Buckley Jr. wrote in one of his most famous odes to that most fundamental American right—the right of white men to hold on to their property and never share it with anyone, especially not poor people of color. "I will hoard my power like a miser, resisting every effort to drain it away from me."[17]

In the 1960s, this language appealed to a certain subset of young anti-Communists who founded an organization called Young Americans for Freedom that would help launch the conservative movement. One of those young people was the future congressman from Maryland, Bob Bauman; another was the future marketing man of the movement, Richard Viguerie, who would later tell me he remembered William F. Buckley Jr. as "ten feet tall," like "a little god."[18]

The little god's less famous older brother had, one November day in 1973, stood on the Senate floor and suggested that if Congress was going to pass the Helms Amendment and ban federal funds from being used to help "foreign women" get abortions, "then at least we could accord the same protection to our own."[19] Buckley appended his proposal to the Social Security Act and it passed the Senate. But in February 1974, the Nixon administration was reported to be "quietly resisting the amendment...by letting it be known it wants further public hearings on the entire package of Social Security amendments."[20] Perhaps that was why, when Paul Haring approached the bishops with his idea for appending an abortion ban on the Health, Education and Welfare appropriations bill, the notes from the meeting observed that "Senator Buckley has advised against this effort."[21]

When I asked Paul Haring about James Buckley's proposal, he said he didn't remember it.[22] But one of the women Haring worked with, Randy Engel, founder of the US Coalition for Life, said the idea for the ban was indeed a more collective one. "Paul talked to other people, let's put it that way," Engel, now in her eighties, told me when I reached her at home in Export, Pennsylvania. "It was a kind of a unified idea that an amendment should take place."[23] Indeed, state policymakers had begun pursuing their own restrictions on public funding of abortion, even before James Buckley introduced his federal version in 1973.

But Paul Haring worked hard on a draft that was far more convoluted than Buckley's—a version that Bella Abzug would denounce with the exquisite term "blunderbuss." The draft that Haring took credit for was introduced by Representative Angelo Roncallo, a one-term Republican Congress member from New York. It was so sweeping that it would likely have impacted federal funding of contraception, because it defined abortion as "the intentional destruction of unborn human life, which life begins at the moment of fertilization." After a member objected that that line would impose new duties on federal officials by forcing them to determine when life began, Roncallo quickly struck it. But that didn't seem to help his case.

"A young girl or any woman who is raped could be denied anticonception drug treatment under this amendment," Abzug fulminated. "Family planning would be prohibited. The morning-after pill would be proscribed. Five to 8 million women who use the intrauterine device as a contraceptive would be denied access to this method of birth control." The amendment was "poorly drawn," complained another member. By a margin of two to one, in late June 1974, the House rejected Haring's proposal.[24]

Then, in September, Oklahoma Republican Senator Dewey Bartlett, an ally of the bat-eared Buckley and the racist Helms, introduced a ban on abortion funding to the Senate appropriations bill; it was stripped in conference on the grounds that an appropriations bill was "an improper vehicle for such a controversial and far-reaching legislative provision."[25]

Federal funding of Medicaid abortions was safe for the time being.

THE ASS GRABBER

There's a saying that Richard Viguerie thought applied to his longtime friend Bob Bauman. "If you're the smartest person in the room," the saying went, "you're in the wrong room." Bauman had become so smart that he was insufferable. During his years as a teenager at congressional page school and, afterward, as a Hill staffer, he had acquired a minute knowledge of obscure parliamentary procedure that he used to obstruct his colleagues after he was elected to Congress in 1973.

He wasn't humble about it.

"Sanctimonious," was how one colleague, former New York Congresswoman Elizabeth Holtzman, remembered him.[26]

"It's hard for me to think of anything nice to say about Bob Bauman," Democratic House Speaker Tip O'Neill reportedly said.[27]

A 1976 *New York Times* profile described Bauman as the "gadfly of the House, its most active nitpicker, its hairshirt, its leading baiter of its most powerful members."[28] But he was smart enough to know how to work around his unpopularity. Understanding that the rules of Congress were approximately the rules of the playground, he got Henry Hyde to introduce the Hyde Amendment, because Hyde was popular.

"Henry was a very dynamic speaker. He was a large man," Bauman, who was stocky and short, told me. "Very, very humorous, and a very friendly person."[29]

Hyde was a jovial giant from Illinois with a penchant for ass grabbing. This appears to be one transgression that Henry Hyde managed to get away with. When he died at the age of eighty-three, his obituaries mentioned his crusades against federal funding of abortion, his leadership of the Clinton impeachment trial, and the embarrassing revelation that Hyde had carried on an extramarital affair of his own. But the obituary said nothing about his propensity to grope women with such cheerful regularity that they developed a specific defensive maneuver for walking past him.

Margaret Goodman worked in Congress while Henry Hyde was a member. I called her up one day while researching the Helms Amendment. When I mentioned Henry Hyde's name in passing, she made a knowing sound and said something about him being "a grabber."

"Hold on, Margaret," I said, pulse racing, "I need to turn on my recorder."

"Oh," she said, like it was no big deal that she had just told me one of the leading conservative figures in modern history had assaulted her in public, "he was just an obnoxious grabber."[30]

The members of House committees sat up on a dais like a row of judges. Goodman had to walk along the dais, past Hyde, to get to the Democratic chairman so she could give him the important things she needed to give him.

"Oh, sweetheart," Hyde said when he grabbed her ass. She wanted to slap his hand away but there was a room full of people watching, so she took a deep breath, steadied herself, and kept walking. After that, she kept her ass away from Henry Hyde.

"You just made sure, you sort of sidled along with your back up against the wall, because Henry Hyde liked to reach out and grab you," Goodman told me. "On your butt, just, surreptitiously."

A man with a habit of humiliating women this way ought to have been disqualified from making laws about their bodies, although that would probably have disqualified many lawmakers from that era, which, come to think of it, might have been fine. Instead, this ass grabber's ban on federal abortion funding has been the law of the land for fifty years.

It all started when Bauman sidled up to Henry Hyde at the rail outside the House cloakroom.

"As a freshman congressman I was an unknown quantity and, Machiavellian that he is, Bob Bauman got me aside one day and said this bill was coming up that appropriated all sorts of money for abortions and wouldn't it be a nice idea if we could just sneak an amendment in there that would halt this nefarious practice," Hyde would later tell an audience at the Maryland Right to Life Banquet. "And I said, 'Great, Bob, I'm with you all the way.' He said, 'No, you—you offer the Amendment.' He said we would really catch them by surprise. I was just a freshman and difficult as it may seem I was attempting to keep a low profile. But in any event we did do it and as sneakily as possible without informing anyone...Bob drafted the amendment and we waited and handed it up and the next thing I knew I was in the well addressing my colleagues on behalf of the right to life."[31]

THE TAX AVOIDER

Bob Bauman warned me he might be slow to reach the phone.

"If I don't answer on the first few rings, be patient," he wrote. "At eighty-six, I don't move as fast."

But when I called him up from my home office at the appointed time, late one morning in early December, he didn't sound slow. His words tumbled over each other in a voice that was deep and resonant, like a stream rushing through a cave. Despite what I'd heard about him, Bauman didn't sound sanctimonious; he was courteous and drily funny, with a tendency to drop deadpan one-liners about his fall from grace, like: "I haven't been asked to speak to any right-to-life conventions lately."

Before meeting with him, I devoured with tabloid-level intrigue his 1986 autobiography, *The Gentleman from Maryland: The Conscience of a Gay Conservative*, which dripped with sordid details about his sad and complicated life.

"I did not want to write this book," Bauman wrote in the preface. "I wrote it because I need the money."

This was one of the contradictions, like being a gay Catholic, that plagued Bauman throughout his life. Although he was a single-minded devotee of fiscal conservatism, a man who believed, above all, that governments should not spend more than they had, Bauman had been profligate with money. Early in his career, he and his wife, Carol, a fellow cofounder of Young Americans for Freedom, had fallen in love with Glebe House, an 1855 farmhouse with green shutters that sat behind two brick gateposts at the end of a long country lane lined with fifty-foot trees.[32] They bought the estate but couldn't afford it, nor could they afford the decision to send their four kids to the area's "best" school. Soon Bauman was underwater, taking out second mortgages and borrowing against his congressional paycheck and falling two or three months behind on bills.[33] Once the family was saved from ruin by a friend, the grand miser himself—William F. Buckley Jr.[34]

"Throughout twenty years of marriage I steadfastly refused to heed Carol's repeated reminder that we rarely had enough income to meet our expenses, a decidedly unconservative economic approach," he acknowledged in his book.[35]

His inability to live up to the dictates of his faith and politics had, during his time in Congress, driven him to alcoholism and paid sex, and to hypocritical behavior, like cosponsoring antigay bills, including the Family Protection Act, which banned federal funding of organizations that treated homosexuality as "an acceptable lifestyle."[36]

"In all my thirty years or more of practice I have never seen a more self-contained, isolated, and alone individual than you," the therapist he consulted during this low period of his life had declared.[37]

Bauman learned that he was adopted when he was eight and his alcoholic father told him in a drunken rage: "You know you're not my son, Bobby." Young Bobby put his hands over his face to hide his tears. The adoption petition he would later discover in a drawer described him as "destitute, unwanted, devoid of parental support and in need of care and protection," which must have been how he felt when his beloved adoptive mother died from stomach cancer, and his father's new wife sent him off to Fork Union Military Academy. He was miserable in this world of Confederate-gray uniforms and took refuge in the only soft place available—sexual encounters with other boys, that made him feel good and bad, like something was wrong with him—something so bad, maybe God had taken away his beloved mother to punish him.[38]

I knew all of this about him from the book, even before we got on the phone. The question I still couldn't answer was why he was willing to talk with a journalist who supported what he called "the right to death."

"I wonder," I asked him, "if you can pinpoint a moment where you came to your beliefs around abortion?"

At first, he meandered, with that deep and resonant voice, through his memories from Catholic school. Then something seemed to occur to him.

"I think, probably looking back on it, maybe it was my own adoption and the fact that I didn't know who my mother was, I could have died, you know, and so on," he said. "But that was not an openly conscious thing; it might have been a subconscious thing."

I tried to imagine Bauman as I listened to him. It was dead winter in Boston where I sat at my desk, the heat blazing through the vents in my home office, but in South Florida, maybe it was warm, and maybe he was sitting on a porch somewhere. On his end of the line, I could hear a wind chime tinkling. *Why did he agree to talk with me?* I wondered, looking down at his out-of-print book with its blue cover showing a photo of twilight over the Capitol Building. The copy I bought online for $6.64 was covered in library shrink-wrap, inscribed with the name of the mortgage executive who once owned it, and stamped on the binding with the red words "BOOK SALE."

"I'm curious how you feel looking back on the Hyde Amendment," I asked. "How do you feel about the lasting impact of this measure that you played such a big role in?"

"Well, if I get any credit when I get to Saint Peter at the gate, I hope that's on my list," he said. "I think it's the most important thing I ever did in Congress was to get the Hyde Amendment through under Henry's name."

The most important thing is we go to heaven.

"What about Rosie Jimenez?" I asked. "What about the woman who died because of it?"

There was a pause that held everything, or nothing.

"Well, I'm sure that's multiplied many times," he said. "You think about that doctor in Pennsylvania who had dead bodies stored in the refrigerator"—a reference to disgraced abortion provider Kermit Gosnell, who was convicted of murder and kept fetal remains in a freezer—"the other side is just as bad. The suffering that abortion causes is immeasurable. And if you can do something to ameliorate it in some way or another, on either side of the issue, I'm willing to do that. But I don't think that we have to spend federal money to support death. I really don't."

"I'm curious," I said, "reading your book, it's really striking, you went through—and you're very open about it—a kind of questioning of your relationship to the Catholic Church, and also to conservative politics, in the aftermath of the Bauman scandal, as you call it. So I'm curious if at any point during that process, you questioned your position on abortion as well?"

Bauman seemed puzzled by the question. Maybe I should have put it more bluntly; maybe I should have said: "How come being gay is OK with your God but having an abortion isn't?"

"That really didn't have anything to do with the issue of abortion," he said. "[It] had to do with my own failings, my own inability to control myself and to deal with the issue of homosexuality.... Interesting that you got that interpretation out of reading it."

"I thought it was a fascinating book," I said. "I felt like you were sort of grappling with some of these big questions... and wrestling with the idea of a forgiving God, the idea of a God who would accept people in their wholeness, and so I guess it's a logical follow-up question for me as a reporter, of whether, if there's an exception for gay Catholics to find wholeness and acceptance, whether that would apply to women seeking abortion as well?"

"Well, you know, that's an interesting parallel that I hadn't really considered as you've articulated it," he said.

The cheapest way to understand Bauman would be as a hypocrite. He's gay but Catholic. He's antiabortion but gay. He's been irresponsible with money but he's a fiscal conservative. He told me, at one point, that he thought the Republican Party's path forward on abortion should be to develop a ten-point plan to support women with unintended pregnancies, and yet he spent much of his young adulthood helping to build a political movement that has cut such support to the bone. In doing so, he helped reshape the Republican Party, which today, he's horrified by.

"Trump is not a conservative, he's—well, I'm not going to start the litany of what describes him properly in front of a lady," he told me. No Republican or Democratic politician today, in his estimation, truly embodies the conservative movement that he helped launch—the party devoted to the rights of misers, but also, to a certain decorum.

He looked down on all the opportunists—Trump and Biden, too.

"He's one of those swinging-door politicians," Bauman said of Biden, who supported the Hyde Amendment for more than forty years, until he was running for president in 2019.

"I think he felt pressured from the Left in his own party; maybe you were the ones who pressured him," Bauman said.

I laughed but secretly thought: *If I could take any credit for that, I'd be as proud as Bauman is of getting the policy through in the first place.*

"I haven't contributed much to your research," he said.

"Quite to the contrary," I assured him.

A more generous reading of Bauman is that people are complicated and damaged and that you can be a true believer and still worry about how you'll be remembered in the end. I thought Miss Marple might have preferred this realistic take on human nature. She had once quipped over her knitting that "so many people seem to me not to be either bad or good, but simply, you know, very silly."[39]

There was a moment in my interview with Bauman that I missed the first time, because his words came out in a tumble. It was only later, listening back to the tape, that I heard it and understood why he decided to pick up the phone when I called. It happened when he was talking about why he thought the Hyde Amendment was such a good idea.

"It just seemed a practical way to limit the number of abortions and, of course, the interpretation of the Hyde Amendment—Bauman Amendment, whatever you want to call it"—and there it was. I paused and rewound the audio to make sure. When I listened for it, it was clear as a Florida morning.

The "Bauman Amendment," he had called it.

Perhaps at the end of his life, he was hoping that he might get credit not just before Saint Peter at the gate, but here on earth. Perhaps, listening to the wind chimes, talking to the pro-death reporter on that December day, he'd briefly glimpsed a world where the ban had his name on it instead.

CHAPTER 3

THE SERIAL KISSER

People who can be very good can be very bad too.
—*They Do It with Mirrors* by Agatha Christie

I WAS ON SUMMER VACATION WITH MY FAMILY IN MAINE WHEN MY FOUR-year-old grabbed the biography of former Oregon Senator Bob Packwood, which, obsessed detective that I was, I had brought with me to the beach. All week I had lain flopped on the faded furniture in this airy farmhouse, alternately transfixed and nauseated by the life story of my next suspect. Packwood hadn't contributed to Rosie Jimenez's death. In fact, he had fought harder than most members of Congress to stop it. He was a suspect because he embodied the twisted motives and contradictions that ran through the history of how *Roe* was killed.

Packwood fit another paradigm of the murder mystery. As Miss Marple moves through her inquiries, knitting and eavesdropping and listening to all the suspects, she soon discovers that just about *everyone* has a motive. The characters all turn out to be flawed human beings harboring sinister secrets—the rosy-faced secretary will turn out to be the daughter of a woman who poisoned three husbands; the blue-eyed German pilot will turn out to be the victim's estranged son.

The murder mystery is at its heart about revealing the complexity of human nature.

And Packwood was a complex suspect indeed.

His story was emblematic of the wider motive that had undergirded the politics of abortion for the past half century: opportunism, both personal and political.

Packwood was first elected to the US Senate in 1968 as a pro-choice Republican, back when that was still a thing. He was the first senator to introduce a bill to legalize abortion nationwide—in 1970, three years before *Roe*. He championed the Equal Rights Amendment to enshrine women's equality in the Constitution and became allies with feminist Gloria Steinem, who raised hundreds of thousands of dollars on his behalf. But even as he promoted legal abortion and hired women to powerful positions on his staff when doing so was unusual, Packwood had a serious habit of forcible kissing. He was such a prolific serial kisser that it's impressive he fit it all in. Between November 1992, when *The Washington Post* ran a front-page exposé on his behavior,[1] and September 1995, when he resigned after a sordid Senate investigation, forty-eight women came forward to accuse Packwood of sexual misconduct. In some cases, the allegations went far beyond kissing.

Incredibly, the investigation into Packwood prominently featured the future senate majority leader Mitch McConnell, who, decades later, would ensure the confirmation of accused attempted rapist Brett Kavanaugh to the Supreme Court. Investigators read Packwood's diary, interviewed scores of witnesses, and concluded that while in the Senate, Packwood had done the following: Forcibly kissed the hotel desk clerk at the Red Lion Inn. Pinned a mail clerk to the wall, bent her head back, and stuck his tongue in her mouth. Grabbed the elevator operator in the Capitol and kissed her on the lips, repeatedly. Chased a prospective speechwriter around a table and kissed her. Slid his hand up the hostess's leg to her crotch in the dark dining room of the Ramada Inn and said with a leer, "Do you know who I am?"[2]

Packwood seemed to have accosted practically every woman he met, from a reporter who came to interview him to a lobbyist who came to advocate for abortion rights to the Senate aide who babysat his kids. He pulled at the panty girdle of an employee and stood on her feet, and when she confronted him, baffled, and asked whether he thought they were just going to have sex on the floor of his office, he muttered: "I suppose you're one of the ones who want a motel." She quit her job.

"Mommy, what's it about?" my child asked, pulling at the book cover with blue-marker-stained fingers. It showed a blurry photo of Packwood's flat lightbulb-shaped face; his lips were parted, revealing his bottom teeth.

Parenting is the delicate art of hiding the world from your child.

"It's about this guy Bob Packwood," I said brightly. "Mommy's going to interview him."

My kid looked at me, their cherub's face deadly serious.

"Is he a Bad Guy?"

The question stunned me for a second. I'd been forcing myself to endure page after page of Packwood shoving his tongue into mouth after mouth because I needed to know the answer to this exact question.

Is he a Bad Guy?

It would be easy to say yes, except that Packwood had played a distinctly *Good Guy* role in the history of abortion rights. He had fought the ban that killed Rosie Jimenez and almost managed to stop it. And he'd done so, at least at times, in the language of intersectional feminism.

"The amendment that is now in the House bill does not prohibit abortions. It prohibits abortions for poor people," Packwood declared in his booming voice on the Senate floor on June 28, 1976, four days after Henry Hyde introduced the ban. "We are not going to stop abortions by retaining passing [sic] this House language. What we are going to do is put [women] back into the butcher shop and backroom, with coat hanger abortionists, and we are going to have many women dying immediately from badly performed abortions or dying very soon afterward from infections resulting from improperly performed abortions."[3]

That, of course, was exactly what happened to Rosie a year later.

My child looked at me expectantly. Good Guy or Bad Guy?

"That's a really interesting question," I said, stalling. In the cartoons I felt guilty about letting my kid watch, the Bad Guy tended to be a cackling villain hell-bent on global destruction. The Bad Guy needed to be vanquished—certainly he should never be extensively investigated by someone attempting to determine the intricacies of his motives.

"Are Bad Guys real?" my kid had been asking me lately, and I heard, in this question, a struggle to grapple with queries that were far more complicated. *How safe is the world?* I heard. *And am I Good or Bad?*

A sea breeze filtered in through the open window, fluttering the filmy curtains. I took a breath and placed each word like a block on the bedspread in front of us, building the world I would like my child to see.

"I would say he's both Good and Bad," I said.

"So he's like us?" they asked.

My heart swelled. My little genius!

"Yes, that's right," I said, beaming with pride at their grasp of nuance.

"Sometimes we do bad things and sometimes we do good things," they added.

"That's right," I said, "and most people are like that."

Bad Guys aren't real. Or so I'd like them to believe.

I took this story, like a little charm, and tucked it into my pocket, knowing that soon I would visit Bob Packwood and decide for myself.

THE BAD GUY

"He's not *exactly* like us," my husband said, deflating my pride, when I told him the story later. It's true that most of us do *not* walk around shoving our tongues into strangers' mouths. But Packwood is at least *more* like us than, say, Henry Hyde, who grabbed women's asses while killing their rights. Henry Hyde was a Bad Guy all the way through.

But the more I dug, the more the lines between Bad Guys and Good Guys began to blur. In Hyde's obituary in *The New York Times*, I found a quotation from his Democratic colleague, then Massachusetts Representative Barney Frank, praising Hyde for breaking with his party to support welfare programs. Hyde had acted, Frank said, "on the view that because he opposed abortion, that children would be born in difficult circumstances, and he felt an obligation to help them."[4]

That sounded like Good Guy stuff.

On the opposite end of the spectrum, meanwhile, were pro-choice Republicans like Packwood who tended to *oppose* government spending on programs that helped the poor. In the long run, opposing these programs made it harder for families to have the kids they wanted. As Sara Matthiesen wrote in her book *Reproduction Reconceived*, the establishment of the right to abortion in 1973 coincided with changes like the decimation of the social safety net and the rise of mass incarceration, so that many low-income people gained the illusion of reproductive "choice" at the very moment when the ability to make a decision about child rearing free from social and economic coercion was becoming more elusive.[5]

In Packwood's time, some of the staunchest pro-choice figures in Congress were Republicans, like Massachusetts Senator Edward Brooke. Even the right-wing icon of his time, Barry Goldwater, who would galvanize the nascent conservative movement, had supported the legalization of abortion on the grounds that the government should stay out of the decision (a common conservative viewpoint at the time). Goldwater had secretly arranged an abortion for his teenage daughter.[6] His wife founded Planned Parenthood's Arizona affiliate and remained a strong supporter of the organization for years.[7] However, Goldwater supported the Hyde Amendment and at the end of his career, facing a tough Senate race in 1980, endorsed a constitutional abortion ban. He seemed to be yet another of the opportunists I was learning to spot.

On the opposite side of the aisle, it wasn't as uncommon as it is today for Democrats to oppose abortion. Catholic Democrats like legendary Senator Ted Kennedy opposed it at first, although he switched his position in the mid-1970s.[8] Catholic Democrat Joe Biden voted in favor of a failed constitutional amendment allowing states and Congress to reverse *Roe* in 1982 while he was in the Senate.[9] Then he condemned Republicans for reversing *Roe* forty years later.

Jesse Jackson, the civil rights icon, advocated for the Hyde Amendment in alliance with the National Right to Life Committee[10] and opposed abortion as a tool of eugenics—a position he abandoned when he ran for president as a Democrat.[11] I learned from former NARAL executive director Karen Mulhauser that even my own trusty progressive Massachusetts Senator Ed Markey was antiabortion until, Mulhauser told me, she was seated next to him on a plane in 1983 and used the trip to persuade him to change how he voted on the issue.[12] As Mary Ziegler noted in her book *After Roe*, between 1973 and 1984, Democrats sponsored most antiabortion legislation in Congress.[13]

Indeed, the senator who would boast of securing passage of a Hyde-like restriction on Title X, the bill *signed by Republican president Richard Nixon* to provide *free contraception to the poor*, was a Democrat named Thomas Eagleton.[14] Eagleton's enduring claim to fame was that he became Democratic presidential candidate George McGovern's running mate for eighteen days in 1972 until it emerged he'd been hospitalized for mental illness. That election year, Republicans made an opportunistic push to use abortion to court Catholic voters. Despite Eagleton's antiabortion achievement and McGovern's own expressed view that the issue should be left to the states, Republicans succeeded in tarring McGovern as the candidate of "acid, abortion and amnesty."[15] Nixon won. But a Gallup poll that year found that more Republicans than Democrats supported the idea that the decision to have an abortion should be left to a woman and her doctor—68 percent of Republicans agreed versus 59 percent of Democrats.[16]

The more I dug, the more complicated it got. Because the man who would seal Rosie's fate by flipping his position on the Hyde Amendment was a Democrat, and the senator who tried to stop the ban was a Republican who liked to stand on women's toes and kiss them.

Packwood never heard about abortion growing up, except when it was used as a synonym for disaster. He remembered people calling things like a bad paint job "a real abortion."[17] His dad, Fred Packwood, was a lobbyist, alcoholic, and frequent visitor to the drunk tank at the Salem, Oregon, city jail. His mother was, in the words of one schoolmate, "a very unpleasant woman who'd say unpleasant things about Bob in front of him and other kids."[18]

Packwood harbored political aspirations from a young age, steeped as he was in the milieu of his father's political career. He joined the debate team at Grant High School and later, the Young Republicans chapter at Willamette University. While he built his political chops he was also gathering with bachelor friends at a bar and imposing an informal rule that each man bring a different woman every time.[19] In 1960, Packwood became the Republican Party's chairman for Multnomah County, where he quickly discovered that hiring women could serve a dual purpose: promoting equality while boosting his political goals. He dissolved the women's auxiliary committees and integrated women into the party itself. It turned out women were productive workers who made his political machine stronger. After gaining a reputation in local politics, Packwood was elected to the Senate, where there were zero women at the time.

Determining if Packwood was a Good or Bad Guy would mean understanding *why* he had supported abortion rights—and the answer was complicated, at least early in his career, when like much of the country he was obsessed with the existential threat of population growth. He served on Nixon's Population Commission and befriended Paul Ehrlich, author of *The Population Bomb*, a best-selling book that predicted widespread global famine as the population exploded. Packwood's early forays into promoting abortion rights were infused with concerns about the environment and overpopulation—but also with feminist arguments. In 1970, he introduced two bills at the same time: one to cap the child tax credit after a family had three kids, and another to legalize abortion in Washington, DC.[20]

"I think many of us have not faced up to the particular problem that is going to have to be overcome if we are to solve what we call the environmental crisis, and that problem is, basically, people," he declared, adding, "I would rather that we face that problem now, and start to undertake a policy of national population restraint whereby we can look forward to limiting the population of this country by voluntary means, so that we do not have to, in thirty, forty, or fifty years, look forward to limiting it by compulsory means." Later that year, when he introduced the first-ever bill to legalize abortion nationwide, he again drew a connection to population growth. "It seems highly illogical, at this point in time, when there is so much concern over population growth, that the state should still be in the business of enforcing what biologist Garrett Hardin has called compulsory pregnancy," he declared.[21] Hardin was a white nationalist who would go on to argue in a book published in 1972 that "supporting children gave the government the right to strip their parents of the capacity to produce more," as sociologist Dorothy Roberts paraphrased it in a blistering synopsis.[22] But in the same speech where he cited Hardin, Packwood cited the pioneering Black Congresswoman Shirley Chisholm, noting that public hospitals often denied abortions to poor Black women, while private hospitals offered them to rich women.

"There is no question but that in our hypocrisy or indifference we have made abortion much more available to the middle class than to the poor," he declared.

Packwood would again defend the abortion rights of the poor in the summer of 1976, when he tried to stop the Hyde Amendment. After Bob Bauman and Henry Hyde conspired to get the ban through the House, Packwood stripped it from the appropriations bill in the Senate.

He thought that would put an end to it.

But the fight was just getting started. And now, the Catholic bishops, who had dismissed Paul Haring's idea two years earlier, were throwing their weight behind the Hyde Amendment. They had their sights set on the influential Congressman Dan Flood of Pennsylvania, who oversaw the subcommittee in charge of the bill. Flood was a Democrat and former repertory theater actor known for his immaculate white suits, handlebar mustache, and the capes he wore for dramatic flourish. And Dan Flood *hated* the Hyde Amendment. He believed abortion was wrong, he fulminated, but the Hyde Amendment didn't prohibit abortion outright.

"It prohibits abortion for poor people," Flood told his colleagues. "Listen: A vote for this amendment is not a vote against abortion. It is a vote against poor people. That is what it is, as plain as the nose on your face."[23]

That would have been that—except that Flood's district was heavily

Catholic, and behind the scenes, the Catholic bishops were rallying the faithful. Carol Werner saw trouble brewing. In 1975, she had turned down a job with the federal government to become a lobbyist for NARAL, the national pro-choice organization that started before *Roe* with state-based efforts to repeal abortion bans. (NARAL's acronym originally stood for the National Association for the Repeal of Abortion Laws; after Roe, it became the National Abortion Rights Action League.) Now, Werner was focused on defending the national right to abortion.[24] When she was hired, she recalled, NARAL's DC operation was a shoestring affair run out of an unfurnished office in a seedy area near the Capitol. The daughter of a Methodist pastor from Iowa, soft-spoken and Midwestern nice, Werner could be blunt when needed. She began typing out missives to the group's supporters on her IBM Selectric in ALL CAPS.

"PLEASE READ IMMEDIATELY!!!" she wrote in a memo about the Hyde Amendment on July 30.[25]

"This is extremely serious," she pleaded. "I cannot even imagine how bad it would be to lose on this."

Dan Flood, she reported, had been deluged by no less than five thousand antiabortion letters.[26]

"So far, the 'right to lifers' have really outstripped us—and it is up to all of us to turn that around," she wrote on August 11.[27]

Even as Werner pleaded, groups like NARAL were shifting their hopes to what would become the movement's primary strategy for the next fifty years: fighting abortion restrictions in court. In a July 21 memo, the pro-choice Republican Senator Ed Brooke wrote that groups including NARAL had refused to accept a compromise that might soften the ban. "The group[s] would prefer leaving the Hyde Amendment in if there is not sufficient support to strike it altogether, for they feel that they would have a strong court case against the Hyde Amendment," he wrote.[28]

Years later, Mark Gallagher, a former lobbyist for the Catholic bishops, would boast of how he used the church's political influence to ensure Hyde's passage. He called the pro-life coordinator in Dan Flood's district and got every Catholic pastor there to sign a letter to Flood. After the letters arrived,

Flood, who had declared the Hyde Amendment "a vote against poor people... as plain as the nose on your face," decided it was a great idea after all.[29]

Carol Werner fumed as she watched Flood cave to political opportunism.

In a conference meeting, he declared that the ban should make no exception for medical necessity, otherwise "any woman with an ingrown toenail or a cold in the head would say she had to have an abortion." Flood's theatrical flourishes, Carol noted, were doubtless appreciated by one observer watching the proceedings that day: Flood's own parish priest.[30]

So in the end it was a Democrat, acting for political expediency, who sealed Rosie's fate.

But the political opportunism that drove Hyde's passage wasn't confined to Flood. In the 1976 presidential race, Jimmy Carter was courting a burgeoning new political force—white Evangelicals. Speaking in the House on August 10, a pro-choice Republican from Washington, Representative Joel Pritchard, summarized the landscape a few months ahead of that election. He noted there seemed to be three groups within Congress—those with strong beliefs either for or against abortion, and a third group who "think that abortions are all right in some cases" but were worried about voting against the Hyde Amendment so close to the election. Some of these members, Pritchard said, realized that "in their districts the majority of people support abortion and allowing women to make this decision," but they also knew "a very hard and very skillful minority" was working to punish those who voted for abortion rights.[31]

In mid-September, after adopting a narrow exception for cases where the life of the woman was endangered, Congress gave final passage to the Hyde Amendment. Of the 256 House members and 47 senators who voted in favor of the ban, about 60 percent were Democrats.[32]

THE GOOD GUY

If Packwood's support of abortion turned out to be motivated by anything other than political opportunism, he would stand as a remarkable exception in the history of abortion politics. The shifting allegiances of leading politicians throughout recent history proved that all too many were willing to switch their position to get elected or keep their seats.

So was Packwood a true believer or an opportunist?

I had a unique angle into his motives, thanks to his wife's decision to share a key piece of evidence: Packwood's diaries.

The diaries were Packwood's undoing. When Senate investigators probed the accusations of sexual misconduct against him, they discovered that Packwood had dictated his life in minute detail and then sent the tapes to a secretary to transcribe. His own record, dutifully typed by this poor woman, included Packwood's accounts of serial misbehavior. One passage seared itself into my memory:

"I have one question—if she didn't want me to feather her nest, why did she come into the Xerox room?" Packwood had dictated.[33]

"Sure, she used that old excuse that she had to make copies of the Brady Bill, but if you believe that, I have a room full of radical feminists you can boff. She knew I was copying stuff in there. I had my jacket off and my sleeves rolled up, revealing the well-defined musculature of my sinewy arms which are always bulging with desire. I know what she wanted. This didn't require a lot of thought."

In addition to exalting his rippling forearms, Packwood recorded his efforts to get his rich friends to give his estranged wife jobs she wasn't qualified for so that he could pay less in alimony. He had even recorded *in* his diary his efforts to remove incriminating material *from* his diary.[34] The Senate managed to obtain damning passages from the diaries as part of their investigation into Packwood. But portions of the material remain sealed at the Oregon Historical Society.

To my surprise, Packwood's wife Elaine, who was first drawn to work for him because of his support of abortion, had agreed to go through the diary for me, sensing, she said, that it would be useful for my pursuit of a topic she cared about. She might also have sensed an opportunity to burnish her husband's troubled legacy by emphasizing his stalwart defense of women's rights. So she had emailed me digital scans of the dates when the Hyde Amendment was debated, and they were a treasure trove of insight into Packwood's motives.

On June 28, 1976, Packwood had gleefully recounted how he defeated the Hyde Amendment.

"I was very good in debate, and we won the amendment about 55 to 28, a much larger and more decisive victory than I would have thought," he crowed. "Hopefully this will kill any efforts of the antiabortionists this session and as I have said before, each day we're further away from that Supreme Court decision and each day abortion becomes more established and more utilized by America, the less likelihood of any change."[35]

The following year, when he tried and failed to stop the ban a second time, Packwood was no less preoccupied with his own performance.

"I gave a damn good speech in the afternoon tracing the history of abortion, the fact that it wasn't illegal or immoral when this country was founded," he said. "Unfortunately, there weren't many people around in the afternoon to listen."[36]

Passages like these spoke to dueling motives: a genuine commitment to defending abortion that coexisted with his own ego.

To figure out which was the real Packwood, I needed to meet him in person. So I headed to Oregon.

THE COMPLICATED GUY

On the phone, Packwood's formerly booming voice sounded querulous, and at the age of ninety-two, he was about as physically threatening as an insect. Yet as I prepared to meet him, I couldn't stop wondering what kind of person assumed a woman wanted him to *feather her nest* because she had walked into a copy room HOLDING PAPERS SHE NEEDED TO COPY.

So I dressed like a Victorian desk clerk in a high-necked black cotton top with a blazer and pin-striped pants. As I drove to Packwood's leafy Portland suburb, the phrase "feather her nest" tumbled around in my head like a bad song.

I turned down a steep hill and parked beside a white-and-tan condo building. Elaine Franklin emerged to meet me, wearing a pink sweater and blue floral pants. I was as eager to understand Franklin as I was her husband.

She had started out as a volunteer and then became Packwood's stalwart chief of staff who stood by him when the scandal broke, making irate phone calls to editors to attack the stories that implicated him and labeling *The Washington Post*'s investigation a "witch hunt."[37] She had denied the rumors they were having an affair. Packwood had filed for divorce from his first wife in 1990. When he resigned from the Senate it was Franklin who sat next to him, quietly sobbing. Three years later, she married him.

Franklin was a slight woman with long lashes and a British accent. She led me to a parking garage beneath their condo, where we got into her car to go to a Starbucks around the corner. She ordered two mocha Frappuccinos, adding whipped cream to Packwood's because, she told me, he needed to gain weight. As we waited for the coffees, she confided that her wedding vows included the phrase "in sickness and in health" but *not* "for richer or poorer."

With Packwood, there was only "richer." After he resigned from the Senate, he made over a million dollars a year as a lobbyist.[38]

We returned to their condo, which looked like a page from an architectural magazine. Elaine's contractor son helped with the renovation after they bought it in 2020. We walked through to the living room with its stunning view of the Willamette River, where a covered boat drifted by. Everything was white—the walls, the armchairs and sofa, the rugs, the marble countertops—except an enormous black pear on the kitchen table.

Packwood walked down the hall toward us, hunched over a walker, smiling, his blue eyes bright. He looked like a hollowed-out version of the man on the book cover. His white hair was combed over his forehead like a feathered bathing cap. His hands were skeletal and purple-veined. He folded them together as we sat on high chairs at the marble counter. Franklin was right about his weight; his vivid yellow sweater with white flowers hung from the bony bulbs of his shoulders. The arms beneath rippled no more.

"Clear your throat, speak up a bit, because I'm behind you and I can barely hear you," Franklin interjected when Packwood began to speak. He suggested they switch places, putting Franklin awkwardly between me and him. Then he launched back into a story about how he picked berries one summer as a Cub Scout, and the berry farmer separated the girls and boys.

"The girls picked more!" he said, his voice deep and tremulous.

"Why?" I asked.

"Who knows why! But ... that stuck with me for the rest of my career. That was an example of equal pay for equal work and they worked more, I guess."

I was confused about the takeaway. Packwood appeared to have concluded that women were efficient—and exploitable.

He told me that the first person who said "abortion" to him as anything other than a synonym for disaster was a woman who served on the Multnomah County Commission—the same commission he reshuffled to put women on equal footing with men. One night in the bar, she told him she'd had an abortion.

"Why do you think she opened up about it?" I asked.

"Well, I'm not sure; she was a slight woman and she'd had a lot to drink."

Ever the chief of staff, Franklin interjected with a more positive spin.

"Bob does have a way of getting information out of people that they might not give to other people," she said.

That first woman "opened the gate," Packwood said, and from then on, when he went out drinking with women, he'd ask them about abortion, and he found they knew all about it, even though it was illegal. He began to persuade his fellow Republicans that they ought to support legalizing it.

"How did you get a bunch of Republicans on board with that idea in 1967?" I asked.

He paused, considering how to phrase his response, before settling on, "Properly prepared, I'm more persuasive in debate than anybody I know."

"You can't tell it now," he added, "but I have a very commanding voice and I know how to use a microphone."

I glanced at the counter where Franklin had assembled a stack of diary entries. She handed me one from the day Packwood introduced the bill to legalize abortion in Washington, DC, and I read aloud from it.

"I really felt on top of it. I did know this subject well, and they couldn't ask me any questions that I didn't know the answers to," I read. "We then cut the television part in the television correspondence room, and I did even better there. I was completely at ease." He added: "These bills have given me such a tremendous lift, I just can't express my excitement."[39]

"He says humbly," Franklin scoffed.

Packwood protested. "Well, but as you know, you also find in my diary when I'll say, 'That was the worst speech I've ever given; it didn't work.'"

"You were very honest about yourself," Franklin agreed.

I gulped. Maybe too honest.

"How much of your pro-choice views were shaped by the population control issue?" I asked.

"Almost none," he said. "I actually would have been perfectly happy if the country had not grown from a population standpoint, but it had nothing to do with abortion."

At the end of the entry, he'd dictated a motive as pristine as our view of the Willamette River: "There's nothing better than being a politician with a cause that's inevitably going to win, and being in the vanguard and having all of the right people with you from the start."

Perhaps this was the real Packwood—full of himself, sure, but driven by a sense of companionable joy at being on the right side of history.

Or perhaps the real Packwood was the one who made a sexist joke while my recorder was rolling. Franklin was explaining how she started volunteering for him in 1980 because of his support for abortion rights.

"I worked for absolutely nothing," she said, and Packwood replied: "Well, that's what women should do." She pulled her hand back as if to slap him in the leg.

"Not funny," she scolded.

Packwood got up to wheel his walker down the hall to the bathroom. I turned to Franklin and asked about the sealed copies of the diaries.

"They cannot be released until after my death," she said quietly.

"Why is that?"

"Um," Franklin began, then paused. "Because, you know, there will be things in there that I don't particularly want to see."

"I don't want to see it and I don't want it out in public while I'm still alive," she added. "I think you can understand that."

Packwood rolled back into the room and took his place with his wife wedged between us. We talked about a passage of the diary from August 1976 when Packwood sparred over the Hyde Amendment with Jesse Helms, the racist senator from North Carolina. Packwood respected Helms because Helms respected the Senate; while senators often wandered the chamber, Helms stood at his desk for every vote.

"Even Jesse came up and said he sure hated to argue with me because I was so damn good," Packwood dictated in the diary entry.[40]

I asked him the same question I had asked Helms's granddaughter: Did Helms care about abortion or was he an opportunist?

"It is hard to tell when somebody is as good as they are at arguing," Packwood said thoughtfully, then added: "I find it hard to believe you can be that good at it if you don't really care much about it. If you didn't really care, I don't think you'd spend the time on it."

It sounded like Packwood was talking not just about Helms, but about himself.

We moved on to Gloria Steinem.

"When all the women came forth with their accusations about me, she was *less* critical," he recalled. "She said, 'If worst comes to worst, you might have to resign and run again.' I said, 'Gloria, there won't be any point in running again if I resign.' She said, you know, 'Stall it off as long as you can.'"

Franklin began to wave her arms as if trying to stop traffic.

"Right, no, we're not going to discuss women," she said sternly.

"OK," Packwood said like a scolded child.

What I wanted to say was, *Haven't we been discussing women this whole time?*

What I said was: "I wonder about how you want to be remembered, about your legacy. You're such a staunch feminist, you were so staunchly pro-choice. And then I think people look at that, and they look at the news headlines around what happened in the nineties and see a contradiction."

"Well, we just saw the same thing with our recent mayor," Packwood said. "Sensational mayor." He meant Neil Goldschmidt, the Portland mayor hailed for making the city pedestrian-friendly who turned out to be sexually abusing a teenager. Or as Packwood put it: "Story finally broke that he'd been having a sexual affair with a fourteen-year-old girl."

Affair seems like the wrong word, I thought.

"When he died, Neil Goldschmidt died, second paragraph, fourteen-year-old girl."

There it was. The obituary. Packwood's secular version of the tally that comes at the end of a life. His judgment would be issued not by Saint Peter at the gate, but by the obituary writers.

Regardless, Franklin was shutting this down.

"I think we should not discuss that," she said with a sense of finality.

But I *needed* him to discuss it, and so, before I could stop myself, I started telling the story about my kid asking whether Packwood was a Good Guy or a Bad Guy, and how I replied that it was complicated.

Franklin stared at me with her eyes wide.

"I think it's up to you, Amy, to decide. How you've framed that—'complicated' might be a good word," she said.

"Does it sound like bad behavior? Yes," she added. "I wasn't there to see any of the incidents."

There was a long pause.

"I've been asked if I have been sexually harassed in the workplace, and, you know, and this was a good while ago, by today's standards, yes, I probably was. At the time, did I think it was harassment? No." She motioned as if shooing away a fly. "A lot of it would be verbal harassment, but I didn't think of it as sexual harassment. I thought of it as, you know, men being kind of jerks. It never rose to a point where I would ever have complained to a superior about it because that wasn't the environment at the time," she said.

"Should I judge that behavior forty years ago by today's standards? I mean, I think that's the question."

That is one of the questions.

After all, the year before the Packwood scandal broke, Clarence Thomas had been confirmed to the Supreme Court even though Anita Hill had come forward to testify he sexually harassed her. In the wake of Thomas's confirmation, journalist Florence Graves went looking for powerful men behaving badly, and sources on the Hill told her to look at Packwood. In one view of history, he was a casualty of feminist rage over Thomas that finally found a target it could take down—a liberal Republican that party leaders were willing to sacrifice.

I asked Packwood if he wanted to add anything.

"I have nothing to say," Packwood said, echoing his wife. "You're going to have to make up your own decisions on that one."

We moved on to Kamala Harris—Franklin was voting for her in the upcoming 2024 election; Packwood felt she was too far left. He remained a registered Republican, loyal to the fiscal conservatism of his forebears, even though he and Franklin were disgusted by Trump.

"The point is, Amy," Franklin said, handing me the conclusion that she hoped I would draw about her husband, "after he left the Senate, he lifted himself up, made a good living, and hopefully had a happy life, and became a really good member of the community."

I wondered, exactly, what this proved, other than that power is something that powerful men never really lost.

Franklin took me down in the elevator. She pushed the button, stood facing me, and sighed heavily.

"It must be complicated for you," I said.

"Only in situations like this," she replied.

I wondered, as I walked to my car, if that could be true.

THE BESTIES

In the book I took to the beach, journalist Mark Kirchmeier reached a cynical conclusion about Packwood, whom he believed ran on abortion only because it helped him get reelected in progressive Oregon.

"Feminist champion Bob Packwood's journey has appeared to be one of the great ironies of American politics," he wrote. "But in reality, there was no inconsistency. Packwood never saw the feminist movement as anything more than a device to advance his own career."[41]

After my interview with Packwood, I disagreed.

Packwood cared about abortion rights, even as he took advantage of women's lower social status. As he said of Jesse Helms, why would he have gone to all the trouble if he didn't care? Yet touting the issue had brought him opportunities—not just in politics. It had brought him the opportunity to get close to women who trusted him—the opportunity to take advantage of them in private even as he defended their rights in public.

He had left it up to me to answer my kid's question. Does the public stand he took for women outweigh his bad behavior?

I put the question to his former ally Gloria Steinem, who told me: "Any leader or any person may be constructive and right in some areas and destructive and wrong in other areas. It's up to us to testify for the difference."[42]

After my meeting with Packwood I headed two hours south to Eugene, to meet two women who could testify for the difference.

Gena Hutton was a budding feminist who got a mass mailing one day from Steinem, asking her to support Bob Packwood. Hutton had grown up Catholic on a cattle ranch in rural Oregon. She grew skeptical of her childhood faith at a young age when her mother explained that her older friends were sinning by living together without being married in the Catholic Church. By the time Steinem's letter arrived, Hutton was only too happy to heed the call to support the senator from her home state. She was young, vivacious, and articulate, and before long she was asked to chair Packwood's reelection campaign in Lane County. She was starstruck by the senator, who stayed out drinking with her at a restaurant one night after the rest of the staff had left. His aides kept popping in and interrupting. Later, Hutton realized this must have been their attempt to stop what happened next. Packwood walked her to her car, then grabbed her and kissed her. Her first instinct, as his campaign volunteer, was to protect him by making sure no one saw. She got him into her car and drove across the parking lot to his motel room, where Packwood cajoled her to come in. She refused, clenching the steering wheel until her knuckles turned white.

Her boyfriend had seen them. When she got home, he exploded, claiming she must have egged him on.[43]

I reached out to Hutton shortly before my visit to Oregon. She told me that she had a visitor coming whom I might want to meet: Mary Heffernan, founder of the Oregon chapter of NARAL. Heffernan had gone to see Packwood to talk about abortion in his office, where he grabbed her by the shoulders and kissed her. Hutton and Heffernan were the most outspoken of the forty-eight women who accused Packwood and they became close friends. On the fridge in the condo where Hutton has lived since the 1990s, nestled in a verdant valley of firs and pines, there are photos of the pair of them, before Heffernan's hair turned gray. They meet regularly to drink margaritas and toast Packwood for bringing them together.

Hutton was bright, birdlike, and blue-eyed, so short her feet didn't touch the deck under the porch swing where she sat holding a glass of fizzy pink lemonade. In 1994, Bob Packwood had tried to discredit Hutton in a speech. He dismissed her claim she'd been harmed by his attempted kiss—after all, if she'd been so hurt, why did she stick with his campaign?[44]

"Why did you stick with it?" I asked her, as we sat listening to the birds, surrounded by Hutton's jungle of houseplants.

"I signed up for this for Gloria Steinem!" she cried, pressing her finger into the swing cushion for emphasis. She cared about women's rights so much that she was willing to sideline her own for the cause.

Heffernan was taller than Hutton, her gray hair trimmed short, her face chiseled. She wanted me to know that she did not, in fact, have a nervous breakdown, although Packwood had once called up a friend of hers to ask if she did.[45]

Revisiting this history seemed to chill Heffernan. It was a sunny day in the seventies, but she got up to wrap herself in a cranberry-colored Patagonia jacket.

We talked about how these women were the early edge of the MeToo movement, three decades before the exposure of Harvey Weinstein sparked a national reckoning over sexual harassment. It was cathartic for them to see the issue explode into national consciousness at last. But the contradictions of the moment were dizzying. Because even as women denounced harassment and watched powerful men like Weinstein pay, they lost the nationwide right to abortion.

Heffernan watched in horror in 2018 as Mitch McConnell, the man who participated in the investigation into her assailant, ensured the placement on the Supreme Court of Justice Brett Kavanaugh, a man who Christine Blasey Ford said had tried to rape her.

Then she watched as the Supreme Court, with Kavanaugh in place, erased a right she'd worked to protect for fifty years.

It was this violation, rather than Packwood's, that seemed to upset her most.

"It's really heartbreaking to have worked that hard and to think that you've done it," she said, and her dark blue eyes filled with tears.

She kept coming back to the motive she saw at the core of all these events: power. It was the motive that drove the political opportunists on either side of the killing of *Roe*. Even people like Packwood who believed in abortion rights had used the issue to get power and keep it.

"I don't know that I could believe what [Packwood's] motivations are about anything other than power," Heffernan said. "I know that he loved power. And that can show up sexually. That can show up, you know, in the US Senate."

Hutton recalled that she got a taste of this power in the wake of the Packwood scandal. For weeks afterward, the media and everyone she had ever known suddenly wanted to talk with her. Then, the media spotlight, and the power that came with it, vanished.

When I told them about my kid's question, they laughed appreciatively.

"It's really simplistic, how a child would think about it," Hutton said. "It's really hard to reduce someone to good or bad."

"Yeah," Heffernan agreed thoughtfully. "Is there a better paradigm than good or bad?"

We talked about harm. About actions and consequences. Hutton, more abstract, posited the need to evolve to a higher vibration of consciousness. Heffernan, more grounded, talked about how capitalism enforced the idea that one person must be down for another to be up. But mostly we kept coming back to power, and power's opposite, love. Sexual assault is always about power, never about sex. Maybe there aren't Good people and Bad people; maybe there are just powerful people and those of us trying to heal from the consequences of their power.

Before I left, I took a picture of the two of them, holding each other like a couple in a prom photo, Heffernan tall and sturdy, and Hutton tiny, clasped in front of her, both grinning.

Hutton thanked Heffernan for her activism, for all those years of work that powerful men have undone.

"I love you," she told her.

"Thank you," Heffernan replied, looking her in the eye. "I love you, too."

They embraced and kissed on the lips.

A kiss can mean power or love. It can be bad or good.

Sometimes spotting the difference is as easy as a summer day.

PART 2

THE SECOND DEATH OF ROSIE JIMENEZ

CHAPTER 4

THE LISTENER

> The young people think the old people are fools—but the old people know the young people are fools.
>
> —Miss Marple in *The Murder at the Vicarage* by Agatha Christie

ON A JUNE AFTERNOON IN 1978, THE PRO-CHOICE ACTIVIST FRANCES Kissling paced the street in a verdant neighborhood in the Texas border town of McAllen. Even now with the plan already well underway, she felt ambivalent about it. A white woman with a blond bob, Kissling wore a loose magenta shirt, white pants, and thick-framed glasses. As a TV camera from a Dallas station rolled, she counted out a stack of $20 bills, marked them with her initials, and handed them to Diana Rivera, a petite Latina woman with flowing brown hair.[1]

Until recently, Rivera had lived next to her friend Rosie Jimenez in a garden apartment complex on McAllen's Hibiscus Avenue. The young women had been drawn to each other by their similar circumstances; both were children of migrant farmworkers who were raising young kids on their own while trying to climb out of poverty. They had supported each other as they worked their way through classes at Pan-American University; Jimenez wanted to be a special education teacher and Rivera, a lawyer. On the weekends, they cleaned houses together.²

Now, Rivera was steeling herself to avenge her friend's death.

She took the bills from Kissling and walked toward a ramshackle wooden house with lavender trim. In the dirt yard, the leaves of a giant mesquite tree reflected the summer sun.

Inside the house was the midwife who had performed Rosie's fatal abortion.

The sting operation was a last resort. Kissling had already tried all the official channels to protect more women from dying. The federal and state agencies that investigated Rosie's death had not stopped the midwife. Kissling felt frustrated that even abortion rights organizations didn't seem to be doing much to publicize Rosie's story. Kissling believed these white-led groups saw an unmarried Mexican American woman as too unsympathetic a figure.³

So the women were about to take the law into their own hands—and create a strange crime scene I would examine half a century later as I traced the missteps of the abortion rights movement that contributed to the death of *Roe*.

Eight months earlier, in October 1977, Kissling had heard that an unnamed woman had died in Texas after the Hyde Amendment caused the state to cut off funding for Medicaid abortions. (A court battle waged by pro-choice groups had put the amendment on hold for a time, but the injunction was lifted two months before Rosie's death.) Kissling tipped off Ellen Frankfort, a white feminist journalist with a mane of curls and an irreverent sense of humor, who had already made a name for herself with a bestseller called *Vaginal Politics*. "Millions of women have begun to question the godlike status of the American medical establishment," a paperback edition declared, making the book "the #1 self-help book for women!" Sensing her next story, Frankfort flew to McAllen. On a chilly day, she stooped over a grave marker near the airport to make out the letters punched in the tin: "Rosaura Jimenez."

The name struck Frankfort as poignant—a rose, the symbol of life brandished in protest by activists who opposed abortion. "If there is to be a symbol, an icon, a rallying cry, a slogan, a saint, a martyr, let it not be the long-stemmed flower with petals of red," she later wrote. "Let it be a real woman—Rosaura Jimenez—who died in 1977 at the age of twenty-seven."[4]

Rosie was already a symbol before the public knew her name. Feminists who learned that someone had died because of the Hyde Amendment rallied in Manhattan to denounce Joseph Califano, the Carter appointee who presided over implementation of the ban, as a "murderer." *The New York Times* ran an editorial about the "twenty-seven-year-old Mexican American, the unwed mother of a four-year-old child," whose Medicaid card "did her little good."

"Congress should use the time to ponder the consequences of the present policy," the *Times* wrote. "The Government cannot stop abortions. It can only stop paying for them."[5]

Meanwhile, Congress was debating the terms of renewing the Hyde Amendment in that year's appropriations bill. The fight over proposed exceptions for health and rape and incest dragged on, forcing lawmakers to hold three emergency votes to keep the government running.

"For the last four months off and on, back and forth, fight and scramble, House and Senate conferees have been trying to reach a compromise—with no luck," a young Jim Lehrer in a brown blazer advised millions of viewers on his PBS news program in November 1977.[6]

Arrayed around Lehrer's table were two of my previous suspects: Bob Bauman, looking bored and complaining that adding a rape exception to the Hyde Amendment could allow *anyone* to claim, even months after the fact, that they'd been raped; and Bob Packwood, that complicated abortion rights champion, looking riveted by the blond, blue-eyed CDC investigator who sat across from him. Just twenty-nine years old, the CDC's Ann Marie Kimball was so nervous about being on TV that her legs jiggled under the heavy wooden table.

She was there to talk about the dead woman in Texas. At the time, investigators believed that the woman had gotten her fatal abortion in Mexico.

"The woman who died was aware that Medicaid would not pay for her abortion," Kimball told Lehrer in a measured voice. "Financial constraints were one of the major reasons she went to Mexico to get an illegal abortion."

The night before, the CDC had called and told Kimball to cancel the appearance; she was never sure exactly why, except that the agency was cautious with the press. She told them to go ahead and call the TV network if they wanted to cancel, but they had balked. So there she sat, with a bored-looking Bob Bauman and an attentive Bob Packwood.

True to form, Packwood had offered her a ride home afterward and invited himself over. Kimball was starstruck by the senator—but she declined.

"I was staying with my fiancé, and I said, 'No, I don't think that would work,'" she later told me.[7]

Bob Bauman was considerably less affectionate.

When Kimball in her measured way estimated the Hyde Amendment would cause between five and ninety excess maternal deaths, Lehrer turned to Bauman.

"Does that concern you?" he asked.

"Of course it concerns me," Bauman said, quickly pivoting to another number: the 300,000 abortions federal Medicaid dollars funded each year before the Hyde Amendment.

"The death of five people or ninety people concerns me a great deal; but the death of 300,000 children concerns me as well."

There it was: the red herring the antiabortion movement would use time and again to defuse the political force of women who died from its policies. They would act as if the death of a woman was equivalent to the end of a pregnancy. And what was one dead woman, or even ninety dead women, compared to 300,000 dead children?

Not long after the episode aired, news outlets began to cast doubt on the idea that the Hyde Amendment was to blame for Rosie's death at all.

"Doubts Arise About Abortion 'Martyr,'" the headline read on a November 27 *Washington Post* article that claimed the woman "may have been simply trying to keep her pregnancy a secret when she slipped across the border to have the operation performed in the back of a Mexican pharmacy."[8] The *Los Angeles Times* concurred: "Serious doubt has been raised about widely reported allegations that a Mexican American woman who died after crossing the Texas border for a Mexican abortion went there because of a cutoff in federal Medicaid funds."[9]

But Ellen Frankfort and Frances Kissling shut those rumors down. Frankfort proved that Rosie had gotten her abortion not in Mexico, but in Texas. Most importantly, Rosie had had two previous abortions covered under Texas Medicaid. One of them was performed by the very same doctor who later claimed on *Good Morning America* that Rosie's death had nothing to do with Medicaid because sometimes Latina women just went to Mexico for abortions out of shame.

Yet even after these groundbreaking revelations, Rosie's friends would despair that her death changed nothing. In December 1977, Congress renewed the Hyde Amendment, adding exceptions for cases of rape and incest that were "promptly" reported and when the pregnancy would result in "severe and long-lasting physical health damage." That same year, the Supreme Court had issued two decisions upholding state versions of the funding ban.

So Rosie's friends and the feminists from New York hatched a plan. Diana Rivera would pose as a woman who needed an abortion. Her friend came with her, wired by a TV crew from WFAA in Dallas with a hidden microphone. The midwife took them into a room and locked the door, Rivera would later tell *The Texas Observer*.[10] Inside the room, she saw a jar of dirty water with medical instruments. She imagined her friend Rosie sitting alone in the same room, seeing the same dirty instruments Rivera now saw, and yet deciding to go through with the procedure anyway. Rivera began to cry. The midwife, Maria Pineda, told Rivera to take off her clothes and lie on the bed. In a station wagon outside, Frances Kissling heard those words crackling through the hidden microphone. She jumped out and called the cops from a pay phone.

"There is an illegal abortion in progress!" she cried as officers descended on the house, "and the girl's life is in danger."

Police raced up the plywood front steps and handcuffed Pineda. They hauled her out to the waiting cruiser as she stared at the ground, wearing a floral print dress and beige sandals. Pineda would spend three days in jail for performing an abortion without a license. She was the only person I could find who paid a real price for the death of Rosie Jimenez.

Half a century later I sat reading the handwritten scrawl on the police report from that June day in 1978,[11] trying to solve a different mystery: How was it possible that the arrest of a middle-aged Latina woman was all that abortion rights activists could do to avenge Rosie's death? Kissling had been doing her best to protect more women from dying. Yet she had also pulled the ultimate white-lady move: She had called the cops on a brown person.

But this strange scene prompted an even bigger question that went beyond the women present that day. Why wasn't Rosie Jimenez's death enough to change the policy that killed her? Not only did the policy survive, it was accepted by politicians as a middle ground on abortion. As the Democratic and Republican Parties solidified their differences on the issue to build their respective bases, the Hyde Amendment remained a rare area of agreement. Whether Republican or Democrat, mainstream policymakers would accept that taxpayers—that code word for "white men"—shouldn't have to pay for abortion.

"As you know there are many things in life that are not fair, that wealthy people can afford and poor people can't," President Jimmy Carter mused when asked about the ban in July 1977. "But I don't believe that the Federal Government should take action to try to make these opportunities exactly equal, particularly when there's a moral factor involved."[12]

More than thirty years later, President Obama would reaffirm the Hyde Amendment to ensure passage of his signature health-care law.

"We reiterated the status quo, and we're comfortable reiterating that status quo," a spokesperson said.[13]

The blame for the fact that Hyde became the status quo lay not only with politicians but also with leaders in the abortion rights movement who could have done more to defend Rosie.

That's why I was now approaching Frances Kissling with the same Miss Marple attitude that had guided me toward Paul Haring and Bob Bauman.

In the book she and Ellen Frankfort wrote about their investigation, Kissling criticized her peers in the pro-choice movement for failing to make more of a cause out of Rosie. "I was told over and over that people are not concerned about the death of one woman," she wrote.[14]

She would describe the arrest of Maria Pineda as an unpleasant and "sordid" last resort, writing, "It has never been my style to call on the police to solve any problem, let alone public health problems."[15]

Yet I found evidence that for at least a moment, she had reveled in this sordid and incomplete victory.

The news station WFAA had pulled the footage of the arrest out of a warehouse for me. I watched it, frame by frame. There was Frances Kissling, handing the bills to Diana Rivera; there were the police converging on the ramshackle house. In the final frame, the news anchor stood in front of the McAllen Police Department. As he signed off, a woman in a magenta shirt strode into the background of the frame. A willowy Ellen Frankfort followed, raising a camera. In the final moment before the screen turned black, Frances Kissling threw her arms into the air in a "v" for victory—the only one she could win for Rosie Jimenez.

"HOW NICE TO HEAR FROM YOU," Frances Kissling replied to my email in all caps. "OF COURSE YOU CAN INTERVIEW ME. PERHAPS YOU'D LIKE TO COME TO MEXICO WHERE I LIVE AND WORK PART TIME." She added in parentheses: "I THINK this is unlikely."[16]

"Frances Kissling invited me to Cuernavaca," I told my husband, pacing the kitchen that evening, "which seems totally insane; obviously, I'm not going to go, but I feel tempted." I explained that Kissling had run one of the first clinics to open in New York after the state legalized abortion in 1970, cofounded the National Abortion Federation, and later ran Catholics for Choice. She knew the movement's missteps and was willing to acknowledge them. Plus, Kissling had launched a second career as a listener who specialized in dialogue with abortion opponents, which meant she was skilled in the deep listening that I was trying to master.

"Did I tell you she entrapped the midwife who killed Rosie and had a

TV crew film it, like the weirdest episode of *Cops* you've ever seen?" I said, pacing like a madwoman. "And she's got this whole shtick now about how you should listen to your enemies and try to find the good in the position of the other."

My husband stared at me across the kitchen table.

"I think you should go," he said, because he could tell I wanted to go.

So I bought a plane ticket to Mexico City.

THE VICTIM

I brought the book *Rosie* with me on the plane. It seemed to contain all the messy contradictions of second-wave feminism in its 173 yellowed pages.

On the one hand, it's a vivid account of a woman's preventable death. On the other, it's a rollicking, self-involved tale of two white women and a blundering team of male CDC scientists quarreling over who should be first to interview Rosie's traumatized Latina friends.

A *New York Times* reviewer called the book "absorbing, poignant and sometimes maddening."[17]

Frankfort died by suicide in 1987, at the age of fifty. Her death occasioned four paragraphs in *The New York Times* that mentioned her five books, including *Vaginal Politics* and *Rosie*.[18] Her former partner, Wesley David Miller Jr., sent me an envelope with everything he had left of Frankfort's records on Rosie Jimenez.

Inside the papers smelled like mildew. They contained signs that prominent feminists had at least tried to make a cause out of Rosie: There was a photo of Gloria Steinem in *The New York Times* holding up a picture of Rosie at a NARAL news conference in January 1979 to commemorate the anniversary of *Roe*. Also speaking at the news conference that day were Ellen Frankfort, who announced the formation of a fund to help women like Rosie; and NARAL executive director Karen Mulhauser. According to a faded NARAL report I pulled from the envelope, Mulhauser was announcing NARAL's new "strategy of refocusing public attention on the ultimate goal of antichoice forces—criminalizing abortion under *every* circumstance via a constitutional amendment and/or a constitutional convention."[19]

Even as the movement remembered Rosie, it was pivoting to a bigger threat.

Frankfort had written a dizzyingly powerful first scene for the book.

"Did you or didn't you?" the doctor asked.

Rosie tried to respond, but it hurt too much. She lifted her arm toward her throat.

The account came from Rosie's friend Paulina Cardenas, whom Ellen calls Pauline. (Frankfort also anglicized Diana Rivera's name to Diane.)

It was hard to look at her. She was a dark greenish-brown and there was blood coming from her eyes. Pauline was surprised Rosie was still conscious. She had been in this state for six days and had survived two operations.

"Please let me die in peace," Rosie wrote on a piece of paper.

Pauline turned her head so Rosie would not see the tears.

When Rosie found out she was pregnant, and that Medicaid would no longer pay for abortion, she confided in a friend who told her she knew someone who could help—a midwife her mother had told her about. The friend, whom Frankfort called Evangelina, took Rosie to the lavender-trimmed house. In a room where a young boy slept, and a rug mounted on the wall depicted Jesus in psychedelic colors, Maria Pineda inserted a rubber tube into Rosie's cervix.

She was OK when she came out; she told Evangelina it hadn't hurt.

But the following evening, Rosie's boss was pounding on her neighbor Margie's door. Rosie was sick, he said. She needed a doctor. Margie rushed across the courtyard to Rosie's apartment. Her friend looked awful. The skin under her eyes was purple and she was in pain, pleading to be taken to the emergency room. A neighbor helped carry her out. On the way to the hospital, Rosie screamed in agony every time they drove over a bump. After dropping her off, Margie held on to Rosie's purse. Take good care of it, Rosie told her. It had her scholarship check in it.

"I heard on TV that the reason she went to have an abortion in Mexico was because she was embarrassed," Margie told Frankfort. "That's a bunch of bull. Just money. All the time it was just money."[20]

Money was a pressing concern—and not just for Rosie Jimenez.

When Karen Mulhauser took over as the executive director of NARAL in 1975, her predecessor, Bea Blair, told her the job would be a cinch. The group had only 7,000 members, but it didn't seem like it would have too much left to do.

"They thought at that time that things were pretty secured...and that there wasn't going to be that much challenge," Mulhauser told me.[21]

It was tempting to believe the issue was settled. Mulhauser had spent the years before *Roe* referring desperate women to safe providers through a confidential underground service. She herself had induced her own abortion with a knitting needle while in college. In a bus station afterward, she had passed out on the floor in a rush of blood. *Roe* was supposed to have put an end to all that horror.

But the women charged with defending *Roe* had underestimated the opposition.

By the late 1970s, the National Right to Life Committee claimed that it had 11 million members and 1,800 local chapters nationwide.[22] They held a minority view; in 1979 just 19 percent of people surveyed thought abortion should be illegal under all circumstances.[23] But they were stronger at mobilizing and by then, Mulhauser knew it. That year, she would tell *The Washington Post*: "We are not outnumbered. We are being out-organized."[24]

NARAL needed money to fight this better-organized adversary. So the organization turned to its intrepid fundraising consultant. Roger Craver was a long-haired former hippie, raised by a firebrand of a mother who once threatened to withhold sex from her husband if he didn't help her picket the post office over its exclusion of Black workers.

No picket, no pussy, she had declared at the dinner table, and her son Roger had learned how to make an irresistible pitch.[25]

He knew the Hyde Amendment was a problem.

He also saw it as an opportunity.

THE LEAD SUSPECT

Roger Craver is the father of the liberal nonprofit industrial complex. He helped progressive groups like Common Cause, Greenpeace, and the National Organization for Women (NOW) get off the ground by building a base of small donors. He did it by writing the perfect fundraising appeal with just the right mix of urgency and substance. Those mailings with "URGENT" on the front that you throw unopened into your recycling bin today were a new technology back then. They helped transform small outfits like NARAL into major professional operations. NARAL would go from a membership of 20,000 in early 1978[26] to 90,000 in 1980 and 140,000 in 1982.[27]

Craver's job was to help NARAL find a message that would make someone sit down at their kitchen table and write a check.

"Dear Friend: What you do in the next 10 minutes will help decide whether or not the story on the envelope becomes a reality," one fundraising letter drafted in 1977 read. The story on the envelope was a fake headline reporting that all abortions had been banned except to save the mother's life. The letter went on to invoke the real and "startling" Supreme Court decision permitting the Hyde Amendment to take effect, accusing abortion opponents of attacking "those women least able to defend themselves—the poor."[28]

As they raised money for NARAL, Craver, Mathews, Smith chose to "capitalize on the Hyde Amendment vote," as the firm put it in a memo.[29] NARAL mailings to donors denounced it as "the most appalling piece of special legislation in years."[30]

"Before the Hyde Amendment went into effect, hundreds of women turned to Medicaid every day for assistance in ending pregnancies," a 1978 mailing read. "Now they find that door closed. Please think of them—and the alternatives they are forced to face—when you write your check."[31]

The Hyde Amendment was a fundraising boon for NARAL.

But like each incremental cut to *Roe*, it wouldn't hold public attention for long.

THE LISTENER

Within seconds of meeting Frances Kissling, I realized that she had invited me to Mexico to argue with me.

We were standing in a high-rise in Mexico City where she had just finished a board meeting for Ipas, the organization that adopted the manual vacuum aspirator after passage of the Helms Amendment. She was wearing an outfit remarkably like the one she wore on the day of Maria Pineda's arrest—a pink linen shirt and flowing white pants. She looked smaller at eighty. Her blue eyes were merry, her hair thin and pale as cornsilk.

"You and I are going to have fun," she said with an impish smile, "because we probably disagree on fifty percent of issues."[32]

She seemed to relish the idea that we were about to fight, and with her wild ride of a book in my backpack, I was ready.

Before we got into the car to drive to her home in Cuernavaca, Kissling introduced me to the executive director of Ipas Latin America and the Caribbean, Maria Antonieta Alcalde Castro. Sitting around a table in the high-rise, we talked about how Mexico had been moving toward progress on abortion for twenty years while the United States moved in the opposite direction. A green bandanna tied onto Alcalde Castro's purse symbolized the "Green Wave" that had sent hundreds of thousands of women surging into the streets to demand decriminalization of abortion across Latin America. When I asked her to assess how the abortion rights movements in Mexico and the United States differed, she chose her words carefully.

"I feel that the US abortion movement is very branded—with all the respect I have for the organizations with big brands," she said.[33]

"In the US... it is hard, I think, for people to be pro-choice and disagree with Planned Parenthood for example," she added. In Mexico, the movement was far more decentralized. A centralized movement can be a strength, she noted. Big organizations like Planned Parenthood and the Center for Reproductive Rights could afford expensive lawsuits and political campaigns. And yet, it was the decentralized movement in Latin America that had succeeded in pressing historic change and making space for young people with radical visions. Meanwhile, in the North, we were being slowly defeated by a better-organized opposition.

Kissling and I said goodbye to Alcalde Castro and got into a car with an unsuspecting driver who was about to spend the next two hours inching through legendary Mexico City traffic on a Friday afternoon while listening to two white women fight about abortion.

This was not so unusual for Kissling, who never shied away from conflict. Raised the oldest of four children in a working-class Catholic family in Flushing, New York, she saw just one path that would keep her free of the duties of children and husband that had made her own mother miserable: She would become a nun. But she left the convent after nine months, deciding a life of spiritual devotion didn't suit her active mind.

"You know, we never wanted you," the Mother Superior told Kissling.

Perhaps it was Kissling's deep thinking the Mother sensed, the appetite for inquiry that would lead her to be dubbed a "philosopher of the pro-choice movement."[34] Or perhaps the Mother had seen a residue of the rage that ripped through Kissling at the age of twelve, when she learned that her mother was not allowed to take Communion in public, because she was divorced. Or perhaps it was that flair for the unexpected that would make Kissling the ideal president of Catholics for Choice, where she spent twenty-five years needling the Vatican with its own theology, haunting Catholic officials in the halls of the United Nations, proffering pro-choice interpretations of holy texts. She showed Catholic theology was less about what the Bible said than about who was reading it.

Kissling pulled her tiny feet in their pink sneakers up onto the car seat, and I pointed my recorder at her and asked: "Why listen?" Why listen to people we disagree with?

That question was about to become highly pertinent.

"The first reason to do it, and this is the simple reason, OK?" Kissling said animatedly, gesturing with her hands. "Is because if you don't understand them, you can't beat them. Period. It's just a practical reality. So that's all I'm going to say in the car." She laughed.

And then, suddenly, as Taylor Swift played on the radio, and the car crawled through highway traffic, she and I were screaming at each other. We were pulled like magnets to the issues we disagreed on, like third-trimester abortions, and whether it's acceptable to limit them; Kissling said it was. I wasn't so sure. The sun set over a slow-rolling exodus of PeMex tankers and battered pickup trucks, and we hurled explanations for the failure of the pro-choice movement across the backseat.

Kissling believed the movement failed because it was too extreme.

"If I'm being asked, why do I think the movement has failed? I think it has failed because it has only one message," she said.

Kissling's nuanced position on abortion has made her controversial within the pro-choice movement. She reaches for a philosophical complexity that the politics of abortion do not allow.

I felt my blood pressure rising as the car moved one-third of an inch forward. It's so *obvious*, I thought, that the movement failed because it was not bold *enough*. Apparently, I was lousy at hiding my disagreement. "I don't think that I have made well the points I have made, because they have had no impact on you whatsoever," she told me in frustration.

Neither of us was really listening.

"My whole coming of age, I've watched us give ground; I've only seen us lose," I told her, my voice rising.

Maybe *this* is why we've lost, I thought, because we've spent so much time *arguing with each other*.

The traffic cleared as we reached Cuernavaca.

Kissling pushed a button and a metal gate slid across a cobalt-blue stucco wall. I felt my face redden with embarrassment.

Where were my manners? I was here as *a guest*.

"Thank you," she called to the driver, noting that he had been getting an earful over the past two hours.

"It was great!" he said with a smile as he bid us farewell.

I tried to summon his accommodating spirit as I walked into Kissling's home, complimenting the artwork that seemed an homage to her career. I saw a cardboard mask of the pope's face with its towering white hat and a wire sculpture of a woman with a fetus in her womb. In the main room was a brightly painted table and four chairs featuring grim-faced cats and dogs playing poker: cats on one side, dogs on the other. Kissling flipped on the outdoor lights so I could see the two blue-tiled swimming pools that sloped down her backyard. Then she sat cross-legged on her couch, energized by battle, and we talked until after 11:00 p.m. We reached something like a détente, agreeing that perhaps it would be better if the movement had more than one strategy, if it was more decentralized, like the Mexican movement. She offered me water, gave me a hug, and reassured me: "I'm having fun."

I closed the sliding glass door to my room, surveyed the poster on the wall of a chubby nun with a stern face wielding a rosary, then listened to the stray dogs of Cuernavaca, barking and fighting, until I fell asleep.

The next day, Kissling suggested we go for a swim. Then she stripped naked beside the heated outdoor pool that sat at the bottom of a verdant slope behind the house. I didn't want to get naked in front of my suspect so I stayed in my underwear and a tank top.

The pool was sheltered by a rubber tree, whose copper-colored leaves floated on the surface of the water. We drifted in the pool, retrieving the leaves and setting them on the concrete edge.

"People see you the way they see you," she mused as her white breasts floated like bread on the surface of the water. She was talking about what makes a writer's description of a person "fair," but it was clear we were circling around a more specific question: How would I write about her? Would I include the details that confirmed my assumptions about white feminists of her generation, like how she allowed her Mexican driver to push the cart for her in the grocery store and carry the armfuls of pink and orange lilies she chose in the outdoor market?

"Biases are not bad and they're not necessarily wrong," she said thoughtfully, circling her arms through the water, "but you see the world in a certain way, and can you see others whom you are interviewing in *their* way, not yours?"

I turned the question back on her, because Ellen Frankfort had, at times, described Rosie's friends in profoundly unsympathetic terms.

"At exactly six o'clock the next evening, there is a knock at the door, announcing the appearance of a woman of surprisingly generous proportions on the patio," Frankfort wrote of Paulina Cardenas, who massaged Rosie's feet as she lay dying.

"Ellen was a good writer," Kissling said pensively when I read this passage aloud to her the next day in her living room.

"It is difficult to calculate the age of women whose appeal is not centered on their gender," I read. "Dressed in a comfortable rayon print dress and a navy sweater, Pauline holds her spacious body as if it were a canopy covering her toes which, in their pointed, low-heeled pumps, look tiny."

I looked up from the book at Kissling, who sat across from me on the white couch. The pink and orange lilies from the market stood nearby in two tall glass vases.

"I read that and I think about our conversation yesterday in the pool. What is fair? How is someone going to feel when they read it?"

"Do I think this would have bothered Pauline?" she said. "No."

"Really?" I asked, surprised. When I tried to picture Cardenas, based on this description, I saw a tent with toes.

Of Evangelina, the friend who took Rosie to the midwife who performed the fatal abortion, Frankfort wrote: "Her body has the pudginess of a prepubescent girl who is frequently called 'fatso.'"

"We'll see what you do," Kissling said, meaning—how would I describe *her* naked body when I sat down to write about this visit? "You've seen that I've reached the stage where there's crepey skin, things like that!" she added, raising her arm and shaking her bicep flab.

Kissling had more power to rebut my narrative than Rosie's friends had to rebut Frankfort's, she acknowledged. But Kissling defended the descriptions because, she said, they were true.

Soon we were hurtling toward our next disagreement: whether we should use gender-neutral language to include trans and nonbinary people who need abortions.

Kissling compared the people advocating for gender-inclusive language to the extreme gun-toting Freedom Caucus within the Republican Party.

"You sure you're going to do this, Frances?" I asked, clenching my jaw.

"Yeah," she said matter-of-factly.

My hands began to sweat as she described how our movement was "killing each other and criticizing each other to death."

"I don't hear anyone saying, 'Never use the word "woman"'!" I yelled.

"Well then you're *deaf*," she hissed.

We were shouting again.

Then Kissling began to describe me to myself.

"You are now a barrier to me," she said, raising her arms in front of herself as if she were pulling up a screen. "I am now the enemy; I am now not politically correct—"

"I *hate* the term 'politically correct,'" I interrupted.

"Shhhh!" Kissling said, like I was a child. "Are you going to listen to me or not? Because this is the only way that change really happens!"

"I'm listening," I huffed in a way that showed I wasn't.

I folded my arms over my chest and glared.

"Your face is bad!" she shrieked.

"I'm angry!"

"Why are you angry?" she asked, catching me off guard.

Then, she listened.

So I told her. How I was just at a major gathering of Christian conservatives where they spent the entire weekend talking about how to retrain the playbook they used to kill *Roe* on transgender people.

She leaned toward me, saying, "Yes, yes," and I noticed my shoulders had dropped down from my ears.

I thought I was good at listening. As a journalist, I listen for a living, often to people with whom I disagree. Around abortion opponents, I never let my face get bad. But listening to people with whom you disagree is easy compared to listening to people with whom you *almost* agree.

Sitting in Kissling's living room I realized that's because those with whom you *almost* agree pose a threat to your worldview. There was little chance Paul Haring would convert me. But when I could unclench my jaw and listen to Kissling, I began to question my own assumptions. That was a good thing. Assumptions are a mystery writer's most reliable way of tricking readers into guessing the wrong culprit. We assume the meek and devoted wife couldn't *possibly* have murdered her husband, or that the sinister gold digger is *far* too obvious. Always, our assumptions are proved wrong in the end. And always, that's the best part.

Kissling taught me to be a better listener. But in another plot twist, it turned out that listening to her would lead me to yet another false assumption in my investigation.

"We were a white, middle- to upper-class movement. That's the reality," she said as the sky darkened in the evening on our second night together. We were sitting around a glass table on the patio outside her bedroom, surrounded by greenery. The branches of a tapachine tree encircled us, laden with forearm-sized pods like giant green beans. Kissling wore a pair of black-rimmed glasses and a red-and-black kaftan. She propped her feet up on a chair and sipped from a sugar-free Coke.

It was time to talk about Rosie's second death.

"There were decisions that needed to be made about what were we going to focus on," Kissling said, "and the decision was, we were going to focus on the risk of a constitutional amendment banning abortion. We were not going to focus on the Hyde Amendment. And the principal person responsible for that messaging decision was Roger Craver, from Craver, Mathews, Smith."

I was caught off guard by the simplicity of this answer.

I had expected Kissling to unmask more than one villain. What about all the leaders of abortion rights organizations that she complained about in her book?

"What Roger told the movement was that people care about the constitutional amendment because it might affect their daughter," Kissling said. "If abortion is banned, then my nice white daughter is not going to be able to get an abortion, and I don't want that to happen."

Kissling never heard Craver say these words, she acknowledged; she heard about his directive secondhand. But it was the most concrete tip I had. So, when I got back to Massachusetts, I spent hours sleuthing through NARAL archives from the 1970s, looking for evidence of a conscious decision to abandon Rosie Jimenez. One day, I found a typewritten memo from 1978 that felt like the closest thing I had to a smoking gun.

It was a note from Robert Smith, Craver's partner at the fundraising firm Craver, Mathews, Smith. He boasted about how NARAL had "the hottest direct mail program in the liberal nonprofit sector." But he warned things were starting to cool.

"We're beginning to see some indications that the great days of growth may be temporarily stalled," Smith cautioned. "We need to push hard in developing a new institutional package for NARAL and it is our judgment it has to be something other than one strictly revolving around the economic issues involved. We need to continue to brainstorm on the question of where will this issue go after the stalemate, which primarily involves the deprivation of rights for the poor."[35]

When I ask Roger Craver about this memo later, he will confirm what I feel in my gut—that moving on from Rosie wasn't the work of one person. But as I sat with Kissling on her porch in Cuernavaca, I let myself believe for a moment that I had solved the mystery.

The sun set as the sound of birdsong mixed with traffic on the busy street outside the metal gate. Somewhere in the distance, church bells rang.

"None of the national organizations maintaining abortion rights (National Abortion Rights Action League, Religious Coalition for Abortion Rights) took any action to bring Rosie's story to the public or to help her orphaned daughter," Kissling wrote in the afterword to *Rosie* in 1978.

"It didn't matter," she told me, "that this person died."

Kissling got up and walked over to the wall to flip on the outdoor light. The sky was dark. Night insects buzzed.

"The question now would be," she said, "has that changed very much?"

CHAPTER 5

THE ACCOMPLICES

> The simplest explanation is always the most likely.
> —*The Mysterious Affair at Styles* by Agatha Christie

AFTER MY VISIT WITH FRANCES KISSLING, ROGER CRAVER WAS MY LEAD suspect in Rosie's second death. It was easy at first to assume that a white man was responsible for the mainstream abortion rights movement's decision to shift its political strategy away from defending poor women. It was a story Miss Marple would have appreciated: A simple explanation is often the most likely, at least in a mystery novel when, quite often, the killer acts alone. Kissling's account validated everything I already suspected about white men being the cause of most historical wrongs. Plus, I already had a hero in this story: Faye Wattleton, the first Black woman to lead Planned Parenthood. I knew from her memoir *Life on the Line* that she had taken a strong stand against the Hyde Amendment in 1978—and faced a fierce backlash from within her own organization that would culminate in an effort to oust her from leadership.[1]

But by the time I confronted Craver on a chilly winter day in a tavern on the water with an atmosphere befitting a mystery novel, I was starting to feel like that famous meme from *It's Always Sunny in Philadelphia*; I was the caffeinated lunatic with purple bags under my eyes, looking at an unintelligible map of suspects, whispering: "They're all in on it." This was of course the plot of Agatha Christie's *Murder on the Orient Express*, and as I investigated the second death of Rosie Jimenez, I was starting to feel like I was living in that novel.

Before long, *everyone* was looking guilty.

THE LEAD SUSPECT

I could not have picked a more dismal day to visit Martha's Vineyard, where Roger Craver was living the stereotype of the East Coast elite. In summertime the island bustles with well-to-do beachgoers drawn to its teal waters and ornate gingerbread-like houses. The island's "well-scrubbed little towns" are "clad in the unmistakable livery of righteous success," the author Thomas Frank wrote in his book *Listen, Liberal*, where he described the island as the hub of the elite meritocratic tendencies that have made the Democratic Party an accomplice in America's deepening inequality.[2] The island is the unofficial headquarters of the liberal ruling class—so much a symbol of liberal smugness that Florida Governor Ron DeSantis shipped a contingent of fifty Venezuelan asylum seekers there in 2022; the community, true to its progressive reputation, donated supplies and welcomed them.[3] The Clintons and Obamas vacationed here. The attorney Alan Dershowitz, who defended Trump and the convicted sex offender Jeffrey Epstein, has periodically reminded the nation of Martha's Vineyard's liberal credentials by complaining of being shunned from cocktail parties or denied pierogis at the farmers' market.[4]

As I sat in a booth on a mostly empty ferry on this freezing January day, I felt as if I was about to confront not just a person, but a phenomenon: the role of the liberal donor class in shaping social movements.

Craver didn't know he was a suspect yet. He had been gracious when I told him about my investigation, emailing me a four-page memo titled, "Some Interviewee Suggestions," with a list of top activists he had met over the years as he helped build the liberal nonprofit industrial complex—people like Faye Wattleton, with whom he erected a grassroots fundraising infrastructure for Planned Parenthood. But at some point I was going to have to confront him with Kissling's allegation.

I reminded myself of my Agatha Christie motto, the one I'd used to understand Bob Packwood: Good people can be bad and bad people can be good.

Speaking of bad guys, to distract myself, I opened a book by Craver's nemesis, Richard Viguerie. Craver and Viguerie were the political tech bros of their day. In a 1982 newspaper photo about their new cutting-edge strategy, Viguerie and Craver stood beside each other—Viguerie prematurely bald, dome-headed, squinting in the sun like a vampire, and Craver, curly-haired, looking like a hippie even in a suit.[5] For decades, these two men undid each other's work. Viguerie built the conservative movement and Craver built up liberal nonprofits, using the same new technology: sending people mail, asking for money.

Somehow, they managed to be friendly with each other the entire time.[6]

The ferry docked and I walked off the boat in the rain. Craver greeted me warmly and I followed him to the Black Dog Tavern, which was mostly empty this time of year. We grabbed a table near the gas fireplace. Craver was neatly dressed in a dark sweater and sturdy black shoes.

He began telling me about how it all started in the late 1960s with a call from John Gardner, who had just quit his job as Johnson's secretary of health, education, and welfare in protest of the Vietnam War. Gardner was sick of raising money from corporations and foundations that had a way of steering an organization's agenda toward the status quo. He came up with an idea most people thought would fail. He wanted to raise money using small donations from regular people. Gardner's advisors pointed him to the one guy they thought might be willing to help—a hippie named Roger Craver who had cut his teeth on the civil rights movement and didn't have a wife or kids yet, and so might be willing to do something stupid.

"I have to figure out a way to get $5 million from individual citizens in $15 increments," Gardner told Craver.

"I said, 'Well, no, John, no one's done that,'" Craver recalled with a gap-toothed smile. "'Well,' Gardner said, 'that's why people tell me you're crazy enough to do it.'"

So Craver racked his brain. To pull this off he would need an enormous quantity of mailing addresses for people who sympathized with liberal causes. But where would he get them? He determined that the mother lode lay in the Library of Congress, which kept archives of newsletters geared toward people with interests in causes like the environment. Craver, who had "hair down to his ass," as he put it, and a wardrobe consisting mostly of shaggy denim shirts and beads, needed someone who looked more trustworthy than he did—someone who could convince these newsletter editors to fork over their mailing lists.

"I'll have someone here tomorrow," Gardner told him.

The next morning, when Craver got to work, a tall, solemn man in a gray suit was waiting. He was the former US consul general in Jerusalem, Evan Wilson, who, according to Craver, promptly dispatched ten foreign service officers to the newsletter editors and to leaders of civic organizations and persuaded them to cough up their mailing lists.

Together, Craver and Gardner used those names to build Common Cause, a pro-democracy organization that was soon doing what everyone thought was impossible—raising its budget through small donations from regular people. Craver used the same model to help organizations like Greenpeace and NOW get off the ground. That is the story of how all your favorite nonprofits were born.

Craver took out his reading glasses and examined the menu. He had just been describing how he spoke at the ninetieth birthday party for his direct mail nemesis, Richard Viguerie, who had given all the attendees a copy of his book about how conservatives should eat healthy to outlive liberals. While Craver surveyed the menu, I read him a passage from another of Viguerie's books that scared me half to death: "'I still work/focus twelve to thirteen hours a day, five and a half days a week (never on Sunday).'"[7]

Craver let out a staccato chuckle.

"I do the same thing," he admitted.

I was relieved to hear it.

"One thing I will say for Viguerie, he does believe in what he does," Craver added as the waitress came to take our orders.

While we waited for our food, we talked about how NARAL became one of Craver's first clients in the early 1970s. On NARAL's behalf, he began writing four-page letters that raised money while shaping how people thought about abortion—like the mailing from 1977 with the fake news clipping on the envelope that read "Abortions Banned in USA Except to Save Mother's Life." Inside, the letter warned that while that story was "made up to show what may happen," this reality had already arrived for poor women subject to the Hyde Amendment.[8]

Almost everyone would throw this sort of mail in the trash, just like we do today, but those who did read the letters tended to be "highly educated" and "committed to the cause," Craver noted, which meant they might donate small amounts regularly their whole lives—something he and Viguerie referred to with the marketing term "lifetime value." The key was to keep hold of these most committed donors. In fact, Craver had a clear image of this ideal donor: She was a white woman, in her sixties, well-educated, who liked to read, and wore natural fibers rather than polyester.

"It was my mother," he told me.

The waitress set down our salads and Craver lit up as he talked about his mom and his upbringing in Gettysburg, Pennsylvania.

"Every Saturday morning, the three of us, my mother, my brother, and I, would picket the Adams County hospital, which was beside our house, because they would not admit migrant farmworkers," Craver told me. One day his mother decided they would all picket the post office to demand the organization hire Black workers. When her husband, who ran a business in town, protested that it would alienate his customers, she gave him that perfect pitch: No picket, no pussy.

It got better.

She wrote her sons a letter every day. Sometimes she scribbled notes in the margins or left a ring-shaped coffee stain on the paper. Later, when he became the direct mail master of the Left, Craver would copy these flourishes from his mom's letters, creating scribbles in the margins and consulting with an artist to get the right Pantone shade for a coffee stain, so that it looked like the mailing had just come out from under a mug on Karen Mulhauser's or Faye Wattleton's desk.

And when Craver wrote his pleas for money for groups like NARAL, he would always fax them to his mother for her approval.

I pulled from the archives the memos I found between Craver's firm and NARAL's leaders—the ones that referred to the need to start moving on from the Hyde Amendment.

I read aloud from a memo dated July 1, 1977, when his firm wrote: "While I believe our decision to capitalize on the Hyde Amendment vote was sound, it is our recommendation that you use the next six months to set in place some fundamental membership systems."[9]

"Right," Craver said between bites. "One of the things I learned very quickly is that people will move on from one issue to another...'OK. We've dealt with the fire of the Hyde Amendment. Now let's hold on to these people.'"

The key for holding on to people was to focus their outrage on a clear enemy who was always on the verge of a major victory. Craver added: "As long as I could find a devil to write about, that's all I needed."

Antiabortion activists were exceptionally compelling devils, especially after they began burning down clinics in the late 1970s. Despite the strong fundraising returns from mail about these burnings, Craver's colleague Rob Smith had issued a warning to NARAL.

Seated in the tavern, I read Smith's smoking gun message aloud to Craver: "Unless we develop a dramatically new approach where the issue breaks out of its current stalemate, the size of NARAL's membership may stabilize by the end of 1978," Smith warned. "In the near future, we need to push hard in developing a new institutional package for NARAL. And it is our judgment, it has to be something other than one strictly revolving around the economic issues involved. We need to continue to brainstorm on the question of where will this issue go after the stalemate, which primarily involves the deprivation of rights for the poor."[10]

Craver's expression didn't change.

"These movements rise and fall on current events," he said, moving his hand up and down in a wave motion. "What Rob is saying there is...we have to institutionalize this in the sense of making these members feel like they're responsible for an institution, not just taking care of an issue here and an issue there."

I told him what Frances Kissling had claimed.

"She told me that there was a moment when you advised the pro-choice leaders that they needed to move on from the Hyde Amendment."

"I probably did," Craver said, sitting forward in his chair. "Because one of the things I've always tried to do is to institutionalize—in the best sense of the word—make permanent, these movements; otherwise, they're just like parades."

"And would it have been because you thought people don't care about poor women?" I asked.

"No, no," Craver said, horrified. "It was either because the issue was starting to die down and we needed to find something else or become more institutional, or it was because it wasn't in the cards politically. It was just so far out of reach it wouldn't be believable.

"The whole Medicaid thing was important to me," he added.

I pressed him. "Her recollection of it was that—and probably the common wisdom of the time—but that your advice was: 'You gotta get to what people care about, and it's their own daughter, it's not some poor person on Medicaid.'"

"That would be unlike me," Craver said. "I would be unlikely to say that."

I believed him. The records showed his message was less about a disregard for poor women than a desire to cultivate the loyalty of donors, who might enjoy the idea of saving poor women but who ultimately wanted to feel they were in a long-haul fight against the devil. These donors needed new material to stoke their outrage and keep their interest. Indeed, in 1980, when the Supreme Court upheld the Hyde Amendment, Craver's firm would once again work with NARAL to "capitalize on the anger over the Supreme Court's decision."[11]

Progressive critics use the term "nonprofit industrial complex" to describe the way nonprofits can unintentionally serve as oppressive arms of the state because they're beholden to the interests of the government and wealthy donors.[12] Those donors might be billionaires like the ones who lived here on Martha's Vineyard and avoided paying taxes by giving to causes that satisfied their conscience without dismantling the unequal system that had enriched them. Or they might be white women in natural fibers who needed a new outrage every now and then to keep their interest. Craver's model democratized the funding landscape by bringing in small donors rather than just the foundations backed by ultrawealthy people that have a history of steering social movements away from radical agendas.[13] That allowed groups that relied on small donors, like the National Organization for Women, to take a more fighting stand against the status quo. Terry O'Neill, a former president of NOW, told me she could be more outspoken because NOW was funded through average donations of $27. Major women's groups could lose millions if they angered a donor, O'Neill said, whereas, "if I piss off a donor, I've lost twenty-seven dollars."[14]

But catering to the conscience of even small donors like Craver's mom could bring its own more subtle pull toward *their* interests.

The direct mail model Craver pioneered had helped bring significant money into the abortion rights movement, allowing groups like NARAL to transform from shoestring operations into professional outfits. The movement's power and money consolidated in the hands of a few major nonprofits that tended to be led by white people. On the one hand, this branded model would help organizations like NARAL grow in their ability to influence elections. On the other hand, it disadvantaged groups that could not afford to hire fundraising consultants, and it created a transactional model of organizing, where donors might see their monthly contribution as their primary form of activism. Today this transactional model has evolved into a rapid-fire digital form that tends to annoy the masses rather than mobilize them.

Craver made money off the technology he developed for nonprofits, as his life on Martha's Vineyard showed. But one story he told convinced me he was a true believer, too. Craver had been horrified when Biden, as chair of the Senate Judiciary Committee in 1991, rammed through the confirmation of Supreme Court Justice Clarence Thomas after Anita Hill testified that Thomas had sexually harassed her. Biden aggressively questioned Hill and refused to call witnesses who might have corroborated her story, ensuring the confirmation to the Supreme Court of a man who, three decades later, was part of the majority that would kill *Roe*. In protest, Craver quit fundraising for the Democratic Senatorial Campaign Committee.[15]

Craver was a skilled political opportunist, to be sure. But like Paul Haring on the opposite end of the political spectrum, he had been taught by his mother to believe in a certain set of nonnegotiable values.

I was stupid, I thought, as I raced across the parking lot to catch the ferry, *to think that the decision to abandon Rosie was the work of one man*. Of course it was more complicated. The way Craver described his thinking made it clear that he was *responding* to the priorities of donors like his mom—older white women with money to spare; if he believed the Hyde Amendment had become a losing issue for this demographic, then these donors shared the blame. And what about the women leading the organizations that Craver was advising?

I needed to ask another person, the closest thing I had to a heroine in this story. So I scheduled a meeting with Faye Wattleton.

In 1978, Wattleton's selection as the thirty-four-year-old president of Planned Parenthood Federation of America sparked a media sensation. She was the first woman to lead the organization since its founder, Margaret Sanger, and the first Black person to lead it, ever. For all its liberal reputation today, Planned Parenthood was once a cause championed by stodgy white men, including Republicans like Prescott Bush, father and grandfather of the two Presidents Bush, who was treasurer of Planned Parenthood's first major campaign in 1947. These men were focused on distributing contraception, something Sanger championed with arguments that were sometimes feminist and sometimes eugenic and racist, in line with the eugenic and racist views of her time. Wattleton's appointment seemed a clear rebuke of this early racism—although, as she was to discover, plenty of people who worked at the organization still harbored it.

"Planned Parenthood's New Head Takes a Fighting Stand," *The New York Times* headline read in February 1978, next to a picture of Wattleton looking tall, thin, and movie-star beautiful. Wattleton had announced that Planned Parenthood would be playing a more aggressive role in the fight for reproductive rights. She outlined three top goals, the first of which was to restore abortion access to the poor under Medicaid.[16]

Her message caused an internal firestorm at Planned Parenthood, Wattleton would later write in her memoir, including among leaders of an affiliate in Texas, who objected to the mere mention of abortion, which less than a fifth of the organization's affiliates provided at the time.[17]

"Abortion may be OK in New York, but abortion doesn't play well in our town," the Texans told her.[18]

Wattleton was taken aback.

But she would later tell me she wondered if framing the Hyde Amendment as more than just an assault on poor women would have made her position harder to dismiss.

"To be perfectly candid with you, over time, I have even thought if I had to do it again I probably would have framed it differently," Wattleton told me during a phone call in the summer of 2025. "I probably would have put it in the context of: This is an assault on all women, and this is where it's starting."[19]

That wider framing is what she used in her memoir in the 1990s.

"I felt that if we didn't secure the right to abortion for the most vulnerable women with the immediate reversal of Hyde, the ability of *all* women to exercise their reproductive decisions, including abortion, would be put in jeopardy," Wattleton wrote.[20]

The daughter of a traveling Evangelical preacher who decried fornication and a father who chauffeured her pastoring mother through the Jim Crow South as God demanded, Wattleton was born in 1943, six years after Paul Haring, and raised on the opposite side of the racial divide. Wattleton's father devised a daring test he performed every time they gassed up their car: He would ask the attendant if they had a bathroom for "coloreds." Once, the attendant said yes, but a young, gangly Faye ran behind the gas station only to find a pit in the ground. Her father drove away without the gas shouting at the attendant: "We're not dogs!"

Wattleton's mother had her own way of defying racism.

"If you can't come under the tent to worship with us because of the color of our skin, I know one thing we can do together, we can all roast in hell for your not doing it," she once preached before a Black congregation in the tiny Louisiana town of Oak Grove, addressing the white people who had gathered around the outskirts of the tent to listen in. Wattleton's father hightailed it out of there, fearful he'd be lynched if he stuck around.[21]

Reverend Wattleton had memorized the Bible and took it literally. She believed women should wear skirts, never pants. Her daughter didn't quite fit her ideal; Faye Wattleton trained as a nurse, became the leader of Planned Parenthood in Dayton, Ohio, and then president of the national organization. She also became famous as a beautiful socialite who graced the cover of *Essence* and *Working Woman* magazines. Once a reporter asked Reverend Wattleton which of her daughter's accomplishments made her the most proud.

"She keeps an immaculate house," Wattleton would remember her mother saying. "I could eat off her floors."

Her mother's call to preach led her to leave her daughter for stretches of time in the hands of fellow Church of God members. One temporary guardian locked Wattleton in a small room all day, beat her, and stuck a bar of soap in her mouth when she suspected her of misbehavior.

Faye Wattleton is made of steel, I thought when I read that passage in preparation for our interview.

The only problem was that in the pro-choice archives, I had come across a document that clouded my image of this steely heroine. Much as I hated to admit it, Wattleton, too, had become a suspect.

On a sunny day in early spring, Wattleton and I sat on the patio at an Upper West Side restaurant near the home on Central Park West where she has lived for forty years. The patio was halfway in the street, decorated with planters full of red and white geraniums. Behind her, taxis rushed by on Columbus Avenue. She was dressed in a colorful polka-dot shirt with a pink linen button-down over it. She was glamorous, perfectly coiffed, and long-lashed.

We chatted about the remarkable arc of her eighty-year lifetime, book-ended by her great-grandmother Mariah, who was born to an enslaved mother in Mississippi, and her own daughter, Felicia, an attorney who graduated from Harvard.

We opened our menus and ordered salads; Wattleton requested shrimp, no dressing. She told me she still attends church, one without the hellfire of her mother's, and that she still believes in an abiding principle learned from her work as a nurse: that poor people deserve care.

Not everyone within Planned Parenthood shared her vision when she was hired.

"This was not an organization that was magnanimously stepping up to 'We want diversity,'" Wattleton said. "This was a white organization, a good portion of which did not want the organization to be involved with abortion at all."[22]

Nor did much of the leadership want the organization involved in politics, which is hard to imagine today, when Planned Parenthood is a major political player that can spend $50 million in a single election cycle. Wattleton commissioned a report from a political analyst named David Garth, who implored Planned Parenthood to move into politics in early 1979.

"What David said was we had to build a structure that would punish our enemies and reward our friends," Wattleton told me.

Their opposition was way ahead in that respect.

"The right-to-life movement is already strong—and growing stronger," Garth warned. "In essence, they are seeking to become an institutionalized political force... [*Planned Parenthood Federation of America*] is not."

Garth warned Planned Parenthood's leaders they were relying too heavily on the courts rather than charting their own vision for the future.

"The Supreme Court decision did more than just legalize abortion,"

Wattleton recalled him saying. "It neutralized you, it robbed you of your rallying cry, your most provocative issue, your activist identity."

But instead of listening to Garth, Wattleton recalled, members of Planned Parenthood's board rebuked him for suggesting the organization get involved in politics. A task force created by the board recommended the organization focus on public relations and litigation.[23] Their opposition seemed to have no such qualms about politics. In 1980, the antiabortion movement would help elect Ronald Reagan as the "first pro-life president."

After the disastrous meeting with Planned Parenthood's board, Garth asked Wattleton to come to his office. He had a word of advice. "I'll never forget," Wattleton told me. "He said, 'The only way that you're going to be successful and to survive these people is this: The camera loves you and you must insulate yourself from them by your public image.'"

Wattleton followed this advice. She hired a makeup artist and trained in public speaking. She traveled constantly for speeches and TV appearances. Her social life was covered in society columns. *The Washington Post* would declare her and legendary reporter Carl Bernstein a "ubiquitous couple" when they dated.[24] Strangers would send her love letters. "I am six feet two inches, Caucasian, and single," one man wrote, appending his phone number, after reading a profile of Wattleton in *Time* magazine.[25] Such missives weren't unusual. In fact, sometimes they came from none other than Senator Bob Packwood, who sent Wattleton what she called "overly complimentary" letters about how beautiful she was. She told her secretary to throw them away.

"Bob Packwood is somebody that was a true stalwart supporter and leader and advocate," Wattleton told me.

"And?" I pressed.

"They're men," she said matter-of-factly. "They're not gods."[26]

Even the father of the Hyde Amendment would shoot his shot. Once, when Wattleton and Henry Hyde were locked in a fierce debate on *Donahue*, Hyde made a pass at her during the break.

I covered my face with my napkin when Wattleton told me this.

"He made *passes* at you?" I asked.

"What about this don't you understand?" Wattleton replied, poised and effortlessly withering.

"You're not the first person that's told me Henry Hyde was a creep," I said, recalling Margaret Goodman's story about the ass-grabbing. "This is like a MeToo scandal that's many decades old."

"It's only scandalous because of what he did, because he was *not* attractive," Wattleton said, like she was reading me the latest tennis scores. In that moment, right there on Columbus Avenue, over two plates of salad, Henry Hyde died his second death—the death that happened when the woman who had dedicated her life to reversing his legacy dismissed him as so wildly beneath her regard that his attempt to bed her was not even worthy of scandal.

"Do you think that we could make an arrangement to meet in Hawaii sometime?" Wattleton recalled Hyde asking her during the commercial break before they resumed destroying each other on TV.

Wattleton told him to leave her alone or she was going to have him removed from the set.

She and I had moved on to pistachio gelato in delicate glass goblets when I took out the papers I had found in the archives. I was so nervous that I kept spilling green droplets onto the white tablecloth, and Wattleton kept pointing this out with restrained disapproval.

On January 14, 1981, six days before Reagan was inaugurated, Wattleton and fellow pro-choice leaders gathered for a meeting. The gathering was convened by Frank Susman, an attorney involved in what had, until recently, been the most promising avenue for defeating the Hyde Amendment—the battle to reverse it in court, which ended with defeat in 1980. Rhonda Copelon, the attorney who argued the losing case before the Supreme Court, never recovered from that loss; she would spend the rest of her life begging people to repeal the Hyde Amendment, her friend the feminist scholar Rosalind Petchesky told me.[27]

Copelon had stood before the Supreme Court while Henry Hyde sat in the front row watching. She argued that the Hyde Amendment represented an unconstitutional imposition of Catholic belief on Medicaid patients.[28]

But a majority of the all-male Supreme Court disagreed, ruling in *Harris v. McRae* that the constitutional right to abortion did not include an "entitlement" to the money needed to pay for that abortion. Poverty, in this logic, was a problem of the individual person's own making, and not the government's responsibility to fix.

Six months later, Republican members of Congress were reviving the idea of a Human Life Amendment to the Constitution that would ban all abortions. The incoming president had endorsed the idea. I tried to picture these advocates—most of them white—gathered around a table on a mid-January day, perhaps decked out in shoulder pads and perms: Karen Mulhauser, executive director of NARAL, and Janet Benshoof, the late, legendary pro-choice attorney. The group identified "four areas in which it wanted to direct further discussion," one of which was: "Poor Women."

"The discussion of poor women produced agreement that this issue must be kept alive but that the larger issue of the Human Life Amendment must take precedence for the time being," the notes read.[29]

It was right there, in black and white, the movement's decision to deprioritize the Hyde Amendment and allow the second death of Rosie Jimenez. The trouble was, Faye Wattleton was part of it.

"Faye expressed a belief that the Medicaid issue is a separate phenomenon. It was a bellwether issue, she said, regarding people's feelings about the poor, public funding, etc. She thinks it best now to hold on to established ground."

I read that part aloud to Wattleton and watched her face for a reaction. She flashed a smile.

"That sounds very smart!" she said. "What else do you want me to tell you?"

She must have misunderstood.

"You can't prioritize people's lives," she added. "You have to fight on all fronts."

"But you're saying here the focus should be on *holding on to established ground*," I said.

"Right, and our established ground was Medicaid funding."

Wrong. The Supreme Court had just upheld the Hyde Amendment.

"Then I don't know why—I would have to go back and rethink that," Wattleton said. "Because I always felt that we fought on all fronts."

"Read that again," she said, and I handed her the paper. She read it, then paused for a moment, reflecting.

"It may have been that I felt strategically we had to fight back on the Human Life Amendment," she said, "but my thinking would never have been one or the other.

"I would never have walked away from Medicaid," she insisted.

But the movement didn't have much of a choice. They had lost the judicial fight against the Hyde Amendment the year before. And now, they were facing a direct threat to *Roe*.

"I don't think we ever completely gave up on Hyde," Wattleton told me when I pressed her on the question later over the phone. "My view would have been: 'Hey, we really are now confronting an even more fundamental challenge.'"

Wattleton was a nurse by training, after all. She knew how to triage: You always dealt with the deadliest threat first.

I asked her about Roger Craver, whom she had hired to do direct mail fundraising for Planned Parenthood, and Kissling's assertion that he was the one who steered the movement away from Hyde.

"Is that something you ever heard from him?" I asked.

"He wouldn't dare say that to me."

"He seems like a very principled person."

"Yeah, but he probably has his biases, and that may have been what he thought. In retrospect, that wasn't so smart now, was it?" she said. "We could have made—perhaps with a different strategy—a beachhead over Medicaid and slowed down their progress.

"I certainly didn't abandon Medicaid," she added.

But I found a more complicated picture in the Planned Parenthood archives. The year after Wattleton became president, a backgrounder on her produced by the organization made prominent mention of the thirty-five-year-old's focus on meeting the unmet family planning needs of people who couldn't afford them and ensuring access to abortion services for all women, regardless of their ability to pay.[30] Another backgrounder from two years later listed a different set of priorities: "to insure funding for the nation's family planning and reproductive research program," and to defeat an antiabortion constitutional amendment.[31] There was no mention in that document of abortion access for the poor. The backgrounders were of course just one small clue to Wattleton's motives. But they reflected the shifting political realities of the time. Her values might not have changed. But the odds against her did. She was fighting not just a hostile federal government but her own board members and donors—for whom restoring Medicaid funding wasn't necessarily a priority.

"I can attest that by and large, donors, board members, people on the street—they were all like, 'Well, you know, funding, that's a different thing; that's different from having a policy that says abortion is legal,'" Gloria Feldt, who served as president of Planned Parenthood from 1996 to 2005, told me.[32]

Wattleton would keep speaking about how abortion restrictions hurt poor women. In 1989, after the Supreme Court in *Webster v. Reproductive Health Services* upheld a Missouri law banning public employees and facilities from being used to perform or assist in most abortions, she stood outside the court and declared: "This Supreme Court decision once more slaps poor women in the face." As Wattleton answered a reporter's question, the president of the National Right to Life Committee, John Willke, shoved her aside so he could speak.[33]

Under Wattleton's leadership, Planned Parenthood would get more political, but its messaging was always shaped by the fact that it was a health-care provider that relied on federal funding for services like contraception. Under Reagan, that funding came under threat, even as clinics were under literal fire by antiabortion extremists. Despite Wattleton's pleas, the Reagan administration had little interest in doing anything about these bombings.[34]

The January 1981 meeting was far from the only time pro-choice leaders would revisit the issue of Medicaid funding. In fact, a month later, at a meeting from which Wattleton was absent, the leaders talked about ways to restore public funding of abortion in states where it seemed feasible.[35]

NARAL's Mulhauser, meanwhile, was facing her own uphill battle to get her organization to recognize the importance of this state fight. She wanted to prioritize NARAL's state chapters. But her board wanted her to prioritize lobbying in DC.

"They said, 'We should be hiring people as lobbyists, not in the states,'" Mulhauser told me.[36] When she refused to fire her organizers and hire lobbyists instead, she told me, the board fired Mulhauser in 1982. One of the board members who made the decision was Bob McCoy, who had propositioned Mulhauser and been soundly rejected.[37] By the 1990s, NARAL was devoting so few resources to its state affiliates that the national field department quit in protest.[38]

Like Wattleton, Mulhauser insisted that she never gave up on the Hyde Amendment either; in fact, in 1979 she had testified against renewal of the ban by sharing her own story of being raped at gunpoint in her DC home while her two-and-a-half-year-old son slept.

In powerful testimony, she took aim at members of Congress who opposed the Hyde Amendment's rape exception.

"There are many Members of Congress who claim that the present restrictions on the Hyde amendment are not enough, that the rape clause is a loophole which allows anyone who wants an abortion to claim she was raped," Mulhauser declared. "Such unconscionable statements by elected officials reflect the insensitivity in Congress to rape victims in general and a complete disregard for the integrity of women."[39]

Mulhauser's horrific ordeal became part of a strategy that the abortion rights movement would use repeatedly in the 1980s and beyond: making the issue of abortion more sympathetic by making it about something broader. If Republicans defending the Hyde Amendment wanted to make the issue about "taxes," feminists who promoted stories like Mulhauser's would make their cause more sympathetic by connecting it to crimes against women.[40] Her story generated sympathy among supporters and cruelty from abortion opponents like Paul Brown, who denied that Mulhauser could have been raped: "Well, let me tell you, Karen is not the most beautiful creature in the world, so when I hear her say she was raped, my response is 'You wish.'"[41]

Groups like Brown's American Life Lobby kept alive the threat of a constitutional ban on abortion until 1983, when the last major attempt at it failed.

The following year would bring the passage of a state law that would result in another dead young woman. She was a teenage girl named Becky Bell who needed an abortion and didn't want to tell her parents. Because of a 1984 law in Indiana, one of the incremental state-level cuts to abortion access, she couldn't get an abortion without parental permission, so she sought an unsafe one instead. She developed pneumonia from a massive infection and died at the age of seventeen. Her parents would dedicate themselves to fighting parental consent laws. But just as had happened with the Hyde Amendment, these laws would still be seen as an acceptable compromise.

White teenagers like Bell were far from the only victims of the coming era. The Reagan administration would take the Hyde Amendment's disregard for those who needed government assistance to its logical conclusion. Perhaps that was why the ending to this chapter felt like *Murder on the Orient Express*. Everyone was guilty because everyone was performing triage as they anticipated the mass casualties to come. None of my suspects within the abortion rights movement seemed to doubt that repealing Hyde was the *right* thing to do. But by then it already felt impossible. Seated around the table on that January day, the women must have glimpsed the horror that was upon them.

Certainly, Roger Craver had.

On election night in November 1980, after watching Reagan sweep forty-four out of fifty states, the largest margin of victory since FDR, and seeing every candidate he had backed lose, Craver was preparing to drown his sorrows in a bottle when the phone rang. It was his friend Richard Viguerie.

"You've just become a rich man," Viguerie said, and Craver had understood what he meant. Many people were about to suffer and even die under the incoming administration. But on that November night, Viguerie was reminding his friend of the fundamental marketing principle they had each spent the previous decade honing—the very strategy Viguerie had used to help bring Reagan to power. When the devil won, it was good for business.

PART 3

THE DEATH OF BECKY BELL

CHAPTER 6

THE SALESMAN

> For a certain kind of person, murder is easy.
> —*Murder Is Easy* by Agatha Christie

As I drove west out of Washington, DC, on a gray winter day, the landscape around me opened into farmland, and I found myself speeding toward the site of the first major battle of the American Civil War. Somewhere around here, on a grassland now overgrown with wildflowers, the bedraggled and untrained Union army met the bedraggled and untrained Confederates for the first time. Young, frightened men fired bullets into each other's bodies and died in the mud.

There were two immediate takeaways from this opening salvo between North and South. The most immediate was that this war was not going to be over quickly. The more tactical lesson was that when you are fighting a war you must arrive prepared and not give your enemy time to ship in reinforcements by train, which is how the Union army lost the battle along Bull Run Creek.

This is all a ham-handed metaphor for the story I'm about to tell you.

That story begins six miles south of the battlefield, where on this March afternoon I turned off the main road and parked next to a cube-shaped building that housed the marketing headquarters of the conservative movement.

I was here to meet the man who had done more to launch that movement than any individual alive. Richard Viguerie had nursed the American right like a snarling little devil baby for sixty years. Viguerie was the salesman that true believers like Paul Haring needed to get anywhere with their ideas. Haring was like the Jehovah's Witness standing next to a cardboard display in a train station, quietly getting ignored. His pitch was straightforward, but he wasn't great at selling it. Viguerie was the juggler standing outside the station with three flaming bowling pins in the air in front of a crowd throwing dollar bills into a hat. For the true believers to succeed, they needed an adman, and Viguerie, who understood from the beginning that he wasn't much of an intellectual, decided that that was the role he would fill.

He was so successful that a myth began to circulate in conservative circles that he had a faucet in his office through which flowed a stream of gold coins. In fact, what Viguerie was doing was sending mail. In the process, he helped organizations involved in the incremental murder of *Roe*, like Judie and Paul Brown's American Life Lobby, get off the ground by offering loans they could use to pay his company for direct mail.[1]

I came here to ask Viguerie how he did it—how he won.

There was no question in my mind that Viguerie *had* won. After all, *Roe* was gone, progress on LGBTQ rights was being rolled back, income inequality had surged since the 1970s as the rich got richer, the climate was burning up because of entrenched deregulation, and democracy—an institution of which Viguerie admits he is fearful—was crumbling.

But the most fascinating and hopeful part of our conversation would be Viguerie's confession that he feels his side is losing after all. He could see the reinforcements coming, the enemy troops clambering off the train, bound for Manassas. He had worked for the devil for his entire career and now, at the age of ninety, he believed he had lost.

Ride on, soldier! For here in the ruins of battle lie the seeds of hope.

THE BIG FOUR

One of Agatha Christie's worst novels, by her own admission, is a thriller called *The Big Four*. It centered on an international conspiracy. Four powerful figures—an American millionaire, a brilliant French scientist, a Chinese crime boss, and a mysterious Number Four: the Destroyer—were using "wireless energy" to unleash violence and mayhem upon the world. One of the novel's weaknesses, besides its glaring anti-Asian racism, was that the motives of this group were never fully fleshed out. The detective Hercule Poirot cryptically concluded: "The Big Four are for themselves—and for themselves only.... Their aim is world domination."[2]

For all its flaws, *The Big Four* gave me a fictional framework for the real-life conspiracy I was about to encounter. Viguerie was the cofounder of a secretive organization called the Council for National Policy (CNP) that coalesced during the first Reagan administration. Like the conspiracy of Christie's imagination, the CNP was secretive and powerful: Its members included the purveyors of "wireless energy"—radio broadcasting magnates who promoted the group's message through conservative media. Then there were plutocrats with bottomless pockets who funded its agenda, and all the major strategists of the conservative right, from Equal Rights Amendment slayer Phyllis Schlafly to the man who controlled the mail—Richard Viguerie. While the Big Four were hell-bent on "world domination," the CNP would settle on a much more humble and specific goal: controlling American politics.

I was now heading deep into the conspiracy's nerve center.

The first thing I saw when I got off the elevator on the fourth floor of this mundane office building was a smiling bust of Ronald Reagan, which was so on brand that I wanted to laugh. I squelched the urge, because the receptionist was looking at me expectantly. She was an amiable woman with whom I traded curly hair styling tips while she told me she had just returned to work after seventeen years of homeschooling her son. She invited me to sit in a blue armchair next to a medal awarded to Viguerie by the private Christian school Hillsdale College, a tiny Michigan institution with close ties to the CNP and a private endowment of around $1 billion.[3]

The receptionist was working away on a desktop, preparing, I suspected, for the thrice-yearly gathering of the secretive Big Four–esque organization that Viguerie cheekily referred to as "the vast right-wing conspiracy."[4] The CNP's members are supposed to be secret, but thanks to journalists like Anne Nelson, author of *Shadow Network*, they're not; I caught a glimpse of a known member on the receptionist's screen as I passed by.

Viguerie hurtled toward me, a small, hunched man in a suit wearing a yellow tie with an *H* on it that he joked stood for Hillary Clinton, though of course it stood for Hillsdale College. He greeted me courteously, apologized for being late, and led me through a wide hallway to his office, past desks where well-dressed women rose to their feet to greet us. Viguerie invited me to sit on one end of a white sofa in a generously sized office crowded with books and conservative kitsch. There was a bobblehead of founding father John Adams, his hero, on the desk, alongside an enormous glass jar of coins and two metal-plated inscriptions in Latin: "Glory belongs to God" and "Fortune favors the bold." On the coffee table in front of us was a hard hat from the Museum of the Bible and a book of Reagan quotations. This place felt like a shrine to Reagan, whose election was arguably Viguerie's crowning achievement, although it didn't come without personal drawbacks. On the wall over Viguerie's shoulder was a picture of his granddaughter in pigtails at the Reagan ranch. I worried Reagan's ghost might rise from the yellow carpet and grill me about the Democratic Socialists of America membership card in my wallet.

Viguerie was exuding *energy*, an attribute he mentioned repeatedly in his 2022 marketing book; he regarded it as a vital political force that conservatives lacked, while it abounded on the Left. To boost his own energy, he ate ten to twelve servings of vegetables a day, although on the day we met, he told me, he had only eaten half a meal after fasting the day before. Despite his determination to outlive the liberals, he bore signs of old age; thread-thin purple veins across his nose, dress pants worn old-man high around his waist, the transparent wire of a hearing aid. A woman brought him a bottle of water with the cap unscrewed, because his fingers are stiff after sixty-plus years of typing conservative missives. I noticed that a spot on the top of his bald speckled head was bleeding and I wondered why none of the women flocking around him had mentioned it.

Like any adman, Viguerie had a standard pitch. As we sat on either end of the couch, he began to recite it, quickly, like we were in an elevator and the doors were about to open. He didn't look at me while he ran through a list of plot points that I had already read in his books; he looked at the coffee table, where I noticed a phone-book-size report on Hunter Biden's laptop. The pitch started with his childhood in Texas.

"I'm thirteen, fourteen years old playing cops and robbers with the kids in the neighborhood; I don't tell anybody I'm not shooting robbers, I'm shooting Commies," he told the coffee table. "I just came into this world knowing Communists are bad people doing bad things."

Viguerie didn't personally shoot any Commies. By the mid-1970s, he was fighting Communism by hosting breakfast. He convened the leading lights of the burgeoning conservative movement in his dining room. A live-in chef cooked breakfast for these people who wanted to ensure people like the chef didn't have unions or a welfare state to fall back on. One of these breakfasters was the Christian conservative icon Paul Weyrich. One day, as a young staffer on Capitol Hill, Weyrich had stumbled into a meeting of Democratic staffers—or so the pitch went.

"He was just blown away with how they strategized and how they divided up—you do this, you do that," Viguerie said in his Texas drawl. Weyrich watched as the Lefties divided up the different components they needed to pass legislation: the Democratic politicians would introduce it; groups like the ACLU would champion it and defend it in court. Weyrich decided: Just copy/paste.

"At that point, very consciously—'74, '75—we began to reverse engineer the Left," Viguerie told me. The secret to the Left's success, as Viguerie saw it, was their cornucopia of single-issue organizations devoted to abortion rights, civil liberties, and racial justice, as well as their unity around a few single issues everyone could agree on, like opposing the Vietnam War.

"The Left, they pioneered that," Viguerie said. But soon, Viguerie and his breakfast crew would copy the playbook.

One later achievement of this reverse engineering was the creation of the Alliance Defending Freedom, the group that would orchestrate the legal strategy that killed *Roe*; it was founded by conservative leaders in the 1990s as a counterweight to the ACLU.

"That's your Richard Viguerie elevator pitch," I said when Viguerie finally stopped after almost twenty straight minutes.

He didn't deny it.

"Did your parents talk about politics?" I asked. "Because your dad was a union man at one point, right?"

"He was," Viguerie said. "I remember going to the union hall with him once."

I imagined Viguerie trying to enter one again and getting cast out by a protective spell. Unions were one of the first causes Viguerie would undermine when he raised money for a campaign to defeat common situs picketing—a form of picketing that involves targeting a worksite used by more than one employer. Reagan, of course, would go on to break the air traffic controllers' strike his first year in office. Viguerie's union-man father didn't shape his politics. Maybe Viguerie's vitriolic conservatism seeped into his mind late at night, when he'd fall asleep listening to the right-wing polemicist John T. Flynn railing against Franklin D. Roosevelt. Or maybe it came from Senator Joseph McCarthy's televised excoriations of leftists that riveted Viguerie, who delighted in watching the Commies get grilled by Roy Cohn, McCarthy's chief counsel, who later served as a lawyer for Donald Trump. Like Bob Bauman, another architect of the movement, Cohn was gay and closeted; he died of AIDS in 1986 while the administration he helped bring to power was largely ignoring the crisis.

When Viguerie found out that William F. Buckley Jr. was hiring a new executive secretary for the nascent conservative organization Young Americans for Freedom, he begged a well-connected friend to get him the job so he could join the battle. Soon, at the age of twenty-six, he was rubbing shoulders with Buckley, the grand miser himself.

"I didn't know Shinola compared to these people there," Viguerie said. "But I had the *energy*... same *energy* as today."

Like Roger Craver, Viguerie started experimenting with ways to raise money through the mail, and discovered he had a knack for capturing people's attention with grand claims about the impending fall of Western civilization. Meanwhile, Viguerie, a good Catholic, was having babies with his wife, Elaine.

"After the first or second baby, I forget, I went to her and said, 'Honey, I've got something I think is really going to change America,'" Viguerie recalled, speeding up as he fell into this familiar tale. "'Could I be relieved of all household duties, no diapers, no trash, no yard work?' She bought into it, hook, line, and sinker; I was a better salesman than I thought—"

I cut him off. I had read this story in his book and marked it with a Post-it labeled "gross." Then I told my husband while watching his face to make sure he thought it was gross, too.

"Did she push back *at all*?" I asked.

"No," he said, reddening a little, "but it paid off for her; it's been a good life for her."

A life that as Viguerie rose to prominence would include dinner parties on the lawn of a sweeping estate where horse-drawn carriages ferried guests to the house. A life that was marred by an aborted legal separation right as Viguerie's crowning achievement was on the horizon.

After getting his wife's alleged permission, Viguerie began to research marketing, and then in 1964, when Barry Goldwater ran for president, Viguerie went down to the clerk's office in the House of Representatives and began copying the addresses of Goldwater's donors.

"Out of my own pocket I hired six women, and I got 12,500 Goldwater names," he said.

"Where did you find these six women?" I asked.

"Kelly Girls," he said. "It was an agency—if you needed a secretary for a day or week…"

"Do they know their role in history, those six women?"

"No, I suspect not," Viguerie replied with a chortle, and I stopped listening for a second and drifted into a hazy vision of these women sitting around a table in their skirts and cardigans, copying out the names of prospective right-wing donors, while Viguerie's wife changed diapers at home alone. It wasn't just direct mail but women's labor that had underwritten this man's quest to undo working-class and women's advancement.

Unfortunately, I couldn't speak with Elaine Viguerie, who had been disabled by a stroke. But records showed that the Vigueries had been through a separation in 1979 before agreeing to reconcile in March 1980. Elaine claimed that her husband had "continually and maliciously berated" her and once restrained her in a guest room of their house.[5]

"I think it's very common for lawyers to write the most inflammatory thing they can think of," Viguerie said when I asked him about these claims later over the phone. He called that period "a serious bump in the road" in what was otherwise a strong marriage.

There were more bumps in the late 1980s, when a dispute over the couple's property prompted Elaine to make a comment that shed light on the motives of this Big Four–esque suspect. The houses the couple owned weren't what mattered to her husband, Elaine told the lawyers. "His company and his politics is what mattered to him," she said. "He had told me that."[6]

"Is that your motive?" I asked Viguerie during our call.

He acknowledged that his company and politics were important but said that "because of my faith and who I am, family is number one." He still visited Elaine in assisted living four or five times a week.[7]

Even without the marital bumps in the road, the 1980s were not easy for Viguerie, whose business struggled with Republicans in the White House and the devil in retreat. "If the truth were known, I'm getting tired," an uncharacteristically unenergetic Viguerie told *The Washington Post* in 1989, during the presidency of George H. W. Bush.[8]

So what were the motives of this "vast right-wing conspiracy," as Viguerie liked to cheekily call it? Was it something more specific than world domination? There was a moment in our interview that day in his office that seemed to solve the mystery of those motives. It happened when he was describing the difference between his conservative forebears, the Old Right—people like Barry Goldwater and the racist senator from South Carolina Strom Thurmond—and the New Right—people like Bob Bauman and Viguerie.

"The only difference between us and them is we were operationally different," Viguerie said, like he had said it a hundred times, which he probably had. "They would show up for a vote, get beat two-to-one, three-to-one, say, 'When's the next vote? Thursday night? I'll be back.'"

Whereas Viguerie and his ilk had that mysterious movement life force: energy. They didn't take time off after a loss. They regrouped.

But my attention hitched on the phrase "the only difference."

Really? I thought. The *only* difference between the conservative movement of the 1980s and the generation that included segregationist leaders like Thurmond was... tactical?

I should not have been surprised. I knew it was an IRS proposal under Jimmy Carter to crack down on the tax-exempt status of mostly white private religious schools that lit the fuse of Evangelical political power, bringing legions of fresh troops into the conservative movement.

"Evangelicals in those days were starting three new Christian schools every day," Viguerie told me. "They were just on fire. And so we just went to war with the government."

The religion scholar Randall Balmer, in a popularly acclaimed thesis, concluded that the "most obvious, commonsense reading of the religious right is that conservative evangelicals were mobilizing in defense of racial segregation."[9] In fact, the father of the Christian right, Paul Weyrich, told Balmer before his death that it was not abortion but the IRS decision to revoke the tax-exempt status of racially segregated schools that galvanized the movement,[10] bringing Evangelical leaders like Jerry Falwell into the fold. Certainly, there was ample evidence the Christian right mobilized in reaction to the civil rights movement. Falwell founded a white "segregation academy" and denounced the Civil Rights Act of 1964 as "civil wrongs."[11]

"The beauty of the abortion myth is that it conceals an uglier truth," Balmer wrote.[12] The truth, in his view, was that the *real reason* for the religious right's existence wasn't abortion, but segregation. I didn't doubt that the roots of this movement lay in part with the desegregation fight. But Balmer's notion that the fight was *never* about abortion nettled me, because it overlooked the true believers. For many in the religious and political coalition that formed the New Right, it was indeed about abortion and women, along with LGBTQ people and divorce, a transgression that Viguerie seemed to have considered but never completed. The conservative movement had reacted not only to the gains of the civil rights movement but to those of feminism. And the fight against abortion wasn't any prettier than the fight against racial equity—in fact, it was ugly and deadly.

Viguerie's way of describing this history was to invoke that red herring used by Henry Hyde to defend his ban on federal funding of abortion. He acknowledged that the fight over Christian schools catalyzed the movement while denying that *racism* had anything to do with it. It was about *taxes*, and that perennial stand-in for white men: taxpayers.

"I don't know of anybody that I can legitimately call—and I've known almost all of the national leaders over my many years—that was a racist," he said, launching into a rant about "soft racism" on the Left via teachers' unions that are "condemning tens of millions of mostly Black kids" to a life as "functional illiterates."

"How many Black babies have we tried to save through abortions?"

There it was: the rallying cry of the civil rights movement for fetuses, the same one that Henry Hyde would invoke to defend his abortion funding ban. *We can't possibly be racists. Look at all the Black babies we've tried to save.*

"OK, but let me counter," I interrupted. "Jesse Helms."

Maybe Viguerie had forgotten about this guy, who no one would dispute was a racist, right?

"Uh-huh."

"You worked with him, right?"

"Absolutely."

"You don't consider him a racist?"

"Not at all."

"I mean, he used to whistle 'Dixie' at Carol Moseley Braun."

"I have no problem with whistling 'Dixie.'"

"Called all Black men Fred because he thought it was a funny joke…"

"He was raised in a culture and time, he was older than the rest of us, of course," Viguerie said. "I've been around Jesse a whole lot; never heard anything that was racist out of him."

"All right, let me try one more possible racist candidate here," I said. "What about Billy James Hargis, who you worked for back in the day?"

"I certainly did." Viguerie paused and I thought maybe I had him at last. Hargis, a right-wing talk radio host, was an avowed segregationist. Everyone who has googled his name knows that. It was in the first paragraph of his Wikipedia page.

"Why would you think he was a racist?" Viguerie asked me, wide-eyed as a baby lamb.

"He was pro-segregation, wasn't he?" I asked, which is an understatement. The man wrote a pamphlet called *The Truth About Segregation*. Spoiler alert: The truth is that it's good.

"I wouldn't—it's news to me," Viguerie said.

It cannot possibly be news to him.

"He had issues, obviously," Viguerie said. "I've never heard anybody say that before. If he was, it's news to me."

I was starting to get that familiar feeling that I was banging my head against a wall of crystallized belief. In Viguerie's case, the belief wasn't only or even primarily religious. After all, he was an adman. He believed in the principle that his book described as *the whole ball game*.

The ball game was: Protect the brand at all costs.[13]

The brand of the conservative movement was built on one issue more than any other: abortion. The issue of abortion, alongside attacks on LGBTQ rights, formed what Viguerie called the "third leg" on the stool of conservative power. (The other two legs were fiscal conservatism and military might.)

"It was the cultural issues that were the engine that drove the Republican successes for decades," Viguerie told me. "It was the cultural issues—the third leg—that changed everything for the Republican Party."

That and Viguerie's ability to raise money through the mail, and his convening of secretive meanings of conservative activists upon whom he believes Western civilization relies.

Now we got to the hopeful part. The *Dobbs* decision had sawed off the conservative movement's third leg. The stool was wobbling. The enemy was regrouping. That's what happened when the devil was defeated. And with the conservative movement's most compelling devil for the past half century, *Roe*, now dead, Viguerie seemed to be sensing trouble.

"So who's winning and who's losing right now?" I asked Viguerie, adding, "We feel like we're losing."

Viguerie waved away my question as if it were a fly.

"I hear that all the time, from my liberal friends, and I've got thirty [or] thirty-five national liberal friends!" he exclaimed. One of those friends was his progressive counterpart Roger Craver, upon whose good word Viguerie had agreed to take this interview with me. He launched into a soliloquy about how every year he hung out with liberals at the Renaissance, an elite gathering attended by the Clintons, where his "best buddy" was the late sex therapist Dr. Ruth.

I guess the real winners are self-important rich people of all political stripes, I thought.

But no, Viguerie said, it was the Left that was winning.

"So anyway, every major institution in America, with the exception of the courts, is controlled by the Left; all of entertainment, most all of the media, higher education, lower education, unions, big business, Wall Street... our own government: the CIA, the FBI, the IRS have been weaponized against the conservatives," Viguerie said. "We've got control of the Supreme Court; that can change very quickly.... If you think about where the power is... we're children, we're just children playing with adults."

Less than a year after our interview, these institutions, most of which were never "Left" to begin with, would be in the hands of an authoritarian government that was hell-bent on purging them of all liberal influence if not dismantling them outright. After our conversation, conservatives would manage to replace the devil of abortion with the devil of transgender people. In the 2024 election, the newly refashioned third leg would stabilize the stool again.

When I asked Viguerie about all of this during our phone call in the summer of 2025, he conceded that perhaps his side had a "better chance of winning now," with Trump in the White House. But the nongovernmental institutions, he said, were still in the grip of the Left.

"The leadership of these major institutions in America, big media, big tech, higher education, lower education, the nonprofit community, they haven't changed their views or values," he said, they were just "playing nice" with Trump. "The institutions are still in the control of our enemies, quite frankly, and we're just engaged in a spiritual civil war."

In Viguerie's office, an alarm that sounded like a grandfather clock chimed on his phone, a signal that it was almost time for him to depart for an event that evening about a new book on the life of President Woodrow Wilson.

I threw my last questions at him.

"What about abortion, is that an issue that was opportunistic—you saw it could move people?" I asked.

"Absolutely," he said.

Indeed, Viguerie had been explicit before about how, once a person was persuaded by the third leg to sit on the stool, they could get used to the other legs.

"The abortion issue is the door through which many people come into conservative politics, but they don't stop there," Viguerie once said. "Their convictions against abortion are like the first in a series of falling dominoes." Those dominoes went from concern about young people's sexuality to morality in schools and secular humanism as a road to Communism, which paved the way for supporting the other two legs: military policy to fight the Communists and promoting free enterprise.[14]

But he and his fellow soldiers had made a crucial tactical error. They failed to sufficiently change the culture, which is more against them, at least on abortion, than it ever has been.[15] Viguerie knew it.

"A lot of my friends [are] still working to this day to change the law in this state or that state. I said, 'It's idiotic; stop it! Stop doing that!'" Viguerie exclaimed. "It doesn't matter what laws you pass now. If we don't change the culture in America, it'll all be undone in three, four, five years."

With his help conservatives waged what would be called a "culture war"—a war aimed at restoring the old cultural order of the 1950s. But even as their political victories mounted, the culture changed despite them.

So maybe we were winning after all.

Viguerie rose from the couch and I followed him out of the office, past bulletin boards decorated with "I'm Catholic and I vote" bumper stickers. He told his deputy he would see her at 6:40 a.m. the next morning; they were flying to California for a meeting of "the vast right-wing conspiracy."

"The CNP," I said.

"That's your guess." He laughed, relishing the secrecy. Outside in the hallway, waiting for the elevator, we ran into Kevin Allen, an antiabortion activist who worked for Viguerie.

"Amy's writing a book ...," he said, looking at me for clarification on what, exactly, it was about.

"I thought it was about how you won, but maybe you've convinced me that we won, so I don't know," I said lightly.

"No," he said as we got in the elevator, at least, not in the long term. "Whittaker Chambers started his famous book *Witness* by saying he had a feeling that he had joined the losing side by leaving the Communist Party... and sometimes, [as] conservatives, I feel that way."

"Do you?"

The elevator beeped, and Viguerie made a last pitch for the brand that mattered most: his own.

"I see things others don't see.... I was on some recent calls with some really, really high-level people that you know of," he said, managing to name-drop without dropping names. "What's happening out there on the Left, they're just rigging the election, it will be amazing if we can win 2024."

The bell dinged; the doors opened. He let me out first.

Is this all a marketing ploy? I wondered. Because if there was one thing I had learned from Viguerie and his direct mail nemesis Roger Craver, it was that losing—or at least, the perception that you are losing—is good for business. If it was a ploy, I had to give him credit for succeeding spectacularly. Conservatives won in 2024 based in no small part on the perception that they were losing to a liberal elite composed of the media and

Hollywood actors and government agencies and immigrants and Black Lives Matter activists and transgender people that were all conspiring against them—conspiring, most of all, against their hero, Donald Trump. The shadowy notion of a conspiratorial Big Four hell-bent on world domination had served Viguerie's allies. Their base of predominantly aggrieved white men believed that the devils were in charge.

"You ever think about switching sides?" I asked as I followed him down the hall toward the door.

"I'm a true believer," he said with a chuckle as he shook my hand and climbed into the black SUV that was waiting to take him downtown. That might be true, I thought, although it was not abortion alone that he truly believed in, but the wider conservative movement, which was inextricably tied to his own personal brand. As I walked to my car not far from the battleground of our country's original Civil War, I pronounced Viguerie as guilty as Paul Haring and Bob Bauman when it came to the killing of *Roe*. He had armed the groups responsible for *Roe*'s death with the money they needed to make their incremental cuts to abortion rights. In the process, he'd helped give rise to the new civil war that was upon us.

CHAPTER 7

THE ACTOR

Women can accept the fact that a man is a rotter, a swindler, a drug-taker, a confirmed liar, and a general swine without batting an eyelash and without its impairing their affection for the brute in the least!

—Murder in Mesopotamia by Agatha Christie

ONE JUNE DAY I WOUND MY WAY UP A LUSH HILLSIDE IN SIMI VALLEY, California, where the fortieth president of the United States sat grinning at me from atop a horse. Ronald Reagan looked dapper and relaxed, his toned body a leathered green-brown. Somehow, his teeth gleamed white. *How can a statue's teeth look white?* I wondered as I pulled my rental car into the packed parking lot. But if anyone's teeth could remain white in death, it was the handsome actor-president's. Vultures circled above the dead president's head. Perhaps they sensed the legacy of bloodshed here at the Ronald Reagan Presidential Library and Museum.

I made my way through the lush courtyard of a Spanish-style estate and grabbed an audio guide from a woman dressed in a red blazer like an old-time movie-theater usher. Then I learned that the first exhibit I would be subjected to in this cursed place was a hologram of Ronald Reagan himself. It was time to meet Reagan's ghost at last. Sweat beaded on the audio guide in my hand. I remembered, too late, Paul Haring's warning. Hell was real after all. It was right here, in an air-conditioned mansion in the hills of Southern California.

It happened to be the week of Juneteenth, the federal holiday marking the end of slavery, so I tried to distract myself from the impending apparition by taking note of the people around me—Asian tourists, German tourists. What kind of person, I wondered, chose *this* time of year to visit a museum dedicated to a man who ran his first campaign for governor in 1966 after coming out against fair housing and the Civil Rights Act,[1] praised the formerly segregated Bob Jones University as a "great institution" when it still had an interracial dating ban,[2] promoted the sole holdout in the Supreme Court decision *against* Bob Jones University's tax-exempt status to chief justice, called African delegates to the United Nations "monkeys," used the racist stereotype of the "welfare queen" to distort how we think about Black and poor women forever, and alienated Black people to such an extent that he won only 9 percent of African American voters upon his second election in 1984?[3]

Who else was here in hell, besides a feminist reporter trying to force herself to take deep breaths in case there was a special room for Commie sympathizers? The answer was: A lot of people. The place felt packed, even by the standards of an institution that, at least before the pandemic, saw up to 1,500 visitors on an average day. Parents had brought their kids to see the "Star Wars" exhibit—a mash-up of memorabilia from the movies and Reagan's nuclear missile defense system. Tourists were getting their pictures taken outside the 1980s-era Air Force One with its startling military aide mannequin. But as I was about to discover, plenty of people came because they just loved Reagan. The Reagan Museum was the most frequently visited presidential library in the country, a docent wearing a watch with Reagan's face on it who called herself a "Reagan groupie" told me as I contemplated hurling myself off the hillside.

These days everyone seemed to be a Reagan groupie. Liberal Democrats like my parents longed for the normalcy of a time when the gutting of the federal government was at least done with a degree of respect for due process. Even the process-smasher-in-chief, Donald Trump, had co-opted the late president's slogan, "Make America Great Again," and favorably compared his position on abortion to Reagan's in 2024.

In fact, when you looked at the forces behind Trump's reelection, Reagan turned out to be the man behind the curtain. The notorious Project 2025 blueprint for Trump's second term, written by the conservative think tank the Heritage Foundation, mentioned the word "Reagan" seventy times.[4] Three of its coauthors were Reagan administration veterans. The foreword explained that this plan to dismantle much of the federal government and ban abortion nationwide was modeled on the inaugural "Mandate for Leadership" presented to Reagan, who, it boasted, turned more than 60 percent of its recommendations into policy in the next year.

Reagan embodied the two grand contradictions that defined the anti-abortion movement's alliance with the Republican Party. But the first contradiction was his own flip on the issue. As governor of California in 1967, he signed a reform bill making abortion legal for victims of rape, statutory rape, and incest or when someone's physical or mental health was threatened. As he set his sights on national office, he would express his regret for signing the legislation, and then become widely known as the first pro-life president.

One of Reagan's first actions after he was inaugurated in 1981 was to sign legislation removing the rape exception to the Hyde Amendment that had been added by Congress in 1977. (A 1980 Supreme Court decision upheld the constitutionality of the original 1976 ban with its exception only for life endangerment.) He voiced support for a constitutional amendment to ban abortion. He hosted a screening of Paul Haring's favorite antiabortion movie, *The Silent Scream*, next to the White House, mentioned abortion in three of his seven State of the Union addresses, waved to the annual March for Life from the White House balcony and addressed them by phone. In 1984 he instituted the Global Gag Rule, also known as the Mexico City Policy, a global extension of the Hyde Amendment that prevented organizations abroad that received US health aid from so much as offering information about abortion services.

But perhaps his most consequential achievement was the solidification of the antiabortion movement's alliance with the Republican Party. Before Reagan took office, abortion was still not a strictly partisan issue. In fact, as scholar Prudence Flowers wrote, the loyalty of Catholics to the Democratic Party meant that "well into the 1980s, ordinary Democrats were more likely to be pro-life than ordinary Republicans."[5] In 1976, the chair of the Republican National Committee and the first lady, Betty Ford, supported abortion rights; yet the party adopted a platform supporting an antiabortion constitutional amendment in an effort to win over Catholics and socially conservative Reagan supporters.[6] The last shot at an antiabortion constitutional amendment in 1983 failed when one-third of Senate Republicans opposed it.

But Reagan would solidify abortion as a conservative issue—in part by vanquishing the leading argument that it could be a progressive one.

That argument came from the same entity that had used its political weight to ensure passage of the Hyde Amendment—the Catholic Church. In a speech at Fordham University in 1983, Cardinal Joseph Bernardin called for a "consistent ethic of life" that included opposing not just abortion but nuclear weapons, war, the death penalty, and poverty.[7] Everything except the abortion part ran against Reagan's agenda. He viewed the Catholic Church as "the political opposition" and sought to cast the antiabortion cause in a way that fit his own conservative frame. When the administration learned that the US Conference of Catholic Bishops was preparing an encyclical that extended the pro-life position to a critique of the nuclear arms race, they rushed to ensure that Reagan's own antiabortion treatise would publish first.[8]

In *Abortion and the Conscience of a Nation*, Reagan drew on the tried-and-true strategy of co-opting the language of the civil rights movement, comparing abortion to slavery, and framing it as *the* civil rights cause of the time.

Conveniently, in Reagan's frame, abortion was a cause *so significant* that it allowed him to overlook all the issues that actually animated the civil rights movement—like economic, gender, and racial inequality. Here was the civil rights movement for fetuses being touted from the presidential pulpit. Reagan effectively erased issues of structural inequality to focus on what he called "the right without which no other rights have any meaning."[9]

This singling out of protection from abortion as *the* right that mattered above all else would allow Reagan to enact the first grand contradiction of the alliance between the Republican Party and the antiabortion movement: He opposed abortion while gutting the public programs that allowed people to afford families. The Supreme Court with its decision to uphold the Hyde Amendment had justified this contradiction by ruling that it wasn't up to the federal government to fix poverty; that was an individual failing that abortion seekers needed to handle themselves.

Reagan would embody a second, defining contradiction of the Republican Party's alliance with the antiabortion movement: He would claim he was making government smaller while extending the government's reach over bodily autonomy. After all, if protection from abortion was *the* right that mattered most, its defense demanded extraordinary measures.

So popular would Reagan's "small government" ethos become that the Democratic president Bill Clinton would adopt it in the 1990s when he ended "welfare as we know it," eviscerating the social safety net by giving states control over welfare and imposing work requirements and lifetime caps.

Mainstream abortion rights groups, too, would begin to ape Reagan's logic. In 1986, a group of pro-choice strategists began to intentionally frame abortion rights as an encroachment of big government on the family, as Will Saletan wrote in his book *Bearing Right*. Like the Christian right before them, pro-choice strategists began to tap into white resentment over school desegregation to defend abortion rights in conservative states like Arkansas. Harrison Hickman, the consultant whose polling and focus groups steered NARAL toward making abortion sound like a conservative issue, would craft a strategy straight out of the Reagan playbook, harnessing racial resentment and sympathy for rape victims to win narrow victories using conservative rhetoric about government intrusion and crime.[10]

Black feminists like Angela Davis had warned that abortion, if severed from a holistic feminist agenda, would accommodate rather than confront economic inequality.[11] Pro-choice groups in their pivot to Reaganite rhetoric in the 1980s and 1990s would prove her right. Reagan's shadow loomed over all this history.

I came to the library thinking about Becky Bell, the teenager who died of an unsafe abortion during Reagan's final year in office, a victim of one of the incremental cuts to abortion rights.

I did not expect to encounter women who would blow up my understanding of Reagan's legacy.

Before I got to them, though, I had to survive my encounter with Reagan's ghost. So I filed into a theater and sat on a backless bench next to a man wearing a pineapple shirt and a cowboy hat.

First came a video of Reagan with a series of horses—brown horses, white horses. I was reminded of the scene in the movie *Barbie* where Ken discovered that patriarchy is, basically, men on horses. There's academic validation of this concept in Kristin Kobes Du Mez's book *Jesus and John Wayne*, about how Evangelicals love nothing more than a swarthy man on a horse.[12] They even like a swarthy man *not* on a horse. Evangelical support of Trump makes sense if you just remember that principle: Swarthy men are good. Horses desired but optional.

Two-thirds of white Evangelicals voted for Reagan in 1980 and now I understand why: abortion and horses. About eight in ten white Evangelicals voted for Trump in 2016 and 2024,[13] and while Trump isn't exactly known as an equestrian, my sleuthing on this point led me to pages and pages of bizarre fan art on the Internet showing a very swarthy Trump on horses.

Back at the library, I watched a dramatic overview of US history that involved swarthy men fording rivers, inter-spliced with footage of Reagan sawing trees. Then, more horses.

Finally, Reagan walked out onto the stage in riding pants and knee-high boots, carrying a leather saddle and a coil of rope, and right away, started talking about horses.

"There you are, in charge of an animal with more muscle in its neck than you have in your whole body," he said. "From the minute the horse takes its first step, every muscle in your own body responds to it."

He looked smaller than I expected as he stared dead-eyed at the emergency exit behind me. Beside Reagan was a hologram of a glossy, panting golden retriever. A disembodied voice began interviewing Reagan. If you ever need to comfort yourself while watching a hologram of a dead president, I recommend imagining the golden retriever is the one asking the questions.

"Are there any messages about the country and its future you'd like to share with us?" the golden retriever asked.

Reagan set down the rope; he needed *two hands* to answer.

"We've got to do a better job of getting across that America is freedom... and freedom is special and rare," he said. "If we forget what we did, we won't know who we are."

That is a line to live by: "If we forget what we did, we won't know who we are."

After the hologram departed I made my way over to a display of photos from Reagan's childhood in Dixon, Illinois. A docent dressed like a flight attendant in a navy-blue blazer and a red-and-blue-striped tie stood explaining that Reagan was nicknamed "Dutch" because his haircut reminded his father of a little Dutch boy. Reagan's mother was a devout Christian and his father was an itinerantly employed alcoholic who relied on a New Deal relief program to feed his family. The exhibit didn't mention this part; instead, the white text on a red plastic panel declared that Reagan "saw self-reliance and big dreams for a better future in his father," a man Reagan, at the age of eleven, had to drag into the house and put to bed after he passed out drunk in the snow.

"He was a cute baby," a woman in black tennis shoes said, admiring a black-and-white baby photo of Reagan.

The docents were everywhere. They paced the hallways and guarded the entrance to the theater where you could see a video reenactment of Reagan getting shot and injured in 1981. They had a disconcerting way of sidling up to you to drop Reagan facts. They were not paid. They did this for fun.

I was standing in front of a display case looking at a photo of young Reagan in a football uniform when a docent appeared over my right shoulder.

"He's just a natural leader," she said.

"What do you admire most about him?" I asked.

"His personality, his strength."

I'll call the docent Martha, because she was afraid that talking to me could get her fired.

I explained that I was writing a book about abortion.

Something changed in the air between us. Her voice dropped a register. Abortion is a *hard* topic, she said, a *sad* topic. She lingered beside me.

"Are you finding more people *pro* or *against*?" she asked in a low voice, and I began to suspect that she did not toe the party line on this one.

Finally, I asked: "What do you think?"

"I'm afraid if it becomes illegal, it's still going to happen," she said. "It's something that's going to happen no matter what." She looked around to see if anyone was watching.

"Things are going to happen in Texas where people are going to die," she hissed.

"Yes," I hastily agreed.

"Women will have to voice the struggle," she added.

I stood there stunned watching her walk away.

Nothing really mattered after that. Not the display called "A Union Man" that sugarcoated Reagan's stint as a highly prolific FBI informant while he led the Hollywood actors' union. Not the male docent's insulting dig at the sight of my notebook: "Are you doing a little school report?" he asked me, a thirty-seven-year-old woman. Not the screen playing a clip from Reagan's famous 1964 speech "A Time for Choosing," wherein he joked that the seventeen million people said to have gone to bed hungry each night in 1960 were probably all just on a diet and condemned the money spent on welfare in such rousing terms that a woman next to me chuckled and exclaimed: "That's awesome!" Not the dark tunnel meant to represent the 1970s with giant white letters spelling out the words "unemployment," "shortages," and "frustration" that made this decade sound like a den of misery from which Reagan would rescue the country. Nothing mattered until I found Martha again. There she was, around the corner, gesturing behind her at a replica of the Oval Office. I stood watching her entertain the crowd with a story about how Reagan always kept a jar of Jelly Belly jelly beans on his desk and thought: *How is it possible that this woman who puts on a uniform each week to volunteer at an institution dedicated to promoting Ronald Reagan's legacy is pro-choice?*

KILLERS OF THE WELFARE STATE

Reagan's hologram said it best: "If we forget what we did, we won't know who we are." This museum had done its best to erase any mention of what Reagan *did* on abortion. I found only one reference to it, in a recording describing how it was one of the topics he discussed in his radio addresses. But by the late 1970s, Reagan was doing everything he could to accentuate his antiabortion commitment. He had ample incentive to do so. The Christian right was rising to prominence thanks to a surging Evangelical base. Televangelists like Jerry Falwell and conservative admen like Richard Viguerie were riling up a new voting bloc, using abortion.

"I endorse you!" Reagan famously told an Evangelical gathering less than three months before the 1980 election. Six million Evangelicals switched from the Democratic to the Republican Party that year.[14]

The nation's leading antiabortion organization had been founded by the Catholic Church, whose broader "pro-life" agenda Reagan opposed. But his opposition to abortion was enough for the church-founded National Right to Life Committee (NRLC) to throw its weight behind him.

By 1984, the committee was hard at work on getting Reagan reelected. On February 8, David O'Steen, director of the Committee for a Pro-Life Congress, part of NRLC's Minnesota affiliate, wrote to Reagan's advisers, outlining a plan to "maximize the pro-life vote for the President within key 'swing' states in 1984," according to NRLC records I reviewed.[15]

O'Steen acknowledged that most people did not agree with the antiabortion movement's goal. In a 1980 Gallup survey, 25 percent of Americans supported abortion "on demand," and an additional 53 percent thought it should be available in a wide range of circumstances.[16]

But as O'Steen put it: "Polls have shown that the pro-life position enjoys as much as a two-to-one advantage over the pro-abortion position in the percentage of the population that will actually base their votes on the issue." O'Steen touted a "clear superiority" of grassroots organizing on his side, which could help reelect the president. "The pro-life movement today has the most extensive volunteer network of any social movement in the country," O'Steen wrote.

Reagan himself seemed to concur with this assessment of the movement's strength. In January 1984 he wrote in his diary of how he had waved from the balcony of the White House at the annual March for Life.

"The leaders & I had a good meeting," Reagan wrote. "They are more united & determined than ever."[17]

As much as I hated to admit it, O'Steen seemed to be right about the superiority of the antiabortion grass roots.

A major study by sociologist Kristin Luker published in her 1984 book, *Abortion and the Politics of Motherhood*, found that most antiabortion activists reported volunteering between thirty and forty hours a week. Their pro-choice counterparts reported such low levels of involvement by comparison, at least from 1977 to 1980, that researchers had to lower the bar for the number of hours that qualified participants as "activists" to even count them.

"Although pro-choice activists reported working similar hours in the 1960s when they were the group seeking to overturn the status quo, by the time of the present study, we had to define the minimum involvement as five hours a week in order to find a sample of pro-choice activists," Luker wrote.

Toward the end of the study, Luker noted an uptick in pro-choice interest. Reagan's election "upset pro-choice people to the extent that it was for the first time possible to find pro-choice activists who worked ten hours a week or more on the issue."

The antiabortion movement had succeeded, she concluded, "in part because it has been intensely committed to the goal of outlawing abortion during a period when the general public has been only weakly committed to supporting it."[18]

In Luker's view, the engine of antiabortion advantage was housewives—conservative women for whom legal abortion and the rise in women's participation in the workforce posed an existential threat.

Soon this engine would go to work to reelect Ronald Reagan.

In the plan he sent to the Reagan reelection campaign, David O'Steen outlined how the movement's volunteer base could form a "parallel campaign" to reelect the president. He suggested that a woman named Marjorie Higgins be paid a salary of $1,650 a month—about $5,000 today—to help deliver antiabortion voters in swing states. It's not clear how much these voters mattered in the end, since Reagan won everywhere except Washington, DC, and Walter Mondale's home state of Minnesota. Only 4 percent of voters in a *New York Times* and CBS poll said they were going to base their vote on abortion, although that didn't stop the NRLC's president from claiming the movement played a significant part in Reagan's victory.[19] As Luker noted, since antiabortion voters were part of a relatively small proportion of the population that regularly voted, their opinions mattered disproportionately.[20]

Marjorie Higgins was another interesting, behind-the-scenes suspect to emerge in my investigation. Records showed she had already helped elect Republican Virginia Senator Paul Trible in 1982 in part by courting Black voters. Like much of the antiabortion movement's propaganda, her efforts relied on racialized language; literature dropped in Black neighborhoods denounced "the use of tax funds to pay for abortions to kill the unborn of the poor."

She and her team had chosen to leave that language out of the literature for white communities, Higgins noted in a report on the campaign, because "there might be plenty of whites who find it acceptable to kill 'welfare babies.'"[21]

These internal memos showed how the antiabortion movement, like Reagan himself with his "welfare queen" stereotype, tried to weaponize racial resentment to their own ends.

Despite working to reelect Reagan, the antiabortion movement would frequently express frustration with the president, including over his appointment of Supreme Court Justice Sandra Day O'Connor. Yet scholar Prudence Flowers suggested that, in large part to demonstrate its own political power, the antiabortion movement would mythologize Reagan after the fact. In 1988, the National Right to Life Committee declared, "The pro-life movement has never had a better friend than President Reagan."[22]

Did Martha know about any of this? I needed to find out.

THE FORGETTERS

I was meandering through a section of the museum dedicated to Nancy Reagan's outfits, admiring a green peacoat in a glass case, when I ran into three sisters from out of state. They had been on the beach in Santa Barbara for an annual sisters' retreat and were wearing matching pink T-shirts that read "Sister's Trip 2024: Apparently we are trouble when we are together." They were wrapping up their vacation here because they *loved* Reagan.

I asked them what they thought about abortion.

"I don't think, as a taxpayer, it should come out of our pocket," the youngest sister, Denise, said.

Denise and Donna, the middle sister, said they believed the federal government should have no role in abortion—it should be left to the states.

"So Reagan, actually, early on, came out in support of the Human Life Amendment to the Constitution, which would have been a ban on all abortion," I told the sisters, as we stood in front of a six-foot-high color photo of Nancy Reagan holding a brown-skinned baby. "Would you guys be for that or against that?"

"I would be against that," Donna said. "I'm a human being; I can make a decision for myself."

The sisters held a range of views—Debbie, the oldest sister, was against abortion and supported her local crisis pregnancy center. Donna thought it should be legal, at least up to a point, although she wished people would give more thought to prevention. When I told them that the decision to take the federal government out of abortion had allowed some states to ban it outright, they seemed shocked.

"OK, wow, I didn't know that," Donna said.

If we forget what we did, we won't know who we are.

I flashed back to this conversation when Donald Trump compared himself to Reagan during the first debate of the 2024 campaign.

"Like Ronald Reagan, I believe in the exceptions," Trump declared. "I believe in the exceptions for rape, incest, and the life of the mother. I think it's very important. Some people don't. Follow your heart. But you have to get elected also."

I flashed back to this moment again when I was in Amarillo, Texas, on Election Day 2024, interviewing voters who believed abortion should be legal and yet were casting their ballot for the president who'd helped kill *Roe*.

Trump remained popular among Americans less because of what he *did* than because of who he *is*—a white, swarthy if horseless man, a *natural leader*, a guy with *personality* and *strength*.

Finally, I gathered the courage to break the news to Martha. As we wandered past busts of Reagan, I told her that her hero supported a constitutional ban on abortion. She winced as if she had tasted something sour. But she seemed willing to overlook it, maybe because Reagan didn't *actually* manage to ban abortion. Or maybe because—in a logic that, if I'd recognized it then, would have allowed me to predict the results of the 2024 election—even people who care about keeping abortion legal don't care enough to change their loyalty to a man they love.

Before I left, I asked Martha to show me where Reagan was buried. She walked me outside, along a patio where visitors rested on benches under the eaves, and directed me past a graffitied slice of the Berlin Wall to a tree-enclosed clearing.

Reagan's final resting place was marked, fittingly, by a hunk of granite in the shape of a horseshoe.

While I stood there listening to the birds, I thought about how I'd learned more from Martha and the three sisters than from the museum itself. I'd learned that people's views on abortion are complicated and often uninformed. Less than half of reproductive-age women in the United States are aware of the current status of abortion policy in their state, a 2024 survey found.[23] Yet a solid majority of people believe abortion should be legal in all or most cases.[24] One plot twist I'll uncover in the hellscape of my Reagan research is that Nancy Reagan was a quiet member of that majority. Nancy and Ronald Reagan's daughter, Patti Davis, revealed in a *New York Times* op-ed in 2022 that she had asked her mother in 1981 about situations in which a woman isn't able to care for a child. "Shouldn't it be her choice? For some reason I turned to my mother with the question, and she quietly said, 'Yes, it should.'"[25]

If the woman who slept next to Reagan every night, and now slept next to him for eternity under this gray stone, was quietly pro-choice, how could I be shocked that the docent was, too?

Patti believed there was nuance to her father's views on abortion, although those nuances didn't come across in public. She attributed his passion for the issue to displaced grief over the newborn baby he and his first wife had lost many years before he became president. "There was a child you never saw, never touched, a child who died out of reach," Davis wrote in a letter to her father published after his death.[26]

"There was complexity to his views on abortion; there was, as he said, 'soul searching,' and I believe to some degree his views remained a work in progress."

Whatever he believed, I thought to myself as I looked at the manicured hedge that adorned Reagan's grave, what mattered is what he *did*, which was to seize the grand opportunity presented by the Christian right's rise. He used antiabortion rhetoric to get elected—and to justify the jarring contradictions of his political project. And in the process, he had solidified the critical alliance between the Republican Party and the antiabortion movement, the alliance that would ultimately kill *Roe*.

A breeze gently rustled the trees. When I turned to look out over the valley below, I noticed a sign in the grass: Rattlesnake Nesting Area.

If hell is real, I thought, *then God is too, and she has a sense of humor.*

CHAPTER 8

THE POLITE KILLER AND THE PERFECT VICTIM

> A mother's love for her child is like nothing else in the world. It knows no law, no pity. It dares all things and crushes down remorselessly all that stands in its path.
>
> —*The Hound of Death and Other Stories* by Agatha Christie

On an August day in 2022, Addie Bell grabbed the denim jacket in her backseat and hopped out of her car outside the green-domed statehouse in Indianapolis. The jacket had been her aunt's, one of the few pieces of Becky Bell's clothing that fit Addie. Becky's 1980s miniskirts and the rest of the clothes Addie's grandparents kept in a bin at their house were too tight.[1]

There were other differences between them—Becky's hair was blond and wavy, while Addie's was straighter. Becky didn't wear glasses; Addie wore round, thin wire frames and a tiny stud in her nostril. But there were uncanny similarities that had always given Addie the sense she and her aunt would have gotten along. They were free spirits who shared a love for animals; Becky did cartwheels down the street to raise money for the humane society and persuaded her parents to keep a stray dog she found on the street. When I reached Addie in the summer of 2024, she had just adopted a goldendoodle puppy that someone was giving away in a park. Both girls played the flute. In middle school, around the time Addie learned the truth about her aunt's death, she'd pursed her lips over the same silver instrument Becky once played.

Then there were the ways that Addie had shaped her life around the absence of her aunt. It was because of Becky that teenage Addie had written a speech denouncing abortion restrictions for the speech and debate team, and because of her aunt that Addie had become a de facto sex educator to her friends, filling the gaps left by their abstinence-only education by telling them how they could buy condoms at the gas station and get tested for STDs at Planned Parenthood. She knew from the inheritance of her family's grief that this information could save lives.

Now, Addie was grown up, and ready to take on the responsibility of that inheritance. She was going to tell her aunt's story and plead with Indiana lawmakers not to ban abortion in the state. Less than two months earlier, the Supreme Court had struck down *Roe*, allowing states like Indiana that had cut away at abortion access for years to ban it outright.

Around her neck, Addie wore a chain with two dog tags—one bearing her aunt's name, the other that of Rosie Jimenez. They were family relics from a fight that was older than Addie. Now, it was her turn to take up that fight. She was nervous, but ready, as she stepped to the podium wearing Becky's jacket.

"Throughout my entire life, I've heard stories about my aunt Becky from my family, stories about how kind and caring she was," Addie said before the packed chamber, hoisting into the air a black-and-white photo of Becky smiling with her blond hair teased on top of her head.[2] The building was filled with people singing and chanting, holding homemade signs like "Abortion Saves Lives." "In 1988, when Becky was seventeen, she found out that she was pregnant. She didn't want to disappoint her parents by telling them and decided that an abortion was the best choice for her."

But when she went to Planned Parenthood, Becky learned she could not get an abortion without a parent's permission because of Indiana's parental consent law. She could have appealed to a judge, but the judge who would have heard her case was said to be antiabortion.

"I don't want to hurt Mom and Dad, I love them so much," she confided in a friend. So, as *The Indianapolis News* would later report, "desperate, terrified and alone, she slipped out of the family's Northwest-side house under the ruse of attending a party, got lost in the dark on the Southside, apparently allowed the insertion of instruments in her body, returned home pale, feverish and weeping at 1:30 a.m. and was dead within a week."[3]

Her last words to her parents were: "Mom, Dad, I love you. Forgive me."[4]

"The restrictive abortion laws that were in place did not stop my aunt from obtaining an abortion; they stopped her from obtaining a *safe* abortion," Addie said, glancing down at her paper, tracking the words to calm her nerves. Her voice began to shake, and a cheer reverberated through the room as if the demonstrators were urging her on.

"I'm asking you to protect the women who so desperately need safe access to reproductive health care in our state," Addie said, speeding up as she reached the end. "Stop this bill from becoming law and let there be no more Becky Bells."

When she finished her testimony, Addie walked straight out of the chamber and went home. Even as relief flooded through her, she knew it was likely futile. The lawmakers who supported the abortion ban had refused to make eye contact when she glanced up from her paper. No one had asked her questions when she finished. They were all acting like they'd heard the story before—which many of them had. Addie's grandparents had stood in this very building before to make the same plea. Half a lifetime had passed since they began their fight, and in those years, Indiana lawmakers had only restricted abortion further. Between 2010 and 2019, the Indiana legislature passed fourteen antiabortion laws, and four of the state's ten clinics closed.[5]

Becky's story seemed to have no impact on lawmakers like Representative John Jacob of Indianapolis. In fact, he didn't believe the abortion ban they were considering on that August day in 2022 went far enough, because it would still allow what he called "baby murder" in cases of rape and incest, lethal fetal anomalies, or to save the life of the woman.

"Sir, I am not a murderer, and my sisters are not murderers either," Representative Renee Pack shot back at him on the last day of the two-week special session called to pass this ban.[6]

The session was grueling. Pro-choice state Representative Carey Hamilton, who grew up with Becky Bell, would leave feeling exhausted and cry in her car.[7] The yells and chants of demonstrators echoed through the chamber.

One abortion opponent noted that pro-choice demonstrators seemed to vastly outnumber those on his side. "I strongly felt the presence of Satan while in the gallery, clutching my rosary as an antidote," he wrote.[8]

On the last day of the session, a vote was called. Indiana's legislature became the first to pass an abortion ban after *Dobbs*. And Addie Bell found she had inherited a sense of despair particular to the families of those killed by public policy. She had stood before her government and asked them to remember her aunt, and then she had watched them do the opposite.

Unlike Rosie Jimenez, Becky Bell was white and blond. In another context, she might have been the perfect victim. But when it came to abortion, even her race and beauty were not enough. So Addie watched the institutionalized disregard of dead women that lies at the core of our abortion politics.

Her grandparents had suffered through the same experience—including five years earlier, in 2017, when Indiana's Republican-led legislature had decided to make it even harder for a minor to access an abortion in the state.[9]

Bill and Karen Bell had stood at the podium before a yellow-white concrete wall.[10] They were a stereotypical Midwestern family; they'd been homecoming king and queen in the same high school, one year apart. He played college basketball and went on to a career selling wholesale office products. She was a homemaker who volunteered as a teacher's aide.[11]

"I remember her mom being one of those moms in middle school who showed up and brought cupcakes and was kind to everyone and had tons of energy, and thinking, 'Boy, how lucky Becky was to have such an involved mom,'" Carey Hamilton told me. Not long after she had that thought, Hamilton joined a group of teenagers to sing Christmas carols outside the Bells' home, consoling them on their first Christmas without their daughter.

The Bells had learned the cause of Becky's death when the coroner called. He said she had contracted a massive infection from dirty instruments used to perform an abortion. The Bells had gone into shock and hiding. Then, remarkably, these two nonpolitical parents had emerged to reveal their daughter's secret. At first, Karen had resisted the idea, not wanting people to speak poorly of her daughter. But they'd decided it was worth it to prevent more teenagers from dying. Next came a whirlwind of public appearances, television interviews on *60 Minutes*, newspaper articles, and events with the Feminist Majority Foundation. Sometimes these efforts helped to defeat proposed parental involvement measures. Sometimes they resulted in threats. Once abortion opponents had even loosened the lug nuts on the Bells' car tires so that they would fly off on the way home from an event.[12]

And as had happened with Rosie Jimenez, the policy that killed Becky Bell became accepted anyway.

Laws requiring parental involvement in a minor's abortion were among the first to pass after *Roe*. In 1974, a young woman whose father had threatened to throw her out of the house and kill her boyfriend if she got pregnant challenged the parental consent law in Massachusetts. In two court decisions issued in 1976 and 1979, the Supreme Court ruled that states could not give parents an absolute veto over a minor's abortion, but they could require parental involvement if they gave minors the option to petition a judge for permission instead. These judicial bypass processes could be time-consuming, humiliating, and sometimes, unsuccessful. But the idea of forcing minors to involve their parents held popular appeal.

These laws "got presented in ways that were appealing to liberals around 'protecting our daughters,' 'making sure they make good decisions,' 'supporting open communication between parents and children,'" Shoshanna Ehrlich, author of *Who Decides? The Abortion Rights of Teens*, told me.[13] Just like the Hyde Amendment, parental consent was supported by Democratic politicians who wanted to seem moderate on abortion. These laws proliferated in most states, including blue ones. By the time the Supreme Court killed *Roe*, all but fourteen states were enforcing laws requiring parents to be notified or give consent for a minor's abortion.[14]

In 2017, an effort to steepen the very law that killed Becky brought the Bells to the capitol. The legislation included a provision allowing parents to be notified of a minor's abortion even when she had obtained a bypass from a judge unless the judge determined the notification wasn't in the minor's best interest. It also banned providers from helping minors access abortion care in states outside of Indiana that didn't require parental consent.[15] (That provision of the law is on hold due to a court battle as of this writing.)

"Good morning," Karen said civilly as she stepped to the mic. She wore a green shirt with a pendant necklace. She had brought with her a photograph of herself with Becky taken the year her daughter died. She was self-conscious about how different she looked now from the young mother in the photograph.

"I would have voted for the parental consent law like that," Karen said, snapping her fingers, "being the mom I was back in 1988. I wasn't educated. I thought if my daughter, who I love more than anything in the world, doesn't come to me, that law will make her come, and I'll take care of her."

But Karen soon realized she was wrong.

"The daughters that love you more than life, they'll die for you. They won't come to you," she said. "I wish that Becky had had an abortion, a safe one, and that I never knew."

Karen didn't mince words about the bill before the legislature that day. She called it a "killer law." When she was finished, she took out the photograph of herself with Becky and showed it to the crowd, displaying it the way a teacher would show a picture in a storybook. She made a crack about how she was twenty-five years younger in the photo, and the crowd gave an appreciative chuckle, although really, there was nothing funny about a woman aging longer than her daughter had lived.

"Bill Bell," the chair called.

The former basketball player stepped to the podium in a gray blazer, his shoulders stooped. He sounded tired. "I don't question anybody's veracity as to their feelings about this," he said. "I would just hope in drafting legislation in the future as it relates to this issue, that the young woman that we're talking about here, whoever she may be in a given situation, that their state of mind and their situation is really considered."

The lawmakers listened, thanked them, and then they passed the killer law.

Five years later, it was Addie's turn to watch the state legislature show its disregard for her aunt's death. She had gone home after her testimony. But as she watched the hearing from her computer, it felt wrong not to be in that room. So she drove back to the capitol to keep up the presence she had maintained day after day during the session.

"I just wanted them to remember, like, they all know her face, so I was standing there in the crowd holding the picture of her face and signs that said 'Remember Becky Bell' and 'No more Becky Bells.'"

Like her grandfather before her, Addie understood that people have strong beliefs about abortion.

"I can appreciate that everybody has their own opinion," she told me. "While I don't think that I personally would have an abortion if I got pregnant, that doesn't mean I don't want anybody else not to be able to."

Addie knew the consequences of making something illegal, even if you disagreed with it. She also knew that the technology is different now. Many people today order abortion pills online from telehealth services or online pharmacies, although some of these services are beholden to state parental consent and notification laws. But the risk of even one more person dying should have been enough to stop the bill, Addie thought. So she kept her vigil.

"It felt necessary to just kind of be like an annoying, constant reminder like 'I'm still here.' And that was the energy that I wanted to bring ... 'Hello, still here, don't forget about me.'" She tried to lock eyes with the antiabortion lawmakers, staring them down as they turned away and looked at the floor. She haunted the gallery, spending so much time there during the two-week special session that she befriended the security guard. When the final vote was called, she asked him if it would be worth it for her to shout, or if they'd just escort her out.

He told her it wasn't worth it.

So she swallowed the words on the tip of her tongue: "Remember Becky Bell."

In the end, she was left with the same question she had had as a child when she first learned about her aunt. "How could the system that we live in let this happen? Like, how could the system that we've built to allegedly protect us let this happen?"

I decided to put that question to one of the few surviving lawmakers responsible for the law that killed Becky Bell.

THE NICE OLD MAN

Of the seventeen lawmakers who wrote and sponsored the parental consent law that led to the death of Becky Bell, at least ten were dead, as was Republican Governor Robert Orr, who signed it. All but one of the lawmakers were men. Five were Democrats. Only one of the living people involved had written a memoir intriguingly called *No Regrets*: a Senate sponsor of the bill, James R. Butcher.

Butcher was raised in the suburbs of Detroit. His parents came from rural east Tennessee and dropped out of school to work in the cotton and tobacco fields to support their large families. His dad drove a grocery truck and sang in traveling gospel quartets, so he was on the road a lot. At one point, Butcher's mother was hospitalized for a nervous breakdown. Nonetheless, Butcher wrote that his mother felt that "her calling in life was to be a faithful wife to my father and a Godly mother to her son."[16] She took him to the Baptist church for Sunday school, morning and evening worship, and Wednesday-night prayer meetings. At the age of nine, Butcher made what he called the most important decision of his life: He fell on his knees beside his bed and accepted Jesus Christ as his Savior.

"Before I accepted Christ as my Savior, I had been thinking a lot about the length of eternity," he wrote. "Even at the age of nine, I decided I wanted to spend eternity with God and my family and friends."[17]

Butcher grew to be six feet two, an avid athlete who played baseball well enough to get two major-league offers after college, which he turned down.

By then he had married a woman named Marvel who shared his faith, and they had a young son.

"All three of our children accepted Christ by the time they were five years of age," Butcher wrote, a remarkable example of the religious transfer rate I'd studied after meeting Paul Haring.[18] Butcher now claimed all of his grandchildren who were old enough had accepted Christ as their Savior, too.

He attended law school and got a job with Youth for Christ International, which brought him close to conservative icons like Billy Graham but forced him to spend stretches of time on the road. In a parallel to his own mother's experience, Butcher came home one day to find his wife removing pictures from the walls, preparing to move back with her mother because she was struggling and Butcher had refused to go to a Christian counselor with her. When they did go, the counselor convinced Butcher to give up his life of travel and pursue his ambition to serve in politics. He was elected to the Indiana senate in 1978, defeating the senator who authored Indiana's no-fault divorce law, which Butcher tried and failed to repeal.[19] In his book, he listed the law that killed Becky Bell as one of his proudest achievements.

On the phone, Butcher was polite. His voice was raspy. He was ninety-two years old. I pictured him sitting in his green-trimmed log cabin–style home in Kokomo. We talked about Reagan, whom he considered the "second-best president."

"He was respectful of other people's views, but he had strong convictions; he wasn't ashamed of them or afraid to put them out there." His favorite president was Abraham Lincoln, whom Butcher liked to dress up as to impersonate.

"What do you think of the current Republican president?" I asked.

"I don't like Donald Trump but I love him," he said. "What do I mean by that?"

"What do you mean by that?"

He laughed.

"I don't like many of the things he does. I don't like many of the things he says. I don't like the way he talks about other people unkindly and things like that," Butcher said in his raspy voice. But Butcher voted for Trump because "I know he loves this country. He loves himself but I know he loves this country." He appreciated Trump's hard-line position on immigration that would make it so "we're not invaded by illegals."

"Do you think he's a Christian?" I asked.

"He's made a lot of mistakes and some of them violate our Christian principles, but that's between him and his Lord."

He cited the late Evangelical leader James Dobson, who called Trump a "baby Christian" ahead of the 2016 election.

"Are you satisfied with him on the abortion issue?"

"Yes, overall," he said thoughtfully, adding that abortion should be left to the states. He's proud to live in the state that, thanks to the law Addie Bell tried to stop, bans most abortions.

"What motivates you?" I asked him.

"I accepted Jesus Christ as my Savior when I was nine years of age, and I'm trying to live my life according to the principles of the book of the Bible," he said. "I think the Bible is pro-life."

"Which passages of the Bible tell you that the Bible is pro-life?"

He laughed. "Dear, I'm sorry; I can't just riff it off like that. I haven't thought about it for years. I just know, overall, the Bible is pro-life."

We talked about heaven, of which he took a practical view.

He proposed a version of Pascal's Wager: A believer and a nonbeliever go through life, and the believer is happy because he knows that heaven is waiting. If heaven's not real, the believer loses nothing.

"But let's assume that I'm right, that the Scriptures are right, that there is a heaven to gain and a hell to shun, and we both die," Butcher said. The nonbeliever "spends eternity in hell. I spend eternity in heaven. Who has been the more smarter person?" he asked.

"Does that make sense to you?"

"Sounds very sensible," I said.

It sounded like a more pragmatic version of what Paul Haring and Bob Bauman and Henry Hyde had all said: that heaven was worth banking on.

Butcher told me he had never heard of Becky Bell, or if he had, he didn't remember her.

"Do you have a message for Bell's family?" I asked.

"As a father or a parent and a grandparent, I have empathy with their loss," he said. "I can't imagine the pain that they have gone through. And tell them as a result of you sharing with me what they've had to go through, I will be praying for them in the days ahead that God will give them comfort, somehow, some way on the loss of their daughter."

"I find it powerful," I added, "the title of your book. 'No regrets.' I mean, does it bring up any regrets for you around sponsoring that legislation?" I asked.

There's that half-second pause, holding everything or nothing.

"Not really. I mean, I don't know how much that legislation impacted their daughter's decision."

"Oh, it did. I mean, they say she told friends that she was seeking an illegal route because she was ashamed to tell her parents, because she loved them too much."

He cleared his throat.

"Well, all I can say is, I'm very, very sorry. That would not be an intended consequence of the bill, and I trust and pray that it has saved many more lives than lives have been prematurely taken like hers."[20]

Butcher sounded like Bob Bauman.

"A death is just as tragic whether it's a mother or a child in my view," Bauman had said during his television appearance on the Hyde Amendment.[21]

Becky Bell's family had lost a child, who worked as a cashier at Cub Foods and whose bedroom was decorated with posters of Marilyn Monroe and who loved animals so much, she quit horseback riding because she couldn't bear to use a riding crop.

Could that really be the same as the loss of a fetus? Butcher's own book seemed to disprove it. In *No Regrets*, he summarized his wife's loss of a pregnancy in two sentences: "On the first Saturday after we moved to Kokomo, Marvel had a miscarriage and ended up in St. Joseph Hospital on the west side of town," he wrote. "However, I did attend Bible Baptist Church that first Sunday."[22]

He didn't remember the miscarriage at first when I asked him about it. So I read him the passage and asked if he really believed an unborn child's life was equal to a woman's.

"Both lives are equal in value to God and to family members," he said. "All life is precious."[23]

Didn't his own experience with miscarriage prove that a fetus had less value? I pressed. He didn't grieve this loss as the Bells grieved Becky. It didn't even disrupt his Sunday routine.

He and his wife hadn't grown attached to her pregnancy, he acknowledged. But he said it would be difficult for any human being to determine which lives were most important. He had made it through life with no regrets by leaving those questions to God.

I felt I had answered Addie's question about how our system allowed her aunt's death to happen. It had happened because enough state leaders like Butcher had truly believed—like the next suspects in my investigation—that by attacking abortion, they were following God's plan.

PART 4

DEATHS IN THE NAME OF LIFE

CHAPTER 9

THE RINGMASTER

> There are things that my profession has taught me. And one of these things, the most terrible thing, is this: murder is a habit.
>
> —*Murder in Mesopotamia* by Agatha Christie

It looked like a scene from the zombie apocalypse. Hordes of doughy white people in T-shirts flopped prostrate on the pavement, forcing traffic outside the clinic in Wichita, Kansas, to stop. When they were arrested, the zombies slackened into human potato sacks.

"Don't do it!" a woman with wire-framed glasses shouted into a car window as a man in jeans and loafers lay in front of the wheels.

"Let it live! Let it be nursed and suckled!"[1]

It was the summer of 1991 and the militant wing of the civil rights movement for fetuses was in full swing. For six weeks, tens of thousands of people laid siege to the city of Wichita, targeting the clinic of third-trimester abortion provider Dr. George Tiller. Journalists would describe that fevered summer as a "fundamentalist Woodstock" when conservative Evangelicals, whipped into a frenzy by the belief that they were fighting a holy war with a demonic enemy, laid down their bodies and were carted deadweight off to jail.² During the first week, the clinics agreed to close at the behest of police, which only encouraged the seething crowd.³ When the frenzy came to an end after forty-six days, police had conducted more than 2,600 arrests. It was one of the last great stands of the antiabortion "rescue" movement.

The parallel was unavoidable yet discordant as a car horn: Wichita was the Selma, Alabama, of the civil rights movement for fetuses, the moment when mostly white demonstrators co-opted the civil disobedience tactics used to fight segregation, reverse engineering them to attack women's rights. The antiabortion group Operation Rescue would claim more than 60,000 people were arrested during its actions in the late 1980s and early 1990s. It was the largest protest movement since the antiwar and civil rights era.⁴

The next step of my investigation was understanding how this movement that co-opted tactics of nonviolent civil disobedience had prompted one of the deadliest strings of domestic terrorism in US history. It was time for Miss Marple to start listening to the extremists. This time, it wasn't just one murder I was investigating. The "rescue" movement had coalesced around a simple logic: Abortion, they believed, was the *murder* of innocent babies being conducted on a mass scale, and urgent action was needed to stop it. It wasn't long before the most extreme followers of this logic murdered eleven people.

The killings started in 1993 when a fundamentalist Christian named Michael Griffin shot Dr. David Gunn,⁵ a man whose face and schedule had been distributed at an Operation Rescue rally. Just months after Gunn's death, and two years after the "Summer of Mercy" descended on his Wichita clinic, a woman named Shelley Shannon shot and wounded Dr. Tiller.

A year later, John Salvi walked into the Planned Parenthood in Brookline, Massachusetts, and opened fire, shooting receptionist Shannon Lowney in the neck. At a second clinic nearby, he shot receptionist Leanne Nichols while shouting: "This is what you get!" Both women died.

In 1998, Eric Rudolph, who had already attacked an abortion clinic, a lesbian bar, and the site of the Summer Olympics in Atlanta, bombed a clinic in Birmingham, Alabama, killing a security guard and half blinding a nurse.

In October that same year, the abortion provider Dr. Barnett Slepian was putting a bowl of soup in the microwave of his home in Amherst, New York, when an assassin's bullet shattered his window and killed him.

In 2009, after a lull in the "rescue" movement, antiabortion activist Scott Roeder walked into the atrium of Dr. George Tiller's church and finished Shelley Shannon's work. He shot in the head the doctor whom abortion opponents including Operation Rescue's founder, Randall Terry, had maligned as "Tiller the Killer."

Police would find a piece of paper in Roeder's car with the phone number of Cheryl Sullenger, an Operation Rescue leader. Randall Terry, who by then was no longer part of the organization, attended Roeder's trial and called Tiller a "mass murderer" who had "reaped what he sowed." Far from repenting of this declaration, Terry would later tell me that he believed defending Roeder was "one of the greatest services I did to the entire pro-life movement."[6]

Five years after Roeder was sentenced to prison, a group of antiabortion operatives released strategically edited videos of Planned Parenthood staff talking about fetal tissue research, inspiring the shooter Robert Dear to proclaim "no more baby parts" after he opened fire and killed a police officer and two civilians at the Planned Parenthood in Colorado Springs.

What these killers and attempted killers shared, besides the fact that they were almost all white men, was a conviction that stopping abortion required radical action.

It was the "rescue" movement that popularized this idea in the 1980s and 1990s. For even as the movement co-opted the tactics of nonviolent civil disobedience, their framing of the movement as "rescue" had a military edge that reflected the "paramilitarization of pro-life politics" in this era, as Carol Mason wrote in her book *Killing for Life*. The shift toward paramilitary antiabortion activism in the 1980s and 1990s was, Mason wrote, "perhaps a logical consequence" of apocalyptic antiabortion language espoused by earlier, more mainstream antiabortion groups that saw abortion as a transgression that would bring down the wrath of God.[7] In the parking lots outside clinics where Randall Terry reigned, the human rights–infused language of the earlier "right-to-life" groups gave way to the language of war.

I would think back to the "rescue" movement's scenes of white bodies flailing in clinic parking lots on January 6, 2021, when I watched Trump supporters invade the US Capitol. Among the masses present that day were numerous antiabortion extremists:[8] John Brockhoeft, a clinic arsonist; Derrick Evans, a state lawmaker known for harassing patients outside West Virginia's sole abortion clinic; and Mark Lee Dickson, a Texas pastor known for his "sanctuary city for the unborn" initiatives. At least some of the extremists at the Capitol that day shared with the rescuers a sense that the laws of man did not matter—for this was a holy war.

This rhetoric had been popularized by my next suspect: a former used-car salesman named Randall Terry.

THE RINGMASTER

Randall Terry was a weedy-looking Napoleon Dynamite of a man who had been raised in a family of Democrats and then born again on the side of the road in upstate New York. One journalist described him as a "charlatan" or modern-day carnival barker whose priority was to get himself in front of the cameras.[9] He was also a true believer whose views about patriarchal gender roles and the demonic nature of his opposition came from reading the Evangelical writer Francis Schaeffer.

Schaeffer believed there were two kinds of people in this world: Christians and secular humanists, and the conflict between these two forces constituted a holy war with apocalyptic stakes. Schaeffer's influential 1979 film series, *Whatever Happened to the Human Race?*, which he produced and screened around the country with future Reagan surgeon general C. Everett Koop, depicted the white fetus and its defenders as *the* most holy victims in this spiritual war.[10]

Terry wept the first time he saw it.

"Apparently in every age there is always someone branded as subhuman," Schaeffer intoned in one scene that showed images of Black people in chains marching slowly toward the Lincoln Memorial. "It once was the Black. Later the Jew. Today, it is the unborn and the child." The film's message was clear: The real, pressing genocide of the time was abortion. The era's heroic saviors, akin to the civil rights icons and liberating armies of old, were the (mostly white) Christians willing to defend this innocent being from extermination. Schaeffer's rhetoric literally replaced Black people and Jews with fetuses. He relegated the struggles of these groups to history, nullifying them as present-day concerns. Soon, Terry and his supporters were following Schaeffer's teachings, focusing their "civil rights movement" on the single issue of abortion, and erasing, in the process, the injustices that animated the movement they were copying.

Before I met Terry, my own Bible for understanding him was a feminist one that he vehemently rejected. The writer Susan Faludi in her seminal 1991 book, *Backlash*, described Terry as part of the backlash against second-wave feminism that gripped the country in the 1980s. In Faludi's telling, popular culture, the media, the fashion and beauty industries, and antiabortion radicals were all part of an antifeminist backlash aimed at convincing women that feminism had made them miserable and unmarriageable. Faludi described how during their interview, Terry loomed over his first wife, Cindy Dean, informed Faludi that Cindy didn't talk, and scolded his wife for burning the beans.[11]

Whether you believed he was a sexist or a religious zealot or a media hog or all three, Terry's legacy was inseparable from the terror that came in his movement's wake. He popularized the phrase "If abortion is murder, then act like it's murder." This claim resounded in movement gatherings and on the national news before a handful of people took it to its logical conclusion.

I wanted to interview Terry not only to understand his motivations—hatred of women, love of God, promotion of self, or all three—but because he was the unapologetic face of the conservative co-optation of the civil rights movement. Terry was the charismatic ringmaster whose theatrics had convinced a generation of Evangelicals that he was the next Martin Luther King Jr. And by this stage of my investigation, the death of *Roe* was starting to look like a copycat killing.

In its first phase, the antiabortion movement copied the rhetoric of the civil rights movement, forming "right-to-life" groups that championed fetuses as human beings entitled to human rights. In the second phase, political strategists like Richard Viguerie had reverse engineered the Left's strategies and structures. In this third phase, the civil rights movement for fetuses would co-opt the Left's civil disobediences tactics.

It turned out the biggest copycat of all was Randall Terry himself. As I dug into the movement's history in the book *Wrath of Angels* by Judy Thomas and James Risen, I learned that he didn't invent "rescue," even though he made it famous. Before long, I started to feel like I was looking at the Congress of the 1970s with its surprising heroes and complicated villains all over again. Because before thousands of zombies crawled across abortion clinic parking lots, back when Randall Terry was just a pot-smoking piano player getting beaten by his dad for dropping out of high school, it was a group of peace activists who had started it all.

THE PACIFIST

John Cavanaugh O'Keefe was raised in a big Catholic family. His turning point on abortion came when a friend confided in him that she had had one. The friend seemed fine with that, but O'Keefe apparently wasn't. His brother had just been killed in the Vietnam War, and he began to see this friend as akin to the soldier who shot his brother. O'Keefe would meld the antiabortion movement's beliefs with the antiwar movement's strategies. It was an extremely niche proposition. He couldn't win the antiwar Left to the cause of fighting abortion, and he couldn't rouse conservative Catholics to civil disobedience tactics associated with the left-wing radicals. But he sure tried. He wrote a pamphlet titled *A Peaceful Presence* that cited Martin Luther King Jr. and held small sit-ins at abortion clinics. He and his followers sang civil rights anthems like "We Shall Overcome" that were retrofitted with antiabortion lyrics. They believed they were saving babies, so they called their movement "rescue."[12]

There were women who bucked the conservative stereotype, too. There was Julianne Wiley, an organizer with Cesar Chavez's United Farm Workers, who protested the war one day and abortion the next, delighting in defying expectations by handing out antiabortion pamphlets at antiwar rallies and vice versa. She would eventually leave the movement because of how Randall Terry subordinated women, yet she continued to see her cause as a progressive one.[13] When I reached her years later, she rued the party divide on abortion and yearned for a bipartisan alliance to support children and families. Yet she had voted for Trump three times.[14]

Most intriguing to me was Monica Migliorino Miller, another suspect on my list, who in the underground ranks of the movement cultivated a special niche: By the time she reached her golden years, she was an expert in how to recover, preserve, and display aborted fetal remains.

But the most famous woman of "rescue" was Joan Andrews Bell, a farm girl from Tennessee whose mother left a deep impression on her when she let twelve-year-old Joan hold her miscarried fetus.[15] It was "Saint Joan's" sacrifice that put Randall Terry on the map.

Of course, the ranks of early rescuers weren't all saintly women and antiwar Catholics. There was John Burt, a born-again Christian and former member of the Ku Klux Klan, and Earl Appleby, an aide to racist Senator Jesse Helms. There was Joe Scheidler, a six-foot-four bear of a man in a white mayor's suit and bowler hat who once defended his decision to try to stop an eleven-year-old girl from getting an abortion by protesting: "Everybody had this image of this skinny little girl. She was a big girl. It wasn't like it was going to kill her to have a baby."[16]

On March 26, 1986, Joan Andrews Bell burst into a clinic in Pensacola. When the police left her alone in handcuffs, she knocked an abortion machine to the ground. In prison, she refused to give her name and languished in solitary confinement to express solidarity with the unborn, refusing an offer by the governor to release her to Mother Teresa. She became a cause célèbre championed by the era's burgeoning Evangelical media outlets.[17]

Into this fray came the ringmaster.

Randall Terry's mother was one of four sisters, three of whom had abortions. One almost bled to death from a procedure before *Roe*. But Terry's mom chose to give birth to her son in 1959. Terry would grow into an itinerant young man, doing drugs and roaming the country with a Gideon Bible, until a chance encounter at an ice cream shop brought him to God and to a vision of himself leading holy warriors into abortion clinics.

In 1986, while Joan Andrews Bell languished in prison, Terry gathered a group of her supporters at a Western Sizzlin' restaurant and began to preach the fiery gospel, identifying himself as the new leader of their movement. He would bring masses into the streets by recruiting worshippers from Evangelical churches. These were not quiet Catholics like O'Keefe, but fire-and-brimstone faithful who were ready for battle.

The public's broad support of abortion rights only fueled this group's sense that they were a persecuted minority. In a NARAL poll released in 1988, two years after Operation Rescue started, only 10 percent of Americans said they opposed abortion under all circumstances.[18] For all Reagan's antiabortion rhetoric, he had at times disappointed abortion opponents, and Senate Republicans had stymied the last shot at an antiabortion constitutional amendment. President George H. W. Bush was a former family planning supporter even if he toed the antiabortion line. So, the disillusioned faithful in Randall Terry's grasp declared war.

THE SHOWMAN

When I met Randall Terry, he was sitting alone on a coral-colored velvet sofa in the lobby of an opulent DC hotel after getting kicked out of a political summit run by his old friends. He was sixty-five, with gray fluffy hair like a dandelion gone to seed. It was fall 2024, and Terry was trying desperately to get back into the spotlight. He was running for president. He was making a movie. He was running ads with graphic images of fetuses that compared popular media figures to Nazis.

Miss Marple had a signature approach to solving mysteries. She would examine all the suspects until some personality quirk or tiny detail in their habits reminded her of a resident in her village. Invariably, these unlikely parallels were key to solving the case.

In a similar form, I sensed that understanding Terry would help me understand the extremists not just of his time, but of today. Was he a circus act, a woman hater, a true believer—or all three? And how did he manage to pass off a co-optation of the civil rights movement as a credible struggle that brought tens of thousands of people from the pews to the streets and into jail cells across America?

He was wearing a blue collared shirt and tie with black jeans and pebbled pointy-toed leather boots. His look was disjointed—part rock star, part businessman—but every element had been curated, including the hair, intended to defy the stereotype of the Bible-thumping zealot.

As Terry and I chatted, a beefy security guard walked over. Terry jumped to his feet and extended his hand like he was meeting a fan.

"What's your name, brother?" Terry asked jovially, introducing himself as the presidential candidate of the Constitution Party.

The guard eyed him warily.

The Constitution Party is a far-right political party with a dubious slate of former candidates that includes the disgraced former CEO of Massey Energy, Don Blankenship, and the Christian nationalist Michael Peroutka. The security guard did not seem interested in the Constitution Party, however. He was there to tell Terry that the organizers of this summit—the leaders of the Christian right think tank the Family Research Council—wanted Terry to leave.

Maybe it was because the night before, Terry had confronted one of the speakers, Evangelical pastor Gary Hamrick, to condemn him for not letting Terry's presidential campaign gather signatures in his church parking lot.

Or maybe it was because his running mate, Pastor Stephen Broden, had approached FRC's president, Tony Perkins, to ask for support, with a ramshackle camera crew in tow.

Or maybe it was because Terry's presence here was an awkward reminder that Trump was backtracking on abortion in the lead-up to the 2024 election.

"I have forty years' history with these people," Terry was telling the security guard. "I used to be the fair-haired child."

The guard departed after Terry promised he would be leaving soon. Then Terry whipped out his phone, called one of the young men who was trailing him around the country, and directed him to make their secondhand tour bus *immaculate*.

I followed him through the hotel's automatic sliding doors into the warm fall afternoon, feeling conflicted about joining his circus. Terry had agreed to speak on the condition that I allow him to film our interview for a documentary about his campaign. I agreed, even though I thought there was a chance he would edit the tape to give me demon eyes. I told myself it would be a valuable chance to watch the showman from inside the show.

It was even weirder than I could have imagined.

Parked outside was a 2008 Fleetwood Expedition tour bus Terry bought for $75,000 on a loan. "DestroyTheDemocratParty.com" was emblazoned on the side in red, alongside a cartoon Terry had commissioned to illustrate his notion that he would steal enough Catholic and African American voters from the Democratic Party to help Trump win. Spoiler alert: This didn't happen. Terry peaked at .2 percent of the vote in the states where he managed to make it on the ballot. A Democrat-linked super PAC would spend almost $2.5 million on direct mail and text messages supporting Terry in an apparent effort to funnel antiabortion votes *away* from Trump.[19]

Inside, the bus was paneled in dark-wood laminate. There was a cross magnet on the refrigerator. A Bible rested on the white-speckled counter next to camera equipment. Two bananas sat tucked neatly in a corner. An image of Jesus hung from the wall and a picture of the Virgin Mary was taped to the GPS screen. Terry had been sleeping in the back on a damaged air mattress that only inflated on one side.

For this DIY campaign, Terry had managed to raise almost $584,000; his most prominent donor was disgraced former Republican House Majority Leader Tom Delay, who declared that not getting rid of abortion was his biggest regret while he was in Congress.

Terry and I sat on a cream-colored bench as three young white men hovered around us. One filmed us from three feet away while a second sat holding a microphone near Terry's feet.

"Guys, please feel free to remind me to not hunch over," Terry coached. "The old man hunch. I hate that look."

His running mate, Stephen Broden, a Black pastor from Texas, lingered at the front of the bus.

Terry leaned toward me with his arm over the back of the couch. His breath smelled like stale coffee. He was fired up about getting kicked out of the conference, ranting about the "grifters" at the event for "kissing the ass of the Trump family because they're more committed to the Republican Party than they are to principle."

"That is what agitates them about me: I put principle first," he railed.

Not that Terry was beyond accusations of grift himself; In the heyday of "rescue," he had raised so much money from supporters during a jail stay that he was able to buy a farm outside Binghamton, New York.[20] But he was correct that it was a rough time for the people inside the conference and their principles. With its $22 million budget, the Family Research Council outstripped Terry's shoestring operation by a long shot; inside the hotel ballroom, giant screens under glittering blue stage lights broadcast high-definition images of well-coifed speakers.[21] But this year's Pray Vote Stand summit was a downer compared to the year before, when legions of faithful in red MAGA hats lined up to see Trump speak. Most Republican candidates had addressed the convention last year as they jockeyed for the coveted white Evangelical vote. This year, Trump wasn't just absent from the summit; he had foresaken its dearest cause, promising just a few days before that he would veto any nationwide abortion ban. Over the summer, the Family Research Council's clean-shaven, dad-joking president, Tony Perkins, had denounced the Republican Party for passing a platform he saw as soft on abortion without giving delegates like him time to weigh in. Abortion, that reliable third leg on the stool of conservative power, had become politically toxic. Even Melania Trump was calling herself pro-choice.

Yet the Christian right's formidable political machine was still turning out voters for Trump.

Terry, on the other hand, was trying to turn out votes for himself. In the process, he was revealing the antiabortion movement's ugly, unrestrained heart. He said in public what many abortion opponents quietly believed. His aggressive and unfettered way of denouncing abortion as the murder of babies and comparing it to the Holocaust was his way of calling the movement's bluff: *If abortion is murder, then act like it's murder.*

Terry has repeatedly run for office so that he can air this message in its most grotesque form by exploiting laws that force TV stations to run even the most gruesome ads from candidates. He packed those ads with images of fetuses.

Why is he like this? was the scariest question of all.

Terry was raised "at the knee of feminists," as Susan Faludi quoted his aunt saying about him.[22] His aunt was a former communications director for Planned Parenthood in Rochester, and she had somehow helped produce the country's most notorious antiabortion operative. It was a terrifying proposition. What if you made a humble contribution to the pro-choice movement and then your nephew founded Operation Rescue? Faludi described Terry as part of a generation of "downwardly mobile sons, condemned by the '80s economy to earn less than their fathers," who blamed "the rise of independent and professional women" for the "economic and social dislocations" in their lives.[23] She based this analysis in part on the fact that Terry's first wife supported the struggling couple with her job at a flower shop.

Journalists Judy Thomas and James Risen dismissed this narrative of Terry.

"If he believed in a male-dominated world, it was a concept he learned in his church pew, not in the unemployment line," they wrote in *Wrath of Angels*.[24]

Regardless of how Terry arrived at his sexism, he was open about it in a way that was rare among my suspects. Paul Haring believed in complementary roles for men and women. Richard Viguerie made his wife change all the diapers while he studied marketing. James Butcher's wife packed up her pictures while he was on the road. But Terry was the first to tell me outright: "I believe in patriarchy." Indeed, he had left the Evangelical fold and converted to Catholicism eighteen years before in part because of its stricter adherence to patriarchal gender roles.

"How did you break with your family?" I asked while the camera rolled, hoping his answer would help me ensure my kid didn't join the Young

Republicans. "I've done research on this, and it's very rare for people actually to break from the political and religious beliefs they were raised with. Most of us just accept what our parents tell us about religion and about politics."

Terry paused the interview.

"Chris, I need you to do me a favor," he said, handing his phone to one of his acolytes. "I want you to get a few shots with this phone from that angle." He gestured behind my shoulder, telling Chris to film his face.

Terry turned toward me again. "I tend to be passionate about what I believe," he said. His break with his family started in 1976, the year Henry Hyde introduced the ban that killed Rosie Jimenez. Terry was seventeen, a wannabe rock star working at an ice cream shop called the Three Sisters.

"I've got to show you this," Terry said, reclaiming his phone from Chris. "You've got to check this out."

"Randall, sit up," one of the men reminded him.

Terry sat up and hit play. On the phone screen was a shaky image of a white shack in a parking lot.

Off camera, Terry was sobbing.

"For me this is hallowed ground," he cried. The camera moved inside the empty shack: "They tore out this wall, but it was cinder block then, baby!"

It was the former ice cream shop where Terry was working one day in 1976 when Mark Saunders from the Elim Bible Institute came up to the window, saw the Bible Terry was reading, and asked if he was a Christian.

"It's kind of hard to be with the friends I hang out with," Terry told him. They began meeting to talk about God until Saunders pulled over by the side of the road one day so Terry could fall to the ground and invite Jesus into his heart. Terry soon claimed he had experienced a vision instructing him to go to the "abortion mills" to save babies and spread a "Bible-based perspective." My favorite part of this purported vision is that Terry swore it included a scene of him being interviewed on *Donahue*.

Like Bob Bauman, Terry seemed to identify strongly with the unwanted fetus.

"My mom didn't want me," Terry said to me seemingly out of the blue during our interview. "I was an unplanned pregnancy. She was nineteen years old when she got pregnant in 1958. This was a crisis."

Terry's hero Francis Schaeffer believed there were two Americas: a Christian one and a demonic one. Across this stark divide, it was amazing Terry and I could communicate at all. One of my questions almost fell into the ideological void that stretched between us on the bus bench.

The question was: Why were *you* the one to lead the movement when people like Joan Andrews Bell were already out there getting arrested?

Terry let out a reedy laugh.

"You don't believe in God," he said.

I might be open to the idea of God, I thought, *but not to a God who, given the option of personally speaking to anyone on this green earth, would choose Randall Terry.*

"God put his *hand* on me to do it.

"I believe in male leadership," he added. "The Bible teaches patriarchy.

"The fact of the matter is," Terry continued, "the vast majority of wars in human history—and this is a war—wars are led by men, and I'm a man.

"The way that I assess any ethical argument regarding child-killing, and our response to it, is I take out the word 'baby' and I put in the word 'Jew,' or I put in slaves," he added later, manifesting verbally the displacement of the Holocaust and slavery that his hero Schaeffer had visualized.

We had moved on to a discussion of murdering abortion providers, which Terry has stopped short of endorsing outright.

"The problem with using lethal force is the separation of powers biblically—to be judge, jury, and executioner is problematic unless you're at war," he added. "And we are not at war. We're in a culture war."

Hold on. Didn't he just *say* we're at war? Here was a lesson in how to be an extremist, one that reminded me of Trump and his followers. You make an incendiary claim, then contradict it, then move on to the next incendiary claim.

Did he take responsibility for the violence? I asked. Didn't he understand, when he said, "If abortion is murder, then act like it," that he might inspire some die-hard believers to kill?

"No," Terry said casually.

"When you look back at the murders that happened, in the 1990s and then, most recently, George Tiller, what do you think about the impact that those killings have had on the movement? Has it been a net positive or a net negative for the movement?"

Terry paused for an uncomfortably long time.

"I don't know."

In the end, Terry's vision came true. The "rescue" movement staged hundreds of blockades. Terry won support from powerful Evangelical leaders like Jerry Falwell. He got his interview on *Donahue*.

Even his opponents would later admit that the abortion rights movement might have something to learn from his unabashed stance.

"If you think abortion is morally just, act like it's morally just," Lauren Rankin, author of a book about clinic escorts called *Bodies on the Line*, told me. "Do not apologize for the thing that you believe in. Do not apologize for that which you are advocating. I think there is power in that."[25]

As for victims, like Dr. George Tiller, Terry believed history would vindicate his killer.

Again, he shamelessly drew the slavery parallel.

"Was John Brown right or wrong?" he asked, referring to the abolitionist who tried to set off a slave revolt at Harpers Ferry.

The cameraman called for a pause. The memory card was full.

They had turned off the air-conditioning on the bus to improve the sound. The air felt close and hot. Terry was sweating, wiping his face with a tissue. "Was John Brown right or wrong?" he asked again. From the front of the bus, Stephen Broden, who had sat silent for over an hour, called out, "He was right."

Weeks after our interview, Terry texted me gleefully; his campaign ads with images of bloody fetuses were running during *The View* and the World

Series and generating headlines in the lead-up to the election. In one ad, Terry made what he said was a joke: "Jake Tapper compared Trump to Hitler but sees no connection between his words and assassination attempts," Terry said. "So words don't matter? Ho! Then I hope Jake Tapper gets the crap beat out of him...in a game of pool!"

In another ad, Terry compared pro-choice celebrities to Nazi propagandists.

I texted back, dizzied by what seemed like an obvious contradiction. If Jake Tapper was promoting violence by comparing Trump to Hitler, then wasn't Terry promoting violence by comparing celebrities to...Nazis?

The difference, he said, was that he had compared the celebrities to the Nazi *propagandists*, not to Hitler himself. People talked all the time about how it might be ethical to murder *Hitler*, but they never said so about the *propagandists*. Certainly, he wasn't calling for *violence* against *Tapper*. Defender of patriarchy, religious zealot, self-promoter, and world-class troll...Terry was all four.

Before our interview concluded, I asked Terry why he had chosen to give up a comfortable life and pursue his convictions even when they put him in jail. Why hadn't he pursued the easier life of the people who sat inside the air-conditioned conference?

He loved this question. He called it the *most important* one I had asked.

Here's how he answered it:

"I live with the daily notion in front of me," he said, pulling his hand up in front of his face like a screen, "that one day I will stand before my maker, and I want to hear him say, 'Well done, good and faithful servant.' That's what I want. And I don't know what he's going to say. I hope he says that. I'd love him to reach out his hand and go: 'Randy. I'm so proud of you. You're a good boy. You did it!'...That's my dream come true."

Is this what's been driving this sweaty bus the whole time? I thought. Terry wanted God to pat him on the head like an approving dad and let him into heaven.

"Well, if I get any credit when I get to Saint Peter at the gate, I hope that's on my list," Bauman said of his decision to promote the Hyde Amendment.

And Paul Haring: "The most important thing is we go to heaven."

Before we concluded, Terry insisted I interview Broden, whom Terry seemed to be using as a prop. Here was the ringmaster's final act, a Black pastor who affirmed that Terry was indeed a hero akin to Martin Luther King Jr. When Broden was done looking me dead in the eye while railing against the "God-hating, man-hating feminists," Terry instructed us to stare at each other so the cameraman could film cutaway shots.

"I don't mind looking at you; you're kind of perty," Broden said in his Southern drawl. Terry interjected, noting that some terms of endearment that *might* fly in the South were *not* accepted in the Northeast, where I'm from.

If Terry was trying to avoid another Faludi-esque moment in which a feminist writer would seize on an incriminating detail to dismiss him as a sexist, Broden wasn't taking the hint.

"The MeToo generation," Broden declared, with a pastor's grand elocution, "has produced a kind of tentative acknowledgment of the glorious beauty of a woman.

"God made you different from us... and he made you different so that we might look at you."

Terry laughed maniacally.

"I mean, not lustfully," Broden said, "but to admire the work of God."

I felt my stomach churn with humiliation.

Had I wasted my time trying to understand these men? Because here it was in its plainest form: the backlash against feminism, just as Susan Faludi described it more than thirty years earlier. These two men were masquerading as civil rights icons, and yet here they were, reminding me I was an object created for men's admiration. As I sat before the cameras, I thought about how the civil rights movement for fetuses was the greatest red herring of all in my investigation. Broden and Terry were using it to inflate their own importance as they put a woman back in her place.

Terry wanted to stage one last scene. He wanted a shot of himself and Broden trying to walk into the conference and getting turned away by guards. He strode into the hotel lobby with the film crew in tow. As he walked, he threw his shoulders back and carried himself with the confidence of a man who believed that he was being watched—not just by the cameras, but by an approving God.

CHAPTER 10

THE FETUS KEEPER AND THE FELONS

Remember, he was a fanatic, and there is no fanatic like a religious fanatic.

—*Poirot's Early Cases* by Agatha Christie

THE "RESCUE" MOVEMENT ENDED NOT LONG AFTER THAT FEVERED SUMMER in Wichita. In 1992, rescuers converged on Buffalo for what they called a "Spring of Life," but this time, a legion of pro-choice clinic defenders led by the Feminist Majority Foundation was ready. In Wichita, clinic administrators had asked pro-choice forces to stand down, fearing their presence would only add to the chaos. But in Buffalo the defenders didn't ask for permission. They encircled the rescuers and screamed in their faces. The "Spring of Life" was a bust.[1] Two years later, President Bill Clinton signed the FACE Act, imposing prison sentences of up to ten years for blockading abortion clinics. After internal drama, Randall Terry had moved on from Operation Rescue.

The militant wing of the civil rights movement for fetuses faded from the news.

But more than twenty years later, a new generation was trying to bring it back.

On October 22, 2020, Jonathan Darnel, a scrawny white man with a military haircut, went live on Facebook outside a glass-fronted building on a bustling DC street.² Behind him was an easel-sized placard with letters in blue, red, and green tape that read "Pro-Life Preborn Rescue Right Now!"

"History is being made today," Darnel declared breathlessly.

The police had already arrived, he noted.

"They may act quickly to arrest people and well, we're going to go down with the ship—most of us will—because these kids are worth it!"

As he broadcast, Darnel checked his phone screen and his enthusiasm seemed to deflate momentarily when he saw that only nine people had so far tuned in to witness this historic moment. At least some of the viewers that day would turn out to be abortion rights supporters who repeatedly interrupted the livestream by calling Darnel's phone. This was not the large-scale "rescue" movement of Randall Terry's time. Still, the blockaders would make history, not because of what they did but because of the price they would pay—and the man who would pardon them.

This depleted effort to relaunch the "rescue" movement involved a multigenerational mash-up of strange allies. Inside, wrapped in chains in the clinic lobby, was Joan Andrews Bell, the martyr of Pensacola, now in her seventies with stringy gray hair. Pacing the hallway was Herb Geraghty, an atheist in his twenties who opposed police brutality and the death penalty. Overseeing the action, like a strange friar dressed in black with a silver cross around her neck, was Lauren Handy, a protégée of Bell and Monica Migliorino Miller and self-described Catholic anarchist who would become famous two years later when police raided her apartment and found fetuses stashed there that she claimed to have recovered from a waste disposal truck.

What they shared was a sense that cutting away at abortion access through state legislation and the courts was not enough. They needed to put their bodies on the line. They were resurrecting Randall Terry's rallying cry: *If abortion is murder, then act like it's murder.*

The blockaders had forced their way through a door into the Washington Surgi-Clinic—pushing and injuring a clinic nurse in the process, the Biden administration would later allege.[3] Four people including Bell wrapped themselves in chains on lime-green chairs in front of an entrance to the medical area. They sang "Ave Maria" and screamed through the door at the patients.

"Just letting you know, ladies out here, if you die in the abortion procedure, you could wake up in a place you don't want to be!" Jay Smith yelled, while Paulette Harlow repeatedly cried: "I love you, Mummy, please don't kill me!"

One woman had traveled from Ohio to get an abortion after learning four months into her much-wanted pregnancy that there was a serious problem with it. She had already taken medication and was having painful contractions when Herb Geraghty informed her and her husband: "There's no abortions being performed here today." She collapsed onto the floor. Another patient sobbed as the rescuers blocked her path. She was ultimately able to get past them by flinging herself through a reception window, according to a detailed account in *Ms.* magazine.[4]

Outside in the hall, Handy agreed to let a young man in to see his partner on the condition that he give her antiabortion literature.

"She has a very hard heart," another rescuer with a blond ponytail wailed, recalling how she had tried to preach the gospel to a crying patient.

Standing in front of the employee entrance was Will Goodman, a former aspiring professional skier with a black bandanna over his mouth. When he saw Darnel's camera, Goodman gave his version of the exchange with clinic workers.

"There have been many cases of assault, members of the abortion center have been violent with peaceful, nonviolent protesters, shoving them, pushing them, blowing airhorns in their faces and in their ears," Goodman declared. "We'd like to press full charges against at least two members of this abortion facility."

But it was the blockaders who would ultimately be charged by the Biden administration for crimes including violating the 1994 FACE Act. They would face up to eleven years in prison at a trial that put their values to the test.

I was preparing to Miss Marple my way into a deeper understanding of people who looked very much like fanatics with a fetish for storing fetuses in their apartments. While press accounts tended to dismiss these blockaders as fringe zealots, I saw them as essential to the antiabortion project that killed *Roe*. These were today's true believers, the stewards of Haring's and Terry's convictions. The mainstream antiabortion movement continued to push for incremental cuts to abortion rights. But these activists were the keepers of the flame. Their willingness to act like abortion was murder lent credibility and urgency to the rest of the cause.

Soon, they were going to lend credibility to the ultimate opportunist, Donald Trump.

I wanted to talk with these modern-day rescuers about their uneasy embrace of Trump. But my first challenge was identifying people among them whom I could stand to listen to. I did not want to spend time with a grown woman who thought screaming "I love you, Mummy!" through a door at abortion patients was a useful way to pass your day.

I was all about deep listening, but I had my limits.

In the end I found three people from this wing of the civil rights movement for fetuses whose presence I found not only tolerable but interesting. One was Will Goodman, the skier; the other was Herb Geraghty, the atheist; and the last was Monica Migliorino Miller, a veteran of the "rescue" movement and an expert fetus keeper.

THE FETUS KEEPER

Monica Migliorino Miller agreed to meet me at a café in February 2023, the day before she was scheduled to go on trial for a "rescue" at a clinic in Southfield, a suburb of Detroit. She was petite, with a short bob of gray hair, a slouching posture, dark, intense features, and no makeup. I doubted she'd object to the comparison: Miller looked like a nun. On the lapel of her purple jacket was a gold pin with two tiny feet, a common antiabortion symbol intended to represent a ten-week fetus.

"It's not my first time at the rodeo," she said wryly when I asked how she felt about the next day's trial. Her voice was deep and threaded with a constant undercurrent of impatience. "But you're always a little nervous."[5]

Like Randall Terry, Miller has stopped short of endorsing the murder of abortion providers. In her book *Abandoned* she wrote that she was "torn and confused" by Dr. David Gunn's murder because "academically speaking," it "could not be condemned on the basis that it was *intrinsically* immoral."[6] After Gunn was killed, the antiabortion militant Paul Hill released a statement calling the murder justified. Miller called Hill, whom she described as "extremely polite," and counseled him that violence might harm the movement.[7] Just over a year later, Hill shot dead Gunn's replacement, Dr. John Britton, and his volunteer escort, James Barrett.

"I wanted to ask you about your manuscript," I said in the noisy coffee shop. Miller had mailed me an unpublished book she wrote in the 1980s titled *Social Liberation and the Pro-Life Cause*. It argued that the antiabortion cause was a progressive one, not a conservative one, because it sought to broaden the boundaries of justice to encompass all members of the human family, which, in Miller's view, included the unborn. By the time Miller and I met, the partisan divide on abortion was solid: 84 percent of Democrats self-identified as pro-choice and 76 percent of Republicans self-identified as pro-life.[8] While as late as 1999 there were forty-three House Democrats who were considered pro-life, in 2024 there was just one, Texas Representative Henry Cuellar.[9] In the end, the argument that abortion was not just a human rights cause but *the* most important human rights cause would be used by Reagan to absorb the issue into the conservative agenda.

"I wondered why—and you mentioned you wrote it in the 1980s—why that felt like an important thing to do? Because [opposing abortion] was in the process of becoming a conservative issue," I asked.

"That is a very good question," Miller replied. "Maybe it's just a personal repulsion I have to being pigeonholed as a right-wing, radical conservative."

Like most Catholics in the 1950s and '60s, she started out as a Democrat. Indeed, Richard Nixon was the first Republican president to win a majority of Catholics in 1972 when he defeated Democrat George McGovern, who had been successfully tarred as the candidate of "acid, abortion and amnesty."[10] Nixon's strategist, Pat Buchanan, would credit "cultural, moral and social issues" with bringing Catholics into the Republican fold.[11] Conservatives were figuring out how they could use abortion as a wedge to separate Catholics from the Democratic Party. They succeeded in part because they convinced people like Miller to downgrade the rest of the Catholic social justice ethic, at least when it came to voting. Liberal aspects of Catholic teaching, like feeding the poor and supporting workers, would need to be suspended in favor of the one Catholic cause that fit the Republican agenda.

"Now of course, the pro-life movement is wedded more or less—because we had no other place to go—to the Republican Party," Miller said.

We talked about her childhood with her nominally Catholic, Italian parents and how she dreamed of becoming an actress. In the early seventies, she went to college at Southern Illinois University or as she called it, "one of the most godless places on earth."

"And then I was in the theater department so it was even more godless."

"Godless in what sense?" I asked.

She laughed. "The students living together, shacking up together, sex all over the place, abortions up the river. Homosexuality: Everybody was out including the professors." She seemed to recoil just remembering it.

In 1974, while Paul Haring was pitching the Hyde Amendment to the bishops, Miller got a part as Sister Felicity in the play *Suddenly Last Summer*. "Here I am in this costume, dressed up like a nun, and it just got me thinking about my religion," she told me. She was riddled with anxiety at the time, obsessed with her success on the stage. To escape, she buried herself in books on religious women. In the library one day a particular book caught her eye: a biography of the French nun St. Thérèse of Lisieux, who died of tuberculosis at the age of twenty-four. In the front of the book was a picture of Thérèse three months before her death. Miller was transfixed.

"The look on her face was so deep and so profound and even kind of grim," Miller told me. "I don't know who you are," she thought, gazing at St. Thérèse. "But ... I'm going there."

In his book on antiabortion activists, sociologist Ziad Munson noted that many such activists entered the movement through social relationships rather than ideology, often during a turning point in their lives that left them open to a radical change of mind.[12] Miller fit this bill; she was in college in the throes of an identity crisis when she found her way to a renewed Catholic faith, and then through a friend, to the militant wing of the antiabortion movement.

She dropped out of school with one semester to go, returning home, where she grated on her parents with her newfound devotion until her father got so frustrated that he declared: "Monica, I don't want to be a saint."

But Miller was heeding the call of St. Thérèse.

"When I went back to school, I felt so liberated; I didn't have to be in a play anymore," she continued. The word "liberated" hit my feminist brain like an off-key chord. It was the height of the women's movement. Miller's peers in the "godless" university were fleeing the cloistered lives of their mothers, finding liberation not just through premarital sex but through career ambitions of the kind Miller was now renouncing.

Except Miller hadn't given up her ambition to become an actress, I was about to learn. She had just found a holier channel for it.

One day in 1976, her friend Sheila, wrapped in a red bathrobe, told Miller she didn't plan to keep the pregnancy she had conceived while on vacation in Mexico. It wasn't Sheila's first abortion. The ability to terminate a pregnancy without risking death was revolutionizing women's lives. Sheila wasn't hung up on this newfound freedom. But like John Cavanaugh O'Keefe when he heard about his friend's abortion, Miller was appalled.

She felt compelled to save the pregnancy Sheila was carrying—but unequipped to persuade her friend to change her mind.

Soon, Miller was pacing the sidewalk outside the local abortion clinic, trying and failing to stop women like Sheila. She read books like *Abortion and Social Justice* that described fetuses in vivid detail. The unborn, to her, became "living, real, and present."[13] Then a friend invited her to a meeting with Joe Scheidler. A father of seven, known for his own theatrical flourishes,

Scheidler would go down in history as the "godfather of the pro-life movement." On that day, he was planning an abortion clinic sit-in.

"In Joe's mind, the pro-life sit-in was a strategy whose time had come," Miller later wrote. "It had worked for civil rights activists across the country, and we all firmly believed that the pro-life movement was essentially a civil rights cause."[14]

At the meeting, Scheidler asked who was willing to get arrested. Miller raised her hand.

She soon found herself on the fringe of the antiabortion movement, following a decidedly different approach than the Catholic-founded National Right to Life Committee, which would work so dutifully to reelect Reagan and pressure him toward incremental progress. Like their counterparts on the pro-choice side, antiabortion groups were often divided when it came to strategy and priorities. Scheidler was fired as director of the NRLC's Illinois affiliate because of his militant tactics.[15]

But Miller was captivated by her new mentor.

She joined the sit-ins, and as she got more involved with the movement, she found a strange new calling—collecting aborted fetuses. One night in 1987, Miller and Scheidler crept toward dumpsters that sat on a loading dock in downtown Chicago. Inside, they claimed, were fetal remains from a Chicago abortion clinic. They retrieved the bags, and back in Scheidler's garage, they unpacked the blood and tissue inside and photographed it. Over a period of two months, they kept going back. And one warm spring day she and Scheidler laid out nearly six hundred aborted remains on a folding table in the middle of a Chicago street, prompting passersby to recoil in horror as the fetuses shriveled in the heat.[16] Miller was hooked on this new hobby. By 1988, she would claim that she and Edmund Miller, a fellow activist whom she would marry the following year, had retrieved two thousand embryos and fetuses. She stacked them in boxes in her apartment, using air fresheners to mask the stench of the formalin that preserved the tissue. Later, they buried the remains.[17]

Displaying images of aborted fetuses had been a tried-and-true part of antiabortion strategy for years. But not everyone was willing to do the dirty work. Nor was everyone willing to give up their freedom for the cause. Most of the antiabortion activists I'd investigated so far, from Paul Haring to Richard Viguerie, lived comfortable lives with a comfortable sense that when they died, their obituaries would include a list of respectable achievements. They had used abortion to advance their careers or win political victories. As a leader in the "rescue" movement, Miller, by contrast, was frequently arrested at sit-ins across the Midwest. Sometimes life and activism collided; while pregnant with her second child she put her eleven-month-old daughter in a car seat and absconded from an arrest warrant with her husband before finally turning herself in.[18] After Clinton signed the FACE Act in 1994, Miller faded from the front lines as she raised her three kids, steeping them in her Catholic and antiabortion beliefs—although she would later complain to me that they didn't understand the significance of her work.

In 2017, once her children were grown, Miller and her supporters launched a new take on the sit-ins of old. They called it Red Rose Rescue. Rather than blockading doors, these rescuers walked into clinic waiting rooms, sometimes posing as patients, and sat down next to unsuspecting women, handing them red roses as they tried to talk them out of their abortions. When the police came, the rescuers refused to leave, disrupting the clinic for as long as possible. Miller and her followers had performed nearly thirty such "rescues" by her count in 2025,[19] leading to a constant churn of arrests and trials, during which they sometimes served short stints in jail, tolerated the disapproval of family and friends, and clung to limited victories, like the rare case where a woman left the clinic after an encounter with them.

Her mentor, Joe Scheidler, was terrified of arrest and often tried to avoid the cuffs even as he roused others to action.[20] But Miller was willing to pay the price. The code of conduct for Red Rose Rescue declared imprisonment to be "a spiritual extension of the rescue."[21]

THE ACTRESS

The morning after my meeting with Miller dawned gray and cold with the looming threat of a winter storm. On the way to the courthouse, I drove past light poles with fluttering maroon flags that read "Southfield, the center of it all," a bold claim for this sleepy suburb. Center or not, the Forty-Sixth District Court was more accustomed to parking violations and petty crimes than the drama that was about to fill this wood-paneled room. Surveying the gallery across a span of brown-and-black checkered carpet, Judge Cynthia Arvant remarked that it had been a while since her courtroom was this full. Miller's supporters, some with criminal records of their own for disrupting clinics, had filled the seats. The city's attorney was Bonnie Fitch, an older woman with frosted brown hair. Miller's attorney was Robert Muise, a thick-necked ex-Marine who had helped launch what he called "the Nation's first truly authentic Judeo-Christian, public-interest law firm."[22]

Exactly one of these attorneys would play by the rules.

The other would kick off some serious histrionics. Admittedly, Muise had a tough job. He needed to somehow make the invasion of a Southfield abortion clinic seem like it wasn't a straightforward act of trespassing.

Whatever your feelings on abortion, most people would agree that a suburban jury trial is a weird place to litigate it. Just how weird became clear during jury selection. Muise grilled the prospective jurors who copped to being pro-choice. But his ears perked up when a man wearing a black kippah asked the judge to excuse him on the grounds that he had fourteen children.

"It would be hard for my wife," the man pleaded.

Damn the wife; Muise simply *loved* the fruitful.

"We'd like to have him on the jury," Muise told the judge. "I have twelve children, so."

Later, on the phone, Muise told me that having children was as close as mortals could get to understanding Jesus's suffering on the cross, by which he seemed to mean not that kids were awful, but that parenting was a form of total self-sacrifice.[23]

Regardless, Bonnie Fitch dismissed the man with fourteen kids from service, sparing the wife.

After the jury was picked, Muise rose to his feet.

"On April 23 of 2022 these courageous pro-life rescuers were advancing the virtues of faith, charity and love," he began, giving his account of the "rescue" at Northland Family Planning.

He whipped out a fake red rose with unnaturally green leaves.

"As a profit-driven abortion provider, those in Northland do not like what the rescuers were telling the mothers," Muise continued. "Every woman that these rescuers spoke to—peacefully, gently—offering them a message of love and hope and charity, would cut against the bottom line—"

Fitch objected. Judge Arvant called the lawyers to the bench.

"I hate to interrupt, but what are we doing here?" she hissed at Muise. She had forbidden him from putting abortion on trial, rejecting his effort to bring a "defense of others" by arguing the protesters were acting to save the unborn.

The judge told Muise to move on and put his flower away.

One of the first witnesses was the clinic owner, Renee Chelian.

Watching the trial from a dock designated for press, which consisted of me and a woman in a bright-red jacket who wrote for the far-right Catholic website Church Militant, I was struck by how alike Chelian and Miller might seem if you didn't know them. They were only a few years apart in age, petite, with short, dark hair. Chelian's was dyed with blond highlights, neatly coifed; Miller's was cut in a practical bob. Chelian wore a soft white sweater with a silver heart on a chain; Miller wore a boxy blue blazer. As Chelian spoke, Miller prayed with her hands folded next to a picture the size of a baseball card that reminded her of her purpose: Jesus, bleeding, on the cross.

The women's lives had run in parallel since 1976, the year Henry Hyde introduced the ban on federal funding of abortion.

That year, Miller had listened in horror as her friend Sheila outlined her plan to have an abortion.

That year, Chelian and her husband had cashed out their savings to buy their first clinic in suburban Detroit. They were ready to fulfill Chelian's dream of helping young women in crises like the one she faced in 1966, when she got pregnant at fifteen.[24] To hide her pregnancy, she wrapped clean maxi pads in toilet paper, faking her period. She considered killing herself but stopped with the razor poised over her skin. Her boyfriend's father managed to find a man who charged $3,000 to perform an abortion procedure. She was blindfolded and taken to a Detroit warehouse, where the man packed her uterus with gauze. Later, she went into labor, screaming through the pain. Her mother's doctor prescribed her antibiotics afterward and she credited the man with saving her life. Her father told her never to speak of the abortion.

"It's illegal, we can't risk jail, and no man will ever marry you," he said.

But Chelian never forgot that feeling of desperation and she dedicated her life to saving others from it. She went to work for the doctor who prescribed the medication after her abortion, flying with him to Buffalo to see patients after New York legalized abortion in 1970. And after she and her husband managed to squirrel away $100,000 by working six jobs between them, "I asked him if I could take our savings and open a clinic," Chelian told me.[25]

Helping women, not making money, was her bottom line.

Chelian was living her dream—but thanks to Miller and her allies, she and her colleagues across the country were soon running defense against the rescuers. Chelian and her husband would wake up at 4:00 a.m. to leave their two daughters with a babysitter so they could camp outside the sit-in meetings, tinkering with spy tools Chelian had bought from *Soldier of Fortune* magazine, listening to hear if her clinic was the next target.

Chelian believed she was saving women. Miller believed she was saving babies. Their lives were on a collision course.

In court on that February day, Chelian sat in the witness stand, looking composed. Muise was trying to twist an NPR article about her clinic into a claim that patients were being coerced into their abortions. No one seemed to be grasping his point, and Miller couldn't contain herself: "It's about *coercion*!" she hissed.

"I'm not hearing from you, Dr. Miller, thank you so much. I don't think you're cocounsel," the judge scolded her.

During a recess Muise huddled with his clients.

"I say this to you every trial," he told Miller, exasperated. "I'm going to put you in the back of the room."

"Your Honor, can I say something?" Miller asked when they returned from break.

"You may not," Arvant snapped.

When court was over for the day, we stood outside as a bitter wind blew across the court steps. I asked Miller what she wanted to tell the judge.

"I wanted to say, 'Your Honor, you have to realize that as we sit here, we are enormously frustrated,'" she said, gripping a legal pad against her chest. "It's like being in an insane asylum."[26]

The jury didn't seem to see it that way. The next day in court the jurors watched video footage from the clinic where patients seemed to back away from the rescuers. Ultimately, they would find Miller guilty of trespassing and resisting a police officer.

Lara Chelian, Renee's daughter, who now worked for the clinic, was there during the invasion. "We worked very hard to make it a safe space, and it still is a safe space, but it felt violating," she told me over dinner one day after court.[27] She recounted a vivid childhood memory of dressing up in her Halloween costume and then seeing antiabortion protesters massing in the trees outside her home. Not surprisingly, given that they've terrorized her since childhood, Lara Chelian bore no sympathy for Miller and her ilk.

"All they do is put harm into the world," she told me ruefully.

Later, I got the transcript of the sentencing hearing, where Muise declared the defendants "the Rosa Parks, Martin Luther King, and Hungarian freedom fighters of today." Renee Chelian, for her part, recounted how the rescuers "have terrorized and harassed my staff," printing their names in incendiary Facebook posts about the trial.

The judge noted many of the defendants had criminal records so long the court's probation department had trouble assembling them.

At last, Miller got to speak.

"The whole problem, Your Honor, with this trial is that the unborn who were about to be exterminated at Northland Family Planning remained invisible," she said.

"My attorney told you that I've taken unborn children out of the trash," she added. "Here's one." She held up one of her fetal images.

"I don't need to see that today."

"You should see it," Miller said. "This jury should have seen this." The judicial system, she said, "props up this lie. And I—I can't—I can't stand—I can't stand the lie."

"This is not theater," the judge said.

"It is a kind of theater in a sense," the actress replied.

"No, it's not."

"We are performing the truth."[28]

After Miller refused to comply with the judge's request to stay 500 feet away from abortion clinics, Arvant sentenced her to forty-five days in jail.

I reached her on the jail phone system soon after.

Her voice sounded tinny as she pressed the receiver to her ear. She had to keep her head inside a small square on the screen or it triggered an error message. She told me that on Easter morning, she'd woken up feeling grumpy, obsessing over not hearing from her kids.

"Their attitude is, oh, this is just something Mom does," she sighed.

"You feel like they don't support it?" I asked.

"I know they don't," she said with that familiar current of irritation in her voice. "They're pro-life, they're against abortion but they don't see the value in what we're doing."[29]

She felt bolstered by stories of women like the one who came to testify during her sentencing that Miller had talked her out of an abortion and later helped her support her son.

Not long after our call, Miller was released.

Two of her fellow rescuers were about to do far longer stints behind bars—and become national celebrities as a result.

THE LONELY ATHEIST

I met Herb Geraghty at the National Right to Life Convention, the annual convening of the National Right to Life Commitee. It was June 2023, a year after the Supreme Court killed *Roe*. He was standing in a hallway in aviator glasses and a collared shirt printed with red and white roses, looking vaguely like a goldfish at a cat convention. In front of him was a table for Rehumanize International, a self-described human rights organization that opposed abortion, the death penalty, stem cell research, assisted suicide, police brutality, torture, and unjust war. The National Right to Life Committee had allied itself with the Republican Party for over four decades. Yet Geraghty was hopefully peddling colorful pins that read "Close Gitmo," "Wage Peace," "Stop Police Brutality," "Legal Assisted Suicide Is Lethal Ableism," and "Feminism: Equality for All, No Exceptions." I stopped at the booth, unable to resist the pull of messaging that felt so unexpected. I had come upon an endangered species: one of the few remaining oddballs who refused to fit into our nation's stark ideological divide. Like John Cavanaugh O'Keefe in an earlier era, Geraghty was too antiabortion for the Left and too left on everything else for the Right. Here at a convention run by a group that had endorsed Trump in the last two elections and would soon do so again, Geraghty was animatedly telling me about the consistent ethic of life—the philosophy that nettled Reagan so much he rushed his own treatise out to get ahead of it.

While Geraghty was talking, Frank Pavone sauntered by. Pavone was a walking Fox News clip, a compact, pugnacious man with a flair for controversy, who had recently been accused of sexual harassment by two women who worked for him at his organization, Priests for Life.[30] (Pavone has denied the allegations.) He had also just been defrocked as a priest by the Vatican for "blasphemous communications" after posting a video of himself on social media displaying an aborted fetus on an altar while praising Trump.[31] As a result of his defrocking, Pavone was dressed in an adapted version of his priestly attire: all black, without the white collar. Pavone greeted Geraghty warmly, and perhaps for my benefit the two of them described how they were willing to work together on abortion even though they were about as different as two people could be. Geraghty is a self-described "member of the LGBT community."[32] Pavone, like most of the Christian right, has denied the existence of trans people, posting: "If today we can't say that a man is a man and a woman is a woman, maybe that's because for fifty years we've been saying a baby's not a baby."[33]

I asked Pavone and Geraghty about the upcoming 2024 election. Even though the primaries were still underway, Pavone had already endorsed Trump.

"I'm friends with them all," Pavone boasted, and Geraghty, barely audibly, muttered, "I'm not friends with any of them."[34]

There it was: the key clue that revealed just how little power this dissenting contingent had within a movement that was now so firmly allied with the conservative Republican Party.

Pavone, who represented the movement's alliance with MAGA, was the one with influence—even if that influence had been dinged by controversy.

Geraghty, on the other hand, was about to be headed to jail—where he and a fellow rescuer, Will Goodman, would find out Trump might be a friend, after all.

THE FEDERAL FELON

Will Goodman was in his fifties with a soft voice and an easy warmth. In the hall outside the courtroom at Miller's trial in Southfield he had joked with me: "You might want to stand back, because I have two federal felonies, so be very careful."[35]

Goodman's college years in the nineties at the University of Illinois sounded like mine; he got involved in Amnesty International, environmental issues, and animal rights. Unlike me, however, Goodman had been raised Catholic, and in college he began to draw closer to his faith. Someone from his Bible study invited him to join an antiabortion group, where he watched a graphic video. Toward the end of Goodman's time in college, Pope John Paul II published *The Gospel of Life*.

"The bishops, commenting on *The Gospel of Life*, used the phrase of

Mother Teresa," Goodman later told me. "They said that the 'poorest of the poor' in the United States are those unborn babies who have been abandoned by their government and even their own mothers and fathers."[36]

He began to see abortion as *the* civil rights cause, more pressing than the rest of the causes that interested him.

"I asked myself a question, you know: Who are the most vulnerable victims?" he told me earnestly. Maybe animals, since they couldn't fight back. Or low-income families victimized by toxic dumping? No, he ultimately decided. "In a certain way, the child in the womb suffers not only an abandonment from the government in recognition of their biological and legal person, but their own parents."[37]

Like Miller, Goodman found his way to antiabortion activism through a social encounter in college at a turning point in his life. Like Miller, he had taken the sweeping Catholic social justice ethic and winnowed it down to the one cause that seemed most urgent.

What interested me about Goodman was that, like Geraghty, he maintained a commitment to social welfare and opposed war and the mistreatment of immigrants. So he was troubled by what he saw as the unavoidable necessity of voting for the most antiabortion candidate: Trump.

But Trump was about to help Goodman in a way he couldn't have anticipated.

In August 2023, Goodman and Geraghty stood trial with their fellow rescuers for the blockade that Jonathan Darnel had livestreamed at the Washington Surgi-Clinic. They were convicted of conspiracy against rights and violating the FACE Act. Afterward, in a subterranean jail, they met January 6 protesters who were there for the deadly riot at the Capitol.

"They were disgusted by our charges, our conviction, and our potential enormous prison sentences," Goodman wrote me from jail.[38] I tried to imagine them there, underneath DC, the activists who invaded the Capitol and the activists who invaded the clinic, finding common cause.

A month after Goodman's conviction, I was watching Trump speak at Pray Vote Stand, the annual Family Research Council summit where Randall Terry and his entourage would be kicked out the following year.

The rescuers were languishing in jail while a smattering of radical supporters kept vigil outside. I hadn't heard a word about the convictions so far at the conference. So my ears perked up when Trump mentioned the rescuers. In fact, he vowed to pardon them.

I wrote to Goodman to ask if he had heard.

"Dear Amy, THANK YOU very much for your message and your update regarding Trump's remarks over the weekend," he wrote back. "I hadn't heard anything about the news yet. Wow! This is quite a surprise. A pleasant although somewhat bittersweet, surprise. You ask how I felt about hearing the news. Here is my response having just now read your full emessage. Pros and cons. Pro- I'm quite glad a former U.S. President has recognized the grave injustice inherent in our case/conviction/possible punishment. Con-TRUMP said it…so that means some partisan ppl may hate us and our cause more since they hate him so much."

Another con, Goodman noted, was that Trump mentioned them alongside the January 6 crowd, who were, he acknowledged, "a very mixed bag" that included "violent rioters (or insurrectionists)."

He ended with a sad face symbol: "Con—Trump may over-politicize the case and create more division, while ignoring the poor unborn victims. :("[39]

In May 2024, Goodman and Geraghty were sentenced to twenty-seven months behind bars.[40]

Goodman called me before he was moved to federal prison.

"Two years out of my life is a lot for kneeling down to pray," he said, "but…if you're going to try to…save someone else's life, how can one or two years even be compared to someone's entire life?"[41]

It was late afternoon, and I was listening to him while I drove to pick up my kid from preschool. Goodman didn't have kids or a partner. He'd never felt that "lightning bolt" of romance, and the hazards of his work made family life feel untenable. "I don't have any income. I don't have any savings. I've been doing this full-time ever since I graduated from college in '96," he would later tell me. His aging parents, like Miller's kids, didn't fully get it.

"I think they would be happier if I didn't do nonviolent direct action and rescue," he said, "but...they think that I see it as a calling and as mission work, and so they respect it."[42]

Goodman would have a rough time in prison. He suffered from persistent tooth pain and sustained a serious head injury when he fell off a top bunk. So despite all the cons he had listed, it was a relief when Trump followed through on the promise to pardon Goodman alongside twenty-two other abortion opponents in early 2025. Soon, Goodman was on the conservative media circuit, appearing on Fox News and the podcast of Steve Bannon, whom he met when they were incarcerated together. ("We'd invite him to our Bible studies; he never came," Goodman told me.)

Goodman and his ilk might rue the partisan divide, but in the end, this divide had saved them from more months in prison. It looked to me like Goodman was paying Trump back by boosting the president's antiabortion credentials with each media appearance. But Goodman said he saw these appearances as a way to serve his cause.

"I'm of the opinion—and this isn't shared in the movement—but I'm of the opinion that we should speak to whoever wants to speak, because it's an opportunity for dialogue and mutual understanding," Goodman said.

After all, that's why he was speaking with me.

Herb Geraghty, for his part, had tried to reject Trump's pardon, so that he could continue to challenge the FACE Act in court. But he was let out anyway. Soon, Trump became even more of a friend to Geraghty. He promised that his administration would only enforce the FACE Act in the most extreme circumstances.

Emboldened, Geraghty was soon leafleting outside clinics again.

On the phone just after his sentencing, Goodman told me he'd spoken directly to the judge and invoked the women's suffrage and civil rights movements.[43] I stopped at a busy Boston intersection. A man wearing jeans and a button-down denim shirt walked up to my window with a cane, begging for cash with a paper cup. Here was someone's baby boy, pleading for coins in the richest country on earth. I thought about the decision Goodman and Geraghty had made about which cause was worth giving your freedom for. These true believers had allied themselves with conservative Republicans, who weren't doing any favors for this man begging for cash outside my window. Perhaps it had been worth sacrificing the rest of their values in order to kill *Roe*.

But for a moment, I saw a flicker of another future, where they had made a different choice, and where we were all working together, shaking our heads in unison about how the world had gone mad.

PART 5

DEATHS BY ABORTION BAN

CHAPTER 11

THE RENEGADES

> I believe, Messieurs, in loyalty—to one's friends and one's family and one's caste.
>
> —*Murder on the Orient Express* by Agatha Christie

NANCY KEENAN, THE PRESIDENT OF NARAL PRO-CHOICE AMERICA, WAS in San Francisco in early 2010 when she was jolted awake by a call from a Washington, DC, area code. It was 4:30 in the morning California time. Half-asleep, Keenan answered. It was Jim Messina, deputy chief of staff for President Obama. Fellow Montanans, Messina and Keenan had known each other for years.[1]

"Keenan," Messina said. "It's Jim."

"Hi Jim," Keenan replied sleepily.

Then she heard President Obama's voice on the line.

In stark terms, he laid out some of the highest stakes Keenan had faced during her six years at the helm of the leading pro-choice political organization. Obama's health reform law, which would extend health-care coverage to millions of uninsured Americans, was nearing passage after months of political struggle. Obama had been fighting not just Republicans, but an influential contingent of antiabortion Democrats including Michigan

Representative Bart Stupak, a heavy-lidded Catholic with a LEGO-style helmet of gray hair.

Obama had opposed the Hyde Amendment on the campaign trail, raising hopes that he would repeal it at last. Yet to win support for health-care reform, he had quickly conceded the Hyde Amendment would stand.[2] Pro-choice lobbyists realized early on that Obama was not going to let abortion get in the way of his wider agenda. Before he was elected, he had promised that signing the Freedom of Choice Act to codify *Roe* would be "the first thing that I'd do."[3] But once in office, with a Democratic trifecta that he would lose the following year, he declared that FOCA was "not the highest legislative priority."[4] His priority was to pass health-care reform.

"He had a lot of bros around him and his goal was to get a bill and if he had to jettison reproductive health care, he was going to do that," one pro-choice advocate told me.

But Obama's surrender on Hyde did not win over abortion opponents. The Catholic bishops sent a bulletin to every American parish, calling for the health-care bill to be defeated unless it included sharp restrictions on abortion.[5] Stupak had pushed the Democratic-majority House to accept an amendment that heavily restricted private coverage of abortion on the new insurance exchanges.

Finally, after months of maneuvering, Obama had struck a deal he hoped would salvage the bill and let antiabortion Democrats save face.

"'Nancy, we're close on the health-care act,'" Keenan recalled Obama saying. "'And as you know, it's all hung up on this issue of abortion. And we have some language we think will get us there.'"

The White House wanted Keenan to give her blessing.

"How long do I have?" she asked.

The reply was startling: "Something like thirty minutes."

Keenan recalled that Planned Parenthood needed to give their blessing, too.

"It was the two big ones, NARAL and Planned Parenthood, that had to really be the ones that said we could live with it," Keenan told me.

Not that they were given much choice.

It was clear to Keenan and her strategists that if they objected, they would be torpedoing a bill that extended health insurance to millions.

Not long after, the House passed a compromise bill, and Obama quietly signed an executive order affirming that the Hyde Amendment's ban on federal funding of abortion applied to the ACA's programs.[6]

It was yet another surrender on Hyde from a pro-choice Democrat.

And in its wake, a new long shot campaign would grow into the abortion rights movement's greatest surprise success story in a generation. It was there that I would find the movement's own true believers.

THE KEY WITNESSES

In a murder mystery, the detective's first step is to interview everyone who was at the scene, to see if they saw anything related to the killing. Ever since the Supreme Court agreed to hear the case that would become *Dobbs*, I had been conducting a postmortem on *Roe*, asking dozens of current and former abortion rights leaders a version of the same question: What are the fatal mistakes that keep you up at night?

It turned out that someone else had begun this digging a decade before I did. In 2010, a Tea Party–fueled backlash to Obama's presidency led to a Republican takeover of state legislatures. Before the election, most state legislatures were Democratic. Then Republicans picked up twenty chambers nationwide and the balance flipped. From 2011 to 2013, state legislatures passed a record 205 antiabortion laws.[7] In 2011 alone, state legislators introduced a staggering 1,230 reproductive health provisions, most of which curtailed access to reproductive health care, and about half of which attacked abortion in particular.[8]

"It was very clear that the pro-choice movement wasn't even bringing any weapons to a gunfight," Sujatha Jesudason, a social justice activist and scholar, told me.[9]

Jesudason and a fellow researcher and organizer, Tracy Weitz, started an organization called CoreAlign and set out to interview movement leaders to determine what was going wrong. Their goal was to unite the movement around a thirty-year plan of the kind their opposition had built to take down *Roe*. They quickly noted a clear vulnerability in red and purple states. The right wing was dominating the middle of the country, while most of the abortion rights movement's resources were concentrated on the coasts. What's more, the abortion rights movement had professionalized and consolidated to such a degree that frontline activists felt disconnected from the levers of power. Yet perhaps because these groups were all competing for scarce foundation funding, their leaders were frustratingly hesitant to change.

"People thought their organizations had the right strategy... it was *other* people who should be doing different things," Jesudason told me. "There wasn't that self-reflection or willingness to shift in strategy even in the face of overwhelming evidence of failure."

Eventually, this effort to unite the movement failed.

But after the death of *Roe*, a decade later, the lack of a state-level ground game was one mistake many former leaders finally seemed willing to acknowledge.

A long-standing lack of progressive investment in red and purple states had left grassroots organizers and lonely lobbyists with groups like the ACLU to fight dozens of conservative state bills, as Meaghan Winter documented in her book *All Politics Is Local*.[10] These state operatives were like overwhelmed Wonder Women deflecting bullets coming from every direction. They tried valiantly but could never stop every bill.

Keenan, who was president of NARAL from 2004 to 2012, acknowledged she could have done more to support the affiliates doing state legislative work.

"Now, as I look back and say, Is there a mistake? Maybe I should have—maybe we should have—invested far more in those affiliates in the states to begin to try to help them fight back at that level," she said.

NARAL's former lobbyist, a sharp-elbowed strategist named Donna Crane, disagreed. For her, the *courts*, not state legislatures, were the key; they were the "goalie" that could stop every bad law. In hindsight, she thought it would have been more efficient to fight for better judges than against hundreds of state bills in dozens of state capitals, year after year.

"If I could do it again, I would use all my breath to argue to take all that time and all those resources and build a better line of defense," Crane told me. "I will take that regret with me to my grave."[11]

Laurie Rubiner, a former Planned Parenthood lobbyist, saw fatal limits in the alliance with the Democratic Party, which treated abortion as a niche issue.

"The other side never does that… it's such a meta life issue for them… it's really about wanting to change the way we live," she said. "And we don't see it that way. We just see it as like: 'Well, how many people can we get out at the polls?'"[12]

Gloria Feldt, who was president of Planned Parenthood from 1996 to 2005, had a more personal regret. She said she was ground down by disagreements within Planned Parenthood.

"It's the internal politics that just wear you down," she told me.[13]

Terry O'Neill, president of the National Organization for Women from 2009 to 2017, surprised me with the breadth of her answer.

"I don't know if it would have made any difference, but it was 2020 before I understood how corrosive capitalism is to feminism," O'Neill told me. If she could go back in time, she said, she'd tell herself: "Working in NOW is not going to make any difference at all, unless you attack capitalism as a feminist project.

"I don't think I would have gone anywhere in NOW if I had had that attitude," she added, laughing.[14]

Not everyone was so willing to admit there *were* mistakes. Eleanor Smeal, a former president of NOW and cofounder of the Feminist Majority Foundation, took issue with the premise of my question.

"Nothing went wrong," she said. "It was like that from the beginning."

"What do you mean?" I asked.

"Abortion was illegal," she said. "When I was a kid it was a swear word."

"But how did we lose the *legal* right?" I pushed.

"How you lost it is because you lost the elections; and they lied, a lot."

"So, something went wrong."

"Well, the election went wrong."[15]

She had a point. The antiabortion movement had found a way to win elections without winning over a majority of voters. James Bopp, the longtime general counsel of the National Right to Life Committee, had spent years fixated on dismantling campaign finance reform. His mission culminated with a win in the 2010 Supreme Court decision *Citizens United* that opened the floodgates to dark money in politics.[16] Corporate donations helped business-friendly Republicans gain seats in state legislatures where they could gerrymander their way into keeping power, even though their economic and antiabortion agendas were unpopular.

Luck had also helped the killers of *Roe*, legal scholar David Cohen argued. If stalwart liberal Justice Thurgood Marshall's health had allowed him to wait two more years to retire, we wouldn't have archconservative Clarence Thomas. If Sandra Day O'Connor hadn't left when she did to care for her ailing husband, we wouldn't have Samuel Alito, the author of *Dobbs*. If Antonin Scalia hadn't died within months of the 2016 election—and the Republican-controlled Senate hadn't held his seat hostage until Trump's election—we wouldn't have Neil Gorsuch. If Anthony Kennedy hadn't retired under Trump, we wouldn't have Brett Kavanaugh. And if Justice Ruth Bader Ginsburg had lasted another ninety days before succumbing to cancer, we wouldn't have Amy Coney Barrett.[17]

Those five justices made up the majority in *Dobbs*.

But power, not just luck, had put them on the bench. The Federalist Society's Leonard Leo had built his organization into such a behind-the-scenes kingmaker that he effectively handed Trump a list of court appointees, chosen in large part for their antiabortion credentials.[18]

When the Supreme Court with its new Trump appointees began to show its willingness to kill *Roe*, the abortion rights movement began to show its woeful unpreparedness to respond. On September 1, 2021, the Supreme Court allowed a six-week ban to take effect in Texas, decimating access in one of the largest states. Planned Parenthood convened a hastily organized Zoom call with more than 400 attendees to coordinate a national response to the crisis. Half an hour in, an infiltrator interrupted the meeting by saying the "n" word. The meeting's facilitator, Planned Parenthood's Brianna

Twofoot, continued talking. (Twofoot later said she didn't hear the slur.) But the Black women on the call knew what they had heard. One described feeling like the wind had been knocked out of her. Another, the founder of We Testify, Renee Bracey Sherman instructed everyone to log off immediately.[19]

I reviewed this incident in forensic detail for a story in *The New York Times* Sunday Review, interviewing the witnesses, bending down and squinting at every detail through a magnifying glass. Because this call felt to me like the movement's own smoking gun. The infiltrator might have been just some juvenile troublemaker, but it felt as if the attack had been designed in a lab to target the abortion rights movement's two greatest vulnerabilities.

The first of those vulnerabilities was an overreliance on the courts that had left organizers scrambling to coordinate a response when the courts finally failed them.

The second was a long-standing failure to protect Black women.

THE SCAPEGOAT

Carol Moseley Braun was the first Black woman in the Senate. Raised middle-class, she had a memorable brush with poverty as a teenager. When her parents divorced, she moved in with her grandmother in the "ghetto," an area of Chicago nicknamed the "bucket of blood" for its violence. One day a teenager ran over from across the street, screaming, "A rat bit my baby!" Shaken, Moseley Braun brought the girl and her baby to Cook County Hospital, where they sat for hours in a hallway waiting for help.[20]

Decades later, the memory of this indignity still made her choke up.

She took from it a simple lesson that she would apply in the Senate, she later told me: "The fact of the matter is that poor women are deserving of the same kind of care we give those who have more."[21]

The year she was elected was supposed to be the Year of the Woman. After the outrage over Anita Hill's treatment by the Biden-led Senate Judiciary Committee in 1991, the 1992 election saw a record forty-seven women elected to the House, and four new women in the Senate.[22]

With new allies in Congress, the Black Women's Health Project was leading a campaign to repeal the Hyde Amendment called CARE: Campaign for Abortion Rights for Everyone.[23] They had reason to hope they would prevail. Clinton had pledged to repeal Hyde on the campaign trail, and in 1993, he submitted a budget to Congress that omitted the ban. Democrats, with a majority in both chambers, had their chance to repeal Hyde at last.

Yet in a raucous debate in the House that, according to one press account, "exploded in a near shoving match," they refused.[24]

"I've been here for five months, and things are still run by white men in blue suits," Florida Representative Corinne Brown, one of 10 Black women in the 435-member House, railed, decrying "White Southern males" who "think they know what's best for poor women."

Meanwhile, Representative Henry Hyde invoked that same rallying cry that Richard Viguerie would use with me in his office. Hyde claimed he was defending Black babies against eugenicist abortion advocates. When another of the body's ten Black women, Illinois Representative Cardiss Collins, expressed her offense, Hyde shot back: "I probably know your district better than you do. Talk to your ministers." He later apologized and had his remarks stricken from the record, but not before offending the Black Caucus and driving at least one member to tears.

Once again, Hyde was clear about the goal of his ban.

"We cannot save the unborn of the rich," he declared. "If the rich pregnant woman wants to destroy the child in her womb, she can. Thank God we can save some of the children of the poor, and that is what I want to do."[25]

But Hyde did make a concession that dealt those agitating for repeal a partial victory—while winning over moderates. He agreed to restore the rape and incest exceptions removed in 1981. In return, the Democratic-led House voted 255–178 to keep the Hyde Amendment.[26]

But Democrats still had another shot to expand abortion rights.

Senator Carol Moseley Braun had cosponsored the Freedom of Choice Act, a bill to enshrine the right to abortion in federal law. The bill took on new urgency after a close call the year before, when the Supreme Court chipped away at *Roe* with its decision in *Planned Parenthood v. Casey*, allowing states to limit abortion unless their laws caused an "undue burden." But the bill soon exposed a rift within the movement over the two perennial third rails of abortion politics: public funding and parental consent for minors. Planned Parenthood and NARAL, the two organizations with the most influence, supported enshrining *Roe* without touching those third rails. But a coalition, including the National Black Women's Health Project, NOW, and Frances Kissling's Catholics for Choice, opposed the bill for not going far enough.[27]

"If we have to continue to fight [the abortion issue] in fifty state capitals, then I am not clear what the point is with moving ahead with the Freedom of Choice Act," NOW's president Patricia Ireland declared.[28]

So Moseley Braun withdrew her support of the bill. The decision aligned with her guiding principle, the same one that guided Faye Wattleton, who had left Planned Parenthood in 1992: Poor women are deserving of the same care.

The backlash was swift.

The New York Times excoriated Moseley Braun for her disunity.

"The Freedom of Choice Act may not accomplish all the goals the pro-choice movement would wish, but it's a constructive start, and it should not be held hostage to Senator Moseley Braun's rigid, all-or-nothing stance," the *Times* wrote.[29]

NARAL's white president, Kate Michelman, agreed.

"If, ultimately, we accept nothing because we cannot get everything, we hand opponents of choice a victory they did not win," she wrote.[30]

Michelman had her own vision of how to win. Under her watch in the mid-1980s, NARAL had begun to tack toward Reaganite language about getting the government out of personal decisions to court moderate voters. The messaging embodied in slogans like "Who Decides?" emphasized protecting taxpayers and letting families choose.[31] Decrying government control succeeded in part because it tapped into white resentment over the government's role in school desegregation and gun control. And while Michelman may not have intended it, the "choice" message could be used to promote parental consent laws and ban public funding of abortion. After all, if the government was supposed to stay out of private health-care decisions, then why should it *fund* those decisions?

Black women, whose choices had been curtailed by forced sterilization and coercive family planning practices, had long pursued a vision more sweeping than "choice." In 1994, after the Clinton administration moved to jettison reproductive health care from its own ill-fated health-reform plan, a dozen Black women gathered to chart a framework they called reproductive justice. It included the right to have children, the right to not have children, and the right to nurture children in a safe and healthy environment. It was a harder framework to sell in the post-Reagan era, because unlike "choice," it wasn't compatible with notions of small government. But it was the frame that met the needs of Black women.

The "choice" framework, on the other hand, could be twisted to justify what was arguably the crowning achievement of Reaganism, which took place under a Democratic president in 1996: the gutting of "welfare as we know it." In his book *Bearing Right*, Will Saletan argued that NARAL's messaging inadvertently bolstered the conservative logic that led Clinton to overhaul welfare, ending cash payments to families in favor of block grants to states. "Protecting taxpayers and passing responsibility to families meant, among other things, welfare reform," Saletan wrote.[32] That reform made it far harder for many people to afford the second tenant of reproductive justice: the right to have the kids you want.

Moseley Braun caught the blame when the Freedom of Choice Act failed. But as I stooped over this moment with my magnifying glass thirty years later, it seemed clear that there were two real culprits. One was the Democratic Party's weak defense of abortion rights. The other was the abortion rights movement's perennial divide over how best to deal with that weakness. Some Democratic politicians might have supported the Hyde Amendment, but movement leaders always wanted its repeal. The difference was about strategy: Should the movement demand what was *right*, or should it settle for what felt *possible*? The bill had died as that conflict flared. And its death was a Rorschach test depending on which strategy you believed in.

You could blame the purists, as some strategists did, for sabotaging the chance to enshrine *Roe*.

"Thanks a lot, that's why we don't have any part of *Roe* codified," one strategist told me, summarizing this argument. "I'm sure the women of Texas are super excited."

Or you could blame mainstream pro-choice groups that had focused for too long on what felt *possible*, so that any compromise on abortion settled further to the right.

"A sure way to disunite your union is to divide concerns along class lines, which is just what will happen if freedom of choice is legislated as a fundamental right for everyone except poor women and teenage girls," *Chicago Tribune* columnist Clarence Page wrote, defending Moseley Braun.[33]

In the end, the lesson that many people took from FOCA's failure was that fighting to repeal Hyde could put even modest gains at risk.

Perhaps that was why, sixteen years later, leading pro-choice groups did not mount a major campaign to repeal the Hyde Amendment through the Affordable Care Act (ACA). But in 2009, even after the concession on Hyde, sixty-four House Democrats voted for Bart Stupak's amendment to restrict private insurance coverage of abortion, too.[34]

Some advocates felt they had been duped.

"We were trying to diffuse the situation, knowing that the time to fight on the notion of federal funding for abortion was not this political moment—the health care reform bill is hard enough," Laura MacCleery, then director of government affairs at the Center for Reproductive Rights, told the Associated Press. "Now I'm thinking we might have recognized that we were going to have this fight, and we should have stood firm a year ago and we might not have found ourselves here."[35]

Instead, the battle lines were drawn not around public funding but around private insurance, and whether millions of people might *lose* it.

On private coverage, pro-choice groups and allies like House Speaker Nancy Pelosi were ready to fight. The late Cecile Richards, who was president of Planned Parenthood at the time, wrote in her memoir that the organization's board voted unanimously to oppose any version of the Affordable Care Act that banned abortion coverage.

"If there is an abortion ban in the Affordable Care Act, there won't be an Affordable Care Act," House Speaker Nancy Pelosi reassured her.[36]

Of course, Pelosi meant a ban on *private* insurance coverage of abortion; that the bill would continue the Hyde Amendment's ban on federal funding was already accepted.

When the Stupak Amendment restricting private coverage passed, Clare Coleman had just become president of the National Family Planning and Reproductive Health Association, an alliance of clinics that provide birth control to low-income patients under the Title X program signed into law by Nixon. Ahead of a meeting with White House Chief of Staff Rahm Emanuel, she urged the movement to take a fighting stand.

"We've all got to go in there and say we'll oppose the bill, and we'll light ourselves on fire in front of the White House, and we'll tell everybody that you've betrayed us," Coleman recalled saying. "This guy only understands arson. You go in and you say, 'We're going to burn it all down.'"[37]

But to her disappointment, not enough movement leaders were ready for arson.

In the end, the ACA would transform health care in this country, ending the exclusion of people with preexisting conditions and granting coverage of contraception with no copay. While the Stupak Amendment didn't make it into the final law, there were concessions on private coverage that felt like a setback for abortion rights. The bill allowed states to ban abortion under policies sold in their new insurance exchanges. As of 2025, half of states do so.[38]

The entire saga had wound up being an object lesson in the limits of the pro-choice movement's alliance with the Democratic Party.

As usual, Frances Kissling was blunter about it than most.

"The conditions that allowed health care reform to totally exclude abortion existed before it happened," she told *The Nation* at the time. "The difference now is that everyone knows we're powerless."[39]

THE TRUE BELIEVERS

But a new way of building power would form in the wake of this defeat.

In May 2010, less than two months after the Affordable Care Act passed, groups committed to abortion funding for low-income people called a convening of abortion rights leaders in Washington, DC. The summit was organized by the National Network of Abortion Funds (NNAF), the National Latina Institute for Reproductive Health, SisterSong: Women of Color Reproductive Health Collective, and Black Women for Reproductive Justice. It wasn't the first time these groups had tackled the idea of repealing the Hyde Amendment.

"Women of color were always saying, 'We need to repeal the Hyde Amendment,'" Dr. Toni M. Bond, a cofounder of the reproductive justice framework and former board president of NNAF, told me. "And women of color were always told, 'Oh, it's not the right time.'"[40]

NNAF joined the first Hyde repeal campaign led by the National Black Women's Health Project in the 1990s and continued to press the issue, which they understood because their member funds were paying for abortions when Medicaid didn't. They launched a repeal campaign in 2000 and then another in 2006, on the ban's thirtieth anniversary. Eighty groups signed onto that campaign, called Hyde: 30 Years Is Enough.

In 2010, the way public funding had been scapegoated in the Affordable Care Act debate created a new sense of urgency for the cause.

"During health care reform, 'tremendous ground' was lost on the issue of abortion funding, as well as on access to abortion more broadly," notes from a summary report of the convening read. "White House could not be counted on and was unwilling to expend any political capital on the issue. Congressional Democrats, even those who are considered pro choice, did not stand up for access to abortion for poor women—nor for middle-class women."[41]

In the aftermath of this defeat, not everyone agreed that tackling Hyde was a good idea.

"People were asked to actually take a position and put their cards on the table: What is your position on going after Hyde for real?" Megan Peterson, who was then the deputy director of NNAF, told me. "And there were people who... did not want it to be a priority." One high-level pro-choice operative got so angry she left the room.⁴²

But organizers from the National Network of Abortion Funds and the National Latina Institute for Reproductive Health were ready for a major push. They formed the Coalition for Abortion Access and Reproductive Equity (CAARE), named for the original 1990s campaign. CAARE would eventually launch a public-facing campaign called All* Above All. Along with NNAF and NLIRH, CAARE's steering committee included Choice USA (now URGE), Advocates for Youth, and the Reproductive Health Technologies Project. They realized that leadership on Hyde would have to come from a set of groups that didn't have political clout to lose, "groups who had no skin in the game, and therefore were going to be able to be a little bit riskier, bolder, and also who represented the communities that are most impacted by Hyde," Destiny Lopez, who would become a coleader of All* Above All, told me.⁴³

It was here that I would find the abortion rights movement's own version of Paul Haring—the true believers with their long shot ideas.

Silvia Henriquez was hired in 2011 as manager of the CAARE campaign. She recruited Kierra Johnson, who was then with Choice USA, and is now president of the National LGBTQ Task Force.

"I'm pulling together some people to talk about the Hyde Amendment," Johnson recalled Henriquez telling her. "I want you there."⁴⁴

Soon CAARE was encountering resistance everywhere.

The ACA's passage had hinged on Democratic assurances that Hyde was the law of the land. And now these activists were questioning that? Even sympathetic Democratic members of Congress were skeptical.

"The number of times I heard 'the law of the land,'" Johnson told me. "The number of times that I heard: 'Well, it's the status quo. We're not changing the status quo.'"

The odds were steep. After the ACA passed, Republicans were fighting even its incremental gains, which they decried as "socialism." Now, this upstart coalition was mounting a campaign that seemed to unite all of Republicans' favorite talking points.

"Our issues sat at the nexus of, like, every social evil: abortion, poverty, racism, sex, and then government programs, and all the racism that goes into who's on government programs," Ravina Daphtary, who joined the campaign in 2012, told me.[45]

The larger pro-choice groups were focused on a bill to enshrine *Roe* called the Women's Health Protection Act, which did not reverse Hyde or parental involvement laws. Laurie Rubiner, the former Planned Parenthood lobbyist, was now chief of staff to Senator Richard Blumenthal, WHPA's lead sponsor. She said repealing Hyde through WHPA just wasn't possible. After all, Democrats who considered themselves pro-choice still supported the ban. It was a third rail.

"It wasn't going to happen, unfortunately," Rubiner told me.

It was the same rift over strategy that had opened in the 1990s.

"It's not unlike a lot of issues that we confront: Do you try to get everything, or do you try to get a piece?" Rubiner said. "They're hard conversations." She added, "And now we get nothing."

Once again, no one within the movement doubted that repealing Hyde was right, but no one thought it was possible, not even Daphtary. In 2012 the group had amassed enough funding to hire her as a state strategist who would take a page from the opposition's playbook, pushing for restoring public funding in cities and states, one by one. During her interview she remembered feeling intrigued but not optimistic. "I was like, 'Sure, I'll get on board,'" she told me. "But I didn't think it was going to happen or go anywhere."

Daphtary felt like the early skepticism surrounding the effort was in part about turf. Two groups had dominated the landscape in Washington for years, and now a coalition that included many young women of color was disrupting the status quo.

"Sometimes it was about Hyde," she recalled, "and sometimes it was just about, 'Who the hell do you think you are?'"

Dozens of reproductive health and justice organizations were rallying behind the idea of repealing Hyde, even if those on the Hill were skeptical. The effort soon grew into a professional operation with philanthropic support, fiscal sponsorship from the New Venture Fund, lobbyists from the top firm Forbes Tate, and a new brand developed with the public relations company Conway Strategic. They called the campaign All* Above All with the slogan "Be Bold."

"I see urgency sweeping reproductive rights and justice groups—and a new commitment to put the lives of poor women, women of color, and young women center stage in a way that was unthinkable a few years ago," Stephanie Poggi, then executive director of the National Network of Abortion Funds, wrote of the campaign in September 2013. "A movement that was primarily focused on not losing more ground is now setting its sights on ensuring that every woman can make and carry out her own decision about abortion."[46]

In November 2013, the campaign planned a major turning point: their first lobby day to educate members of Congress about the need to repeal Hyde. On the same day, Planned Parenthood convened a press conference to promote WHPA. It felt to some like an effort to undermine the nascent campaign.[47] (A former Planned Parenthood official who was there at the time told me the organization would not have undermined a coalition partner that way.)

To deal with resistance, All* Above All developed a Do No Harm code, asking Congress members and pro-choice groups who didn't wholeheartedly support the strategy to at least not actively sabotage it.[48] In exchange, they agreed not to seek support from Democrats facing tight reelections. They began to poll voters and to test new ways of framing the issue. Instead of talking about taxpayer funding of abortion, they talked about how someone's ability to access abortion shouldn't be determined by income or ZIP code. While members of Congress might consider the issue settled, polls showed, "the American people don't consider it settled," Kimberly Inez McGuire, an early leader in the effort, told me.[49]

Soon, incremental victories began to mount. In 2012, Florida voters rejected a ballot amendment that would have banned the state from spending public funds for abortion. In 2016, a Boston city councilor named Ayanna Pressley partnered with All* Above All to pass a city council resolution urging Congress to repeal the Hyde Amendment. She would go on to become one of the campaign's greatest champions in Congress. In 2017, Illinois Republican Governor Bruce Rauner signed a law that repealed state restrictions on Medicaid coverage of abortion. Right away, at the Chicago clinic Family Planning Associates, Dr. Allison Cowett noticed a change. She started to see patients with seven or so kids coming in for the first time.

"I'm thinking…'What's bringing you?'" Cowett told me. "And they're like, 'What's bringing me is now I can get an abortion.'"[50]

There were incremental wins at the federal level, too. In 2012, Congress loosened the ban on abortion coverage for military personnel and their dependents, allowing it in cases of rape or incest; and in 2014, they did so for Peace Corps volunteers. By then All* Above All had settled on a bolder strategy to change the conversation around the Hyde Amendment: introducing a stand-alone bill to repeal the ban and all related federal restrictions. The bill was a way to send a strong message and to educate Congress and the public about the harms of the ban. But their doubters didn't think they could get even fifteen or twenty sponsors in the House. As a lead sponsor, they courted California Representative Barbara Lee, a Black woman with a compelling story of traveling to Mexico for an abortion before it was legal. Lee had been a congressional aide when the ban passed and could remember Henry Hyde's patronizing words about saving "little ghetto kids" from abortion. But she would be swimming upstream by introducing a bill to repeal the Hyde Amendment. Right before she was supposed to do so in early 2014, Lee learned the CAARE campaign hadn't won all the support from Democratic leaders that she believed they needed. In a tense meeting, Lee chastised the campaign for being unprepared. Jessi Leigh Swenson, the federal policy director for the National Abortion Federation, had been called into the meeting because she was being considered for a leadership role with the CAARE campaign.

"We got reamed out," Swenson told me. "Barbara Lee is a wicked-smart politician and she knows how to do hard things correctly."

Later that year, Swenson became coleader of CAARE's federal strategy coalition. The team conducted a "forensic analysis" of the setback with Lee. They determined that they needed to build grassroots momentum while further educating progressive and pro-choice members of Congress. Even among their allies, "'Hyde is law of the land' comments still pepper floor and committee debate," an internal strategy memo noted. "This needs to be fixed."[51]

The summer after their setback, the campaign rented a truck decked out with lime-green accents and the words: "Unite to lift the bans that deny abortion coverage." The Be Bold Road Trip visited twelve cities, including Oakland, where they gathered signatures from Lee's constituents.[52]

By July 2015, they were ready. Defying the doubters, they had amassed a stunning seventy-one cosponsors. Planned Parenthood and NARAL signed on at the last minute, a leading advocate at the time recalled.

"They realized, OK, the train was leaving the station and they weren't going to be on it," the advocate said.

(A former senior Planned Parenthood official who was with the organization at the time said it was not unusual for the group to sign on to campaigns at the last minute because they always review the final version of any language.)

I was working in the *Democracy Now!* TV studio in New York when I saw the press conference. "They just touched the third rail!" I yelled into the newsroom. After years on the beat, I was surprised to see a campaign disrupt the conventional wisdom of abortion politics.

"It required us to make shifts nationally, locally, within the coalition, within Congress, within the way we do field work, communications," Lydia Stuckey, one of the organizers of the campaign, told me. "That required a lot of true believers...and that was what was so heartening. There were a lot of true believers who were ready to go."[53]

The following year, two leading Democratic presidential contenders, Bernie Sanders and Hillary Clinton, denounced Hyde on the campaign trail, and in a major shift, the Democratic Party's platform called for a repeal of the ban.[54] By 2019, when he was running for president, even Joe Biden, a longtime Hyde supporter, was forced to flip, declaring, in line with the campaign's messaging, "If I believe health care is a right, as I do, I can no longer support an amendment that makes that right dependent on someone's ZIP code."⁵⁵ In 2021, the EACH Act was introduced in the Senate, and for the first time in more than forty years, the House passed a version of the appropriations bill that didn't include Hyde.

Finally, the movement was on offense, playing not according to what was possible but according to what was right.

Neither EACH nor WHPA gained enough momentum to pass. But the conversation on public funding had transformed.

"We made some serious headway and shift faster than I've seen any campaign in the repro movement, ever," Johnson told me. "The way we changed the whole game," she added, laughing, "now these members of Congress act like they always supported [Hyde's repeal]. I mean, it's the cutest thing."

Clare Coleman, who worked as chief of staff to the late pro-choice stalwart Representative Nita Lowey from 1999 to 2005, agreed.

"There was no appetite, I can tell you, among House Democrats at least, to try to undo Hyde," Coleman told me. "And it was really funny, when All* Above All came to be… and began to lead from a reproductive justice perspective, and talk about how racist Hyde was, there were lots of House members who suddenly went to the floor with some version of: 'We've always known that the Hyde Amendment was racist.'"

The makeup of power in the movement changed, too.

"The work on the Hyde Amendment was a huge part of kicking the doors down for women-of-color-led reproductive justice policy organizations," Kimberly Inez McGuire, who is now the executive director of URGE: United for Reproductive and Gender Equity, told me.

In 2023, All* Above All would face its own racial reckoning over accusations of anti-Blackness that culminated in layoffs of its staff. Today the organization's president is a Black woman named Nourbese Flint. In the summer of 2025, I asked Flint what her side could learn from the killers of *Roe*.

"I think they have radical imagination," she said. "Their radical imagination is why we are here; they dreamed it to believe it...I think there's a lesson learned in having a radical imagination for our communities."⁵⁶

The abortion rights movement's response to the slow killing of *Roe* had been to fend off the cuts with defensive maneuvers, mostly by challenging state laws in court. Finally, the movement's true believers had started making their own incremental cuts that might one day kill Hyde. In the process, All* Above All broke the loop through which abortion politics usually played. They had started with what was right, and then, step-by-step, they had made what was right feel possible.

CHAPTER 12

THE GOOFY BASTARD

It's astonishing in this world how things don't turn out at all the way you expect them to!

—*Endless Night* by Agatha Christie

It was Election Day 2024 and I was trafficking an unborn child across North Texas. That is, I was driving from Dallas to Amarillo while five weeks pregnant, an act that the chinstrap-bearded antiabortion activist Mark Lee Dickson would deem "abortion trafficking of an unborn child"— if I was on my way to an abortion clinic. Instead, I was on my way to a polling place in the Texas panhandle to meet Dickson, the Johnny Appleseed of the antiabortion movement, a thirty-nine-year-old virgin who had spent the past five years traveling through Texas and beyond in a button-down shirt, black backward baseball cap, and sneakers, sowing the poison fruits of antiabortion innovation. His "Sanctuary City for the Unborn" ordinances proved the legal framework that was used to ban abortion at about six weeks across Texas in 2021. The Supreme Court allowed the ban to take effect in what turned out to be a preview of the murder of *Roe*.

Not only did Dickson help kill *Roe*, but the ban he helped pass, Senate Bill 8, was implicated in the death of a woman in Texas, ProPublica had reported just days earlier.¹ I was setting out to investigate the latest round of deaths caused by antiabortion policies. Women in states that had banned abortion were dying, sometimes while suffering miscarriages of wanted pregnancies. Meanwhile, Dickson was trying to address a major vulnerability of abortion bans to emerge since *Dobbs*—the fact that women knew how to drive. More than 35,000 Texans managed to leave the state to get an abortion in 2023, the first full year after the state banned abortion outright.[2] Many of these abortion travelers drove through the panhandle, the part of the state that jutted up like a middle finger.[3] Many thousands more went online and ordered abortion drugs from online pharmacies or from telehealth services like Aid Access—because sadly for Dickson, people who need abortions know how to use the internet. Even worse for him, the Biden administration was allowing the shipment of abortion medication by mail, and Democratic-led states had passed laws to protect providers who sent these medications to states like Texas. Medication abortion was now the most common form of abortion nationwide, and logistically, it was easier to get than ever, even in states where abortion was banned—although, thanks to Dickson and his allies, accessing it could pose legal risks. In the year after fourteen states banned abortion outright, the number of abortions recorded nationwide *increased*.[4] The bans weren't working. Of course, sometimes they worked all too well, and women died.

I had made a decision I would soon regret: to spend Election Day with Mark Lee Dickson, in part to better understand this zealous and lonely man. I was imitating Miss Marple and looking for clues in human nature.

I had been trying to wrap my head around the human nature of Mark Lee Dickson for years, interviewing him as he traveled through airports or crisscrossed the country in his pickup truck, stopping at stores to buy a new button-down for his next city council meeting.[5] He seemed to have little social life. He spent his days and nights on the road, alone, showing up in places where he was warmly welcomed by like-minded believers but sometimes loathed by residents and officials who saw him as a self-interested carpetbagger. His ordinances turned municipal councils accustomed to discussing the finer points of wastewater management into crowded squabbles over freedom and sin. His critics described him in colorful terms: "a dork," "a loser," "dangerous," a "goofy bastard," and a "nasty little gremlin man."

Yet I found Dickson affable. He seemed to appreciate my coverage in *The Nation* because I was accurate, even when I described him in unflattering terms—like the time I quoted him comparing himself to the nineteenth-century antivice crusader Anthony Comstock and boasting that the moniker made him sound "like Batman."[6] He always picked up when I called.

But I'd seen another, more aggressive side of Dickson, too, in records of his correspondence with local politicians, which the legal organization Democracy Forward shared with me.

His early writings, however, revealed that he was harshest on himself.

Mark Lee Dickson grew up in the Northeast Texas city of White Oak, on the outskirts of the larger city of Longview. His grandfather Glenn Canfield Jr. was a metallurgist and fixture in local Republican politics who ran Right to Life of East Texas.[7] As a child, Dickson was fascinated by Canfield's displays of fetal models at the Gregg County Fair. He marveled at how he himself was once the size of the dolls.

As he grew into his teenage years, his online writing revealed a self-flagellating religious devotion.

"I must tell you the dangers of being a lustful minded sinner," he wrote in a blog post around 2003.[8] "With my very own mind I have committed adultery with almost every appealing actress that has been on television."

These normal adolescent longings were a terrible sin to Dickson, who was steeped in Southern Baptist fire and brimstone and channeling the eighteenth-century preacher Jonathan Edwards's sermon "Sinners in the Hands of an Angry God."

"This I am very ashamed of, for I myself have been a sex-crazed teenager desiring that which is not to be tasted until the joining between a man and a woman in marriage," he wrote. "This is such a hideous sin to admit."

Dickson condemned homosexuality. "Even if you claim to be a Christian homosexual you spit on God's word by ignoring the very truths that God clearly taught on the matter," he wrote.

Throughout the post, he excoriated himself.

"Because of my sins, I deserve death," he wrote. "I deserve to burn in Hell for eternity.

"I would almost question if we actually should cut our very own eyes out from our skulls to avoid committing adultery."

As he grew older, Dickson seemed to avoid not just adultery, but all intimacy.

"I'm twenty-seven years old and I've never cuddled with a girl," he wrote on Facebook in June 2013. "The only things I have cuddled with thus far in life have been stuffed animals and BBQ, but I am completely OK with that. I just wish the BBQ cuddled back."

By then, Dickson had begun to describe himself as the pastor of Sovereign Love Church, and had channeled his fascination with superheroes into starting a comic book club. People who attended the club told me it was a haven for nerdy, outcast kids who lounged on couches, socializing with one another and the spiny-tailed lizard named Papias Rex that Dickson kept in a terrarium. Ironically, given Dickson's view that homosexuality was a sin, the club attracted queer kids like Savannah Bronson, who shared with me a series of alternately goofy and earnest Facebook messages she and Dickson exchanged in 2012, when she was eighteen and he was twenty-six, up late working shifts as a hotel security guard.

To me, these earnest late-night exchanges with someone eight years younger than him—alongside Dickson's long-standing fascination with superheroes—spoke to something fundamentally childlike about Dickson. He often quoted Batman in our interviews. Once I interviewed him over lunch at a café in DC and he ordered grilled cheese and didn't eat the crusts.

Bronson told me she would later come to feel uncomfortable with these messages because of their age difference and Dickson's position of authority running the comic book club. In one message, Dickson confessed to making missteps while pastoring the church.[9]

"Is SovereignLove still up and running?" Bronson typed early one morning as Dickson stood guard over a hotel lobby.

"After about six months of pastoring the church start, I made some mistakes," Dickson typed back. "I ended up buying alcohol for some people who were underage, lost an insane amount of funding...but did not believe that it was worth giving up on because of a few stupid mistakes that I made.

"I've spent over 20,000 of my own money in the past two years on that building, so it hasn't been easy," he added.

Today, Sovereign Love is at the center of questions about where Dickson gets the money for his activism. *Texas Monthly* found that the church has paid well over $100,000 in legal fees to Dickson's attorney, Jonathan Mitchell.[10] Yet the church building appears abandoned. In photos taken by a visitor in 2024, moldering leaves lay alongside Jesus pamphlets on the floor. A toddler-sized action figure stood on a wooden desk. Nearby, stacked in front of a collection box and an enormous pillar candle on a lime-green stand were cardboard cutouts of superheroes and of the blond actress Kaley Cuoco as Penny Hofstader from the sitcom *The Big Bang Theory*.

(Dickson told me the congregation still meets elsewhere.)[11]

Some of the comic book club attendees struggled with mental health, as did Dickson. His antiabortion beliefs, he told me, grew out of a link he saw between suicide and abortion.[12] Like Randall Terry and Bob Bauman, he seemed to identify with the unwanted fetus. He believed that all people deserved to feel wanted—a feeling he struggled to experience himself.

"Some nights the thought of dying is much more desirable than the thought of living," he wrote on Facebook in June 2017, when he was thirty-one. "As morbid as this may sound, it is the truth. I long for the day when I get to close my eyes and wake up to Jesus Christ."

So Dickson set out to save the unborn who were unwanted.

In 2012, he began protesting outside a clinic in Shreveport, Louisiana. Sometimes he held a white plastic bullhorn and a sign that read "We will adopt your baby" on one side and "Babies are murdered here" on the other.[13] Sometimes he could convince an "abortion-minded" woman from the clinic in Louisiana or one of the clinics he frequented in Texas to come with him to a 4D ultrasound facility where he asked the technician to record the sound of the fetal heart tones and implant it into two teddy bears: one for the woman; one for him.

Perhaps there was a teddy bear sitting in the cab of his white Ford F-150 pickup truck on the day in 2019 when he and Jonathan Mitchell devised the first "Sanctuary City for the Unborn" ordinance. Dickson was at his favorite dining spot, Chick-fil-A.

As he munched his French fries, he mulled the possibility that new restrictions on abortion in Louisiana might prompt the clinic in Shreveport to move to East Texas. Abortion was still a constitutional right. But Dickson wanted to find a way for towns to ban it anyway. So he called up Bryan Hughes, a Texas state senator who had been a pallbearer at his grandfather's funeral.

On a three-way conference call, Hughes introduced Dickson, the eager ambassador, to Jonathan Mitchell, the legal mastermind. A graduate of University of Chicago Law School, Mitchell had clerked for the conservative Supreme Court Justice Antonin Scalia. His ideas about how to nullify the role of courts by resurrecting "zombie laws" from history books were so fringe that his former teacher called them dangerous and compared the idea to "a land mine."

"Jonathan always puts the fear of God in me, because God forbid he should be right on this particular question," Richard Epstein, the former teacher and a leading conservative legal scholar, told a Federalist Society panel in 2018.[14]

Mitchell told Dickson he thought that cities could ban abortion and avoid having their bans declared unconstitutional if they outsourced enforcement of the bans to private citizens. It was a wild idea—but true believer that he was, Dickson was ready to sell it door-to-door. Mitchell wrote an ordinance to ban abortion in Waskom, Texas: population 1,900. When five white men on the Waskom city council raised their hands to pass the ordinance in June 2019, a few Texas abortion rights groups noticed but most people didn't take the threat seriously.

"We did underestimate the power of a man in a backwards cap driving around in his car to spread the gospel about antiabortion," Drucilla Tigner, an attorney who worked for the Texas ACLU at the time, told me.

"I think we soon learned that lesson."[15]

Dickson and his teddy bears were soon crisscrossing Texas. He always presented the same proposal: If a city passed the ordinance and agreed to participate in Jonathan Mitchell's legal experiment, then Mitchell would represent the city for free if they got sued.

In 2020, Dickson pulled into the West Texas city of Lubbock. Lubbock, unlike many small towns Dickson visited, actually had an abortion clinic. Lubbock's city council voted the proposal down. So he and his supporters put it on the ballot for voters to decide. By then, more people were paying attention. Planned Parenthood's national office spent $430,000 to defend the clinic. Their supporters knocked on doors and made almost 200,000 phone calls.[16] But in May 2021, residents of the city of Lubbock approved the ban. Pro-choice groups filed a lawsuit to defend the Planned Parenthood clinic, which gave Mitchell a chance to defend his unconventional theory in court. Just as he had hoped, a federal judge allowed the ordinance to stand. The clinic in Lubbock stopped performing abortions. In a corner of West Texas, access flickered out, the first sign that *Roe* itself was dying.

Meanwhile, state Senator Bryan Hughes, who for at least part of that year was living at home with his parents,[17] had copied the private enforcement mechanism into Senate Bill 8. The law banned abortion when embryonic cardiac activity could be detected, around six weeks. On September 1, 2021, the Supreme Court let the ban take effect. Abortion clinics across Texas began turning away anyone whose embryo sounded like Dickson's teddy bears.

After *Dobbs*, states including Texas banned abortion outright, and Dickson and Mitchell formulated a new experiment to make the bans work: They had begun to commune with ghosts. It was not the first time Dickson had encountered the undead. Over a decade before, he posted on a message board that as a child, he had "seen what many people would classify as 'ghosts' as well as 'shadow people,'" including "a woman in my hallway" and "a witch-like woman who was floating above my window staring down at me."

"The instance where I witnessed the witch-like woman I could not move at all," he wrote. "If you would like to talk to me about your experiences feel free to shoot me a message."[18]

Finally, someone had answered. Jonathan Mitchell was about to help Dickson bring the antivice crusader Anthony Comstock back from the dead.

THE CRUSADER

Anthony Comstock was a post office inspector and secretary of the New York Society for the Suppression of Vice whose crusade against obscenity would make him "one of the most important men in the lives of nineteenth-century women," Amy Sohn wrote in her book on Comstock, *The Man Who Hated Women*. He had been raised on a farm in New Canaan, Connecticut, to revere the "Victorian ideal of womanhood—a saintly, pure wife and mother whose domain was the home." It was an ideal embodied by his own mother whom, as a child, Comstock found dead in her bed after she had given birth to his younger sibling. In one of sexual history's most impactful psychological twists, Comstock channeled this trauma into a lifelong crusade to purge the country of prurient longings. He went to Washington, DC, where he staged a spectacular display of sex toys and parlayed his one-man crusade against immorality into the first federal obscenity law to link pornography with contraception. The 1873 Comstock Act made the distribution, sale, and mailing of obscene materials including contraception and abortion drugs and devices a crime. The federal law spawned a series of "little Comstock" laws in the states, including one in Comstock's home state of Connecticut that criminalized anything that interfered with conception—even the withdrawal method.[19]

Comstock terrorized Planned Parenthood's founder Margaret Sanger and the well-to-do nineteenth-century abortion provider Madame Restell, who operated openly and ostentatiously in an era when abortion was illegal, yet common. When Restell committed suicide while awaiting trial after he orchestrated her arrest, Comstock bragged about it.

Today, this law would never get through Congress, but that was the point. Instead of passing a new law, Dickson and Mitchell would try to revive the section of the Comstock Act that made sending abortion pills and devices through the mail a federal crime punishable by up to five years in prison. While the optics of resurrecting a Victorian-era zealot who boasted of driving people to suicide weren't ideal, the law's appeal was obvious: It didn't require democratic support from the American people, who broadly support abortion rights. Yet if the courts took it literally, as Mitchell did, it would operate as a de facto nationwide abortion ban, because it could prevent the shipment of all pills and supplies needed for abortion. As far as Mitchell and Dickson were concerned, the ban was valid law, even though it hadn't been enforced for decades, and most people had forgotten about it. Even Justice Samuel Alito, who cited several Victorian-era abortion laws in *Dobbs*, had overlooked Comstock.

As usual, Dickson played Johnny Appleseed. He took his antiabortion road show to New Mexico where he convinced towns and counties along the Texas border to pass ordinances that declared the Comstock Act in effect within their lines. Women in the area who fought back against Dickson told me these local hearing rooms were so packed and rowdy they felt intimidated; after one hearing in the city of Clovis, a fire marshal had to escort the pro-choice women to their cars.[20] Dickson and Mitchell hoped that lawsuits generated by these ordinances would help prompt the Supreme Court to resurrect Comstock.[21] (In early 2025, the New Mexico Supreme Court ruled that local governments couldn't restrict abortion.)[22]

Their next major battleground was Amarillo—the Texas gateway to legal abortion.

The Amarillo ordinance declared any organization that mailed abortion drugs or devices a "criminal organization." It allowed any private citizen to sue anyone who helped someone travel through the city to get an abortion, and it banned abortions performed on any *resident* of the city of Amarillo, even if the abortion happened in a state like New Mexico where abortion was legal. There was a carve out exempting the person who had the abortion from being sued, an attempt to avoid the taboo of targeting pregnant women. Dickson and his supporters called it an "abortion trafficking" ordinance, an effort to imply that pregnant people were being "trafficked" to clinics.[23] Yet the language of the ordinance revealed that the true victim of "trafficking" was the "unborn child" itself. Opponents were calling the ordinance a travel ban.

In 2023, Jonathan Mitchell pressed Amarillo's leaders to pass the ordinance in time for the city to join a federal lawsuit by antiabortion groups aimed at taking the abortion drug mifepristone off the market.[24]

But the Amarillo city council balked. At least part of the reason was Dickson himself.

He rubbed some of them the wrong way.

"He's trying to create, in my opinion, Mark Lee Dickson's Law of Humanity," former Amarillo Councilman Tom Scherlen told me.[25] "It's all about him." ("If it was all about me, I would not have fought as hard as I have fought," Dickson told me in response to Scherlen's comment.)[26] Fellow Councilman Don Tipps, a State Farm agent and outspoken conservative, agreed.

"I didn't care for him, to be honest," he said. "My relationship with him, or my, whatever you want to call it, started with like a two-hour rebuke. I told him to get out of Amarillo."[27]

Not that Tipps disliked the idea of the ordinance, which he voted for.

"I appreciate what he does," Tipps added. "But man, he can be polarizing, for sure."

("I did not come to Amarillo to make friends," Dickson told me in response to Tipps. "I came to Amarillo to help...save pregnant mothers and their unborn children from the tragedy of abortion.")

In other words, Dickson was heeding a deeply felt call to save the unwanted, and he was not going to back off just because some people didn't want him around.

"I understand that there are a lot of people in this world who hate me," Dickson wrote to me after I shared these criticisms from public officials. "On a regular basis I get messages to my inbox that tell me how horrible of a person I am, or how my mom should have aborted me, or that the world would be better off if I killed myself." He consoled himself with Bible verses like Matthew 10:22, where Jesus told his followers, "You will be hated by all for my name's sake. But the one who endures to the end will be saved."[28]

Driven by these convictions, Dickson was so persistent it could verge on bullying.

In the West Texas city of Abilene, as records I obtained through a public records request show, Dickson warned a cautious council: "The last thing we would ever want [to] do is to battle with the City of Abilene as we have with the abortion industry—which will be done if necessary."[29]

Hesitant to pass the ordinance outright, the council referred it to the ballot, where the residents of Abilene passed it in November 2022.

Sometimes Dickson's approach backfired—like when he came to Hillsdale, Michigan, in 2021. Here at last I was getting my chance to experience the American version of Miss Marple's approach to studying people. She believed human nature was best observed in a small town. "Human nature is much the same everywhere," she declared, "and, of course, one has opportunities of observing it at closer quarters in a village."[30]

As I traced Dickson's path, I encountered some of human nature's best plot twists. I talked to Mayor Adam Stockford, a former boxer who had worked as a carpet layer and then managed to become the rare native of the blue-collar city of Hillsdale to attend the Christian conservative school Richard Viguerie advertised on his tie: Hillsdale College. There, Stockford was mentored by conservative luminaries and steeped in veneration for the founding fathers. He seemed like a natural audience for Dickson's antiabortion ordinance. But after Dickson pitched him the idea over lunch one day, Stockford told me he found Dickson to be "a little bit of a braggart, a little aggressive." When he read the ordinance, Stockford was even more skeptical.

"There was things in it that were, like, encouraging you to snitch on your neighbors, which in a small town, that's poison," Stockford told me.[31]

Nor did Stockford like the section calling for the prosecution of anyone who so much as donated money to an abortion fund.

When Dickson heard Stockford had doubts, he messaged him on

Facebook. Records shared with me by Democracy Forward showed he name-dropped antiabortion operatives like Frank Pavone, who supported his ordinance, and warned that an upcoming hearing on the measure would be "packed out with pro-life advocates."

"It will be a very big surprise if anyone who is truly a conservative stands against this ordinance," Dickson wrote.

"Let's just remove the part about snitching on your neighbors and donating money and pass it," Stockford proposed. "I'm good with that."

But Dickson wasn't satisfied. "If you guys go with a weaker version it will be noticed," he wrote.

After several such exchanges, Stockford finally wrote: "Mark, you've made a few vague threats to me since you came to town."[32]

Ultimately, the city didn't pass the ordinance.

"Hillsdale, Michigan, may have been the first place where I ever encountered a Republican Party whose leadership were a lot more Libertarian than I was accustomed to," Dickson later told me.

More than 1,000 miles away in Eastland, Texas, with its population of less than four thousand, Ben McNabb felt his own reservations with Dickson's ordinance. McNabb, a former city commissioner who runs a pharmacy with his wife, confided in text messages that he found the proposal "overreaching."[33] He wasn't alone; a colleague, the late Commissioner Cecil Funderburgh, told a rowdy room during an initial hearing in June 2021: "I am against abortion. Period. But what we are talking about here is passing a legal document that cannot and will not be enforced." In a revealing detail, the meeting minutes noted: "Commissioner Funderburgh's comments were then drowned out by the crowd."[34]

Dickson's supporters packed the meetings in Eastland with standing-room-only crowds. McNabb told me he tried three times to recruit someone to speak against the ordinance in order to encourage a more balanced discussion, but no one was willing to do so. By August, all the commissioners voted for the ordinance, including Funderburgh and McNabb. But McNabb would not run for council again; he had decided after his run-in with

Dickson that local politics was not for him. Three years later, he told me he still felt conflicted about the vote.

"I wish our community had chosen not to take up this matter," he said.[35]

By the time Dickson got to Amarillo in 2023, he had left behind a trail of galvanized opponents. From Lebanon, Ohio, to Lubbock, Texas, people who had fought Dickson in their towns had formed a private channel to compare notes on how to defeat him. When they combined forces, they often found they could succeed. Texas activists including Drucilla Tigner, who had joined Planned Parenthood Texas Votes, and Blair Wallace, of the Texas ACLU, created the Texas Abortion Advocacy Network, a training ground for local efforts to protect reproductive freedom.

Residents of Amarillo caught wind that Dickson was coming to town in the summer of 2023. Two women, Lindsay London and Harper Metcalf, infiltrated the meeting, wearing long skirts and covering their tattoos to blend in. They helped form the Amarillo Reproductive Freedom Alliance, packing the speakers lists at city council meetings with emotional presentations that dragged late into the night.

In June 2024, they won. The council rejected the ordinance. Only Don Tipps voted for it.

But Dickson and his supporters had a backup plan. They would put the ordinance on the ballot. Dickson had done this five times in Texas when councils balked. Every time, he'd won.

To Tigner, it seemed like he would win again.

"When I first met the Amarillo folks, my question for them was, 'What is your goal?'" Tigner recalled. "And they said their goal was to win, and I said, 'OK, well, what is your secondary goal?'

"I just felt like this was going to be Lubbock 2.0."

She wasn't wrong to be skeptical. This was one of the country's most conservative areas; the two counties that encompass Amarillo had gone to Trump by about 70 and 80 percent in 2020. But Dickson's opponents believed they had a way to win. They leaned hard into the pro-choice movement's use of conservative talking points, which dated back to the Reagan era. They framed abortion as an issue of personal liberty and Mitchell and Dickson's ordinance as "government overreach." They circulated door hangers with eagles and quotes about freedom from Texas Republican Governor Greg Abbott. Conservatives seemed to respond.[36]

This was the final reason I had decided to spend Election Day with Dickson. I knew it was a long shot, but I thought he might lose.

So on the morning of Election Day, I drove past tractor supply stores and trucks with cheese-grater sides packed with sad-eyed cows. I felt hopeful in part because of the secret joy I was trafficking. My excitement over my pregnancy had cast the world in a soft light. Plus, Trump had been backtracking on his opposition to abortion. His base of Christian conservative voters was angry over this betrayal. I believed, as I drove through the Texas prairie, that Trump might lose, too.

I passed white crosses and signs pointing off into the high grass to unseen churches. The crosses loomed over the landscape, some taller than houses, more constant than the Trump signs. I passed a field where a crane the height of a building sat with a white cross suspended by a cord. There was something haunting about it, hanging there like a body in the morning light.

I pulled into a travel center in Jolly, Texas, where a brown-and-white bull statue stood outside in a rectangle of fake grass, his eyes downcast. Inside the bathroom stall I tried to read our country's future in the graffiti. Travelers had etched white crosses into the brown-green paint. Next to one was the word "Jesus" and then the words: "Trump is a traitor."

The next day, on my way back to Dallas, Trump would be the president-elect. I would pass the cow trucks again, and they would be empty, and I would feel empty, too, and terrified as the cows, hurtling, sick, across this landscape of crosses.

But today, I was in such a naive headspace that I had confidently chosen to spend election night surrounded by Trump supporters who wanted to stop pregnant women from riding in cars. I entered Amarillo, passing the Big Texan steak house with its custard-yellow facade and a sign out front that said "Go vote, eat a steak." The restaurant offered a deal where if you could eat a seventy-two-ounce steak the size of a trash can lid in under an hour, it was free. If you vomited into the container they provided, then you were disqualified and required to pay full price: $72. Twelve percent of those who attempted the challenge succeeded.

I was not in Massachusetts anymore.

I pulled into the parking lot outside the Randall County Annex, a bustling precinct with a curved white front where signs for and against the ordinance jutted out of the ground, alongside reminders that there was a presidential election: "Protect personal privacy—vote against prop A," "Vote for Life—vote for Prop A," "Trump/Vance," "Harris/Walz," "VOTE HERE TODAY."

The first person I ran into was a supporter of Dickson's who told me she discovered as an adult that her mother had tried to abort her by "taking a bunch of medication.

"She says that I'm the greatest thing that God has ever given her so she was very happy that it didn't happen," she told me.[37]

I wandered over to a corner of the parking lot where two pickup trucks sat a few yards apart. In the back of one truck was Harper Metcalf, dressed in a flannel shirt and cowboy boots, with a sign that read "Vote Against Prop A." A puppy she found crying in the streets the night before was napping in the cab.

"I'm cautiously optimistic," she told me. "Even pro-life conservatives—Trump supporters—realize this is not the way to go about this."[38]

Nearby in his own truck, holding a sign for Dickson's ordinance, was Alex Deanda. He was the plaintiff in a lawsuit filed by Jonathan Mitchell that affirmed the rights of Texas parents to prevent their children from accessing birth control without permission.[39] Deanda was a big-headed man prone to "dad" jokes, like eyeing my press pass and asking me if people ever stuck out their fingers to "press" it. I asked him if his daughters, now twenty-one, twenty, and seventeen, shared his opposition to birth control.

He looked out over the parking lot. "I would imagine; I'm not too sure," he said. "We have communication pretty constantly, every day; they've mentioned some things that show me that they still support it."[40]

Dickson strode by in the uniform he said God told him to wear when he debuted his ordinance: black-and-white Vans sneakers, jeans, a collared shirt, and a black backward baseball cap. His God not only deplored lustful-minded sinners but had the taste of a '90s teenager. Dickson's cap read "Make America Great Again." He was outside the Capitol on January 6, 2021, during the insurrection, although he didn't go in. But the last time I saw him, a month earlier, he'd expressed disappointment over Trump's promise to veto a nationwide abortion ban.

"I believe President Trump's statements on abortion have hurt his chances at winning the 2024 election," he told me.[41]

I was naive enough to think he was right.

As we stood under the hot sun in the busy parking lot, surrounded by cars honking their support for one side or the other, I asked Dickson about the women who had died in Texas.

Six days earlier, ProPublica had reported on the death of Josseli Barnica. She was grieving the loss of the pregnancy she was losing to a miscarriage at seventeen weeks, when doctors delayed her care for forty hours, exposing her uterus to infection. Her husband rushed to her side from his job on a construction site. She told him that her medical team had told her "they had to wait until there was no heartbeat," and "it would be a crime to give her an abortion." Three days after delivering a dead fetus, she died. Barnica had sought care in September 2021 just two days after the Supreme Court allowed the six-week ban Dickson helped pioneer to take effect. But Dickson blamed the doctors for misinterpreting the law.

"When you read the stories about these women," I asked, "even if the doctors made a mistake in the moment and interpreted the law too conservatively, obviously the law was a factor. I mean, does that weigh on you?"

"These people are misinterpreting the law and the problem is with them"—he paused and coughed—"the problem is with them not following the law."

"Abortion is an elective procedure," he continued. "It is in the same category as breast implants. It's not an essential—"

"Why do you compare it to breast implants?" I interrupted.

Dickson blushed. "Just an elective—"

"But why that? There's tons of elective procedures."

"Well, that's just," he stammered. "That's one of them that's out there."

"I know, but why choose that?"

"Well, because people view abortion as necessary."[42]

Dickson is part of a long tradition in the antiabortion movement of denying abortion can ever save a life. The antiabortion organization American Association of Pro-Life OBGYNs, has for years attempted to get around the issue of life-threatening pregnancies by redefining abortion in emergency situations as a "premature delivery" or "maternal-fetal separation."[43] Abortion opponents prefer these "separations" to be performed via inducing labor or performing a cesarean section rather than through simpler and safer procedures that have the direct effect of terminating the pregnancy. Today, doctors across Texas are balking at performing these procedures, even when a patient is very sick. A 2025 ProPublica investigation discovered this trend has resulted in a surge in sepsis cases in Texas.[44]

"The women in these ProPublica stories, they needed an abortion," I pressed.

"No, they didn't," Dickson said, and the dead women stood between us, like ghosts in the parking lot.

This parking lot was holding a lot—including the contradictions that would define this election. One woman I interviewed seemed to carry all those mysteries in her small frame: Dexie Organ, a sixty-year-old white woman who stepped out of a beat-up rust-colored Nissan in black leggings and a red top. She voted against Dickson's ordinance.

"It was kind of a tough decision but I have eight daughters," she told me in her Southern drawl, adding, "I have six sons, too."[45]

Organ wanted her daughters "to have what they want," she said. "We're women. I don't know why they think they need to suppress us."

"I hear that," I said, adding that it might surprise people that she voted against the ordinance, when she has fourteen kids.

"I've also had an abortion," she said. "I've had that experience, too."

"Thank you for sharing that," I replied. "And can I ask how you voted in terms of the president?"

"I voted for Donald Trump," she said, and I felt the sudden urge to lie down on the hot pavement.

"Our country is such a mess under Kamala and Joe Biden," she continued. "I would like to see a woman president but I just don't think she's the one; she's not strong enough to lead. We've got all these foreign wars going on and the men in the other leadership roles in our world would just annihilate us."

"You feel like Trump is stronger on foreign policy?"

"Yes I do," she said. "And I think he's a businessman... I mean our country's in ruins financially. I work three jobs. I wait tables, I'm a registered nurse midwife and then I have a side lick that I breed small dogs... Chihuahuas and American bulldogs."

"Do you have any concerns about Trump's position on abortion?"

"I don't," she said. "He gave it to the states."

This will be a common refrain among pro-choice Trump voters in 2024. Most people in this country support the right to abortion and yet, the majority will vote in favor of Trump and his fellow Republicans responsible for ending that right. I thought back to the sisters at the Reagan library, and how support for abortion rights can so easily be trumped by loyalty to a swarthy white man.

Later, I will interview Jackie Payne, who studies moderate white women voters like Organ through her organization, Galvanize Action, and she will make me feel silly for believing abortion could sway a presidential election. It was true that 86 percent of moderate white women said the decision to have an abortion should rest with women and their doctors, not politicians—the highest number Payne had ever seen. Yet abortion never ranked as the top issue for these swing voters; the economy was always first, with abortion ranked third or fourth.[46]

These women were mad about *Dobbs*—but not mad enough.

I wandered over to Dickson. He was standing with a supporter named Cathy Welch who had blond curly hair and the general vibe of an irate bulldog. I pressed them on another contradiction that had been irking me—the way the ordinance implied that women are trafficking their own unborn children, and yet didn't penalize them. Aren't we the real traffickers? If the ordinance were honest, wouldn't it go after us?

"We don't want to penalize the mom; we want to walk with the mom," Welch told me. "We want to counsel the mom."

"What if the mom doesn't want your counseling? What if she wants to get an abortion?" I asked.

"Well, then she can drive herself to New Mexico," said Welch, who was holding a sign for a proposal to prevent women from driving to New Mexico.[47]

"For too long, we have treated women as if they are always the victim," Dickson chimed in. "The unborn child is truly the victim of the abortion; they're the one who is being killed."

I found his honesty refreshing. In an era where two-thirds of abortions involve the simple act of a person taking medications at home, it's implausible for abortion opponents to claim *everyone* who takes these pills is an unwitting victim. Indeed, it seemed to aggravate Dickson when women showed that they were *not* victims—like when the group Shout Your Abortion took the abortion drug mifepristone in front of the Supreme Court during the *Dobbs* arguments.

"Clearly, the woman who takes abortion-inducing drugs in front of the Supreme Court and says that they are ending their pregnancy, why aren't we treating that person like we would treat the mother who drowned her two-month-old baby in the bathtub?"

Dickson paused and added, "Which is not the death penalty, by the way."

Then he wandered over to coach his supporters to change the order of their chants. The proper order was: "Vote for Life! Vote for Trump! Vote for Prop A!"

The sky began to darken. We were hours away from any belief I had left in America. Supporters and opponents of the ordinance gathered in the waning light.

A man in a blue T-shirt surveyed the scene. "I vote: How about get a life?" he muttered as he got into his car.

Dickson was pacing, cradling two of his fetal models in his hand. A crew had shown up to film him.

"They're going to make you a star," I joked.

"I'm already a star," he said wryly, and then imitated a high-pitched baby voice, making the fetal models speak: "Us too!"

In that moment, I felt ready to render my Miss Marple verdict on Dickson's nature. All the contradictions about him were true. He was dangerous, indeed, if he wanted to treat women who have abortions like they had drowned a baby in the bathtub. He was a true believer, too, who believed that he was saving the unwanted. He was also a goofy bastard.

The polls closed and Dickson's team of volunteers headed across town, filing into the carpeted sanctuary of Covenant Church. Fluorescent lights shone overhead. The weary volunteers loaded up paper plates with homemade enchiladas and brisket and baked potatoes with shredded cheese, salsa, and sour cream. A whiteboard in front of the stage listed the eleven cities or states with abortion ballot initiatives, with Amarillo on top. Dickson strode over and wrote the word "Victory!" next to Florida, where a ballot initiative to restore abortion rights had failed.

"Florida baby!" someone called out.

"That may be our retirement state now."

My heart sank. I had spent a day over the summer in the waiting room of the Planned Parenthood in Sarasota, watching patients get turned away in tears because they were past the state's six-week cutoff. *Now that will keep happening*, I thought, *every day, in every waiting room, in a state where 84,000 abortions were performed the year before the ban took effect.*[48]

It was the first sign that the country was going to hell. The map on the Fox News screen over the stage was red as blood.

Texas Senator Ted Cruz won reelection. The room erupted in cheers.

"Pennsylvania's close," Alex Deanda called out hopefully.

I felt my dread rise like water, and wished I was at home in my living room with my husband and not sitting next to Peggy Thomas, a sixty-two-year-old Trump supporter who bore a striking resemblance to Hillary Clinton.

Then I noticed Dickson had disappeared.

I took out my phone. And my heart skipped: He'd lost.

I dialed Fariha Samad, a curly-haired former paralegal and president of the Amarillo Reproductive Freedom Alliance.

"Are you guys declaring victory?" I asked, incredulous.

"I've been celebrating for a while now," she said, sounding breathless, although she was waiting for another news outlet to call it.

I surveyed the forty or so people in the room eating their brisket and potatoes. None appeared to have heard yet.

Then I went hunting for Dickson, pushing through a wooden door into a hallway. I followed him back into the sanctuary as he strode over to his easel of ballot initiatives and wrote "loss" next to Colorado, one of seven states that voted for abortion rights, a bright spot on this terrible night.

"We'll talk about that," he said, pacing and scrolling on his phone when I asked if he'd noticed that he'd lost.

Christian right stalwart Josh Hawley won reelection to his Missouri senate seat. Dickson clapped halfheartedly.

"Trump's going to win!" someone yelled, and I wanted to lie down and scream with my teeth in the carpet, but instead, I dogged Dickson like a basset hound to see if I could smell the loss coming off him. I trailed him through a set of doors into the church café where he seemed to be hiding.

"Can you give us a minute?" he asked, sending me away.

I waited in the sanctuary until he came out to face his flock, standing beside his half-completed easel that now read "Victory! Loss! Loss! Loss!" On a table, the fetal models lay like an offering.

"So guys," Dickson said at last. "Tonight is not a night with results we were hoping for." He listed cities where he had won before: Lubbock, Plainview, Abilene. "Very different results. So we gotta be honest. What happened?" he asked.

The answers to that question were dancing their asses off across town, and suddenly I wanted him to finish so I could get over there.

"This is our Alamo in the pro-life movement in Texas!" Dickson declared.

"Remember the Amarillo!" a supporter shouted.

Dickson took a seat at the back of the room as his supporters rose to their feet. One played the rousing Christian anthem "Battle Belongs" on a guitar. A few lifted their hands in the air. I turned to ask Dickson a question and noticed that his eyes were filled with tears. He was a true believer indeed. This was his life. And while he might be feeling crushed on this night in Amarillo, he was still guilty in the incremental murder of abortion rights. By his own count at the time of this writing, eighty-two cities and eleven counties have passed versions of his ordinance.[49]

I left the church and trafficked myself and my unborn child out of there to join the celebration across town. Joy was about to become hard to find, and I had temporarily suspended my investigation in order to spend a few minutes with people who could help me remember that in the darkness to come, there might be hope.

"I would describe the atmosphere as jubilant," Fariha Samad had told me on the phone, and I pressed my foot to the accelerator and almost blew a stop sign in the dark. Light emanated from the burger bar and I could hear the music before I opened the door. Inside, the women were drunk and exuberant. Harper Metcalf's eyes shone.

"How do you feel?" I shouted over the music, and she looked me dead in the eye and said: "I don't know if I've ever been this happy." Behind the bar a TV was mutely playing our descent into authoritarian rule on MSNBC, but they were ignoring it, so I did, too.

"I feel validated as fuck," Samad said.

Late that night, Blair Wallace texted her friend Drucilla Tigner: "We fucking won in Amarillo," she wrote. And Tigner, exhausted, demoralized, and staring down the barrel of four long years, texted back: "I can't believe it. I'm sobbing."

They had done the impossible. They had broken Dickson's string of victories in the heart of the Bible Belt. Inadvertently, Dickson had become the Johnny Appleseed not just of abortion bans—but of much-needed abortion rights organizing at the local level. Perhaps the activists sensed, as I did watching them dance, that this kind of winning—tiny, limited, local—was the way forward, the only way we would win for the next four years.

It was about to get dark, I knew. But tonight, the GoldenLight Cafe lived up to its name, the stage lights shone and the streamers overhead sparkled, and the music bumped, and the Texans who had defeated Mark Lee Dickson danced.

Soak it up, I told myself. *You are going to need this joy.*

I didn't know yet just how soon the darkness would come and how personal it would get.

CHAPTER 13

ALL THE KILLERS WHO WERE NEVER CAUGHT

I have sometimes been wildly despairing, acutely miserable, racked with sorrow, but through it all I still know quite certainly that just to be alive is a grand thing.

—*An Autobiography* by Agatha Christie

SIX DAYS AFTER THE 2024 PRESIDENTIAL ELECTION, DURING A PERIOD OF collective despair, I lost my own little ray of hope: my pregnancy. I was about to walk down the aisle at my friend's wedding when I went to the bathroom and saw blood. As my friend and her husband exchanged vows, I stared at the backs of the other bridesmaids in their blue velvet dresses and wondered if they had ever lost a pregnancy.

I was trying to feel less alone.

The truth was that I knew how common this was. I understood that as many as one in five pregnancies ended this way, because for years it had been my job to investigate these endings. *You are like Alison now*, I consoled myself. *You are like Kate. You are like all those women you have interviewed.*

In the days to come, the horrific stories of women I'd reported on formed a strange circle of comfort. They reassured me that I was not the only one who had endured the shame and isolation that comes with failing to carry a pregnancy to term in a society that has never really lost its Comstockian reverence for ideal Victorian motherhood. It was my turn to go through the painful steps that I had heard sources describe to me—except that, in their cases, antiabortion policies made an already upsetting experience traumatic or even dangerous.

"Do you want me to turn the screen away?" the tech asked before scanning my empty uterus.

"No," I said, because I am an expert. I *know* about this; I even *knew* she was going to ask that because they *always* ask that, and anyway, what would be the point?

I was already frozen and cracked like a winter pond.

There was so much I knew and yet, so much I did not, like how miscarriage can make you feel like you might explode into a flock of shrieking bats when a stranger asks, "How are you doing?"

"I've had better weeks," I said through gritted teeth when the medical assistant asked me.

"I've had better weeks," I told the phlebotomist during a blood draw to confirm my hormones were dropping.

So many people must be walking around secretly feeling this way all the time, I marveled.

I knew so much, but I did not know that.

I did not know that losing a pregnancy, even in the early weeks, when a procedure to treat it was not required, would make me feel like I was living in a basement. The light felt muted, and no matter how close I got to the window, it wouldn't get brighter.

After the ultrasound of my empty uterus, I walked in the park through winter trees and felt a loss that I couldn't name. This loss felt so different from losing a *person*. When my grandmother died, in 2020, I wanted to tell everyone I knew everything that I loved about her, like how, when I'd ask how she was, she'd sing out: "I have no special complaints."

She was a hundred, I told everyone who would listen, and once she pretended to disown me for piercing my lip. I wanted them to know *her*. I wanted to share my grief, to disperse it.

With this loss, all I knew for sure was that if anyone tried to tell me what it meant, or what I needed to do about it, I would turn them into stone.

Which is why, while I was in the basement, I thought about Alison.

She was a counselor with long blond hair. When she was three months pregnant with her second child, she began to bleed. It was 2013. *Roe* had been the law of the land for forty years, but in her town, in her blue state, where abortion is robustly protected, it did not matter.[1]

It still doesn't.

The suspect in Alison's case was the same one that had dogged me through this entire investigation. It was the Catholic Church.

In 2019, I sat in a cozy living room at the foot of the mountains in Washington while Alison told me the story.

Alison went to the only hospital in her hometown of Bellingham, near the Canadian border. An ultrasound showed the fetus was still viable. So they discharged her and told her she should return if she bled more heavily or ran a fever. Like me, Alison had been pregnant with her second child. Now, I understood just how hard she and her husband must have hoped that the pregnancy was safe, and that Alison would be safe, too.

When Alison began to bleed through her pads she returned to the emergency room. They discharged her again. Alison's only hospital was a Catholic facility that followed rules written by the Catholic bishops. The rules said: "Catholic health care institutions are not to provide abortion services."

Alison passed a blood clot the size of a jawbreaker. She spiked a fever. She returned to the hospital a third time. Asked to describe her pain, she said it was a seven out of ten. She showed classic signs of infection.

"Appears anxious," the staff recorded in her chart. They said her pain might be the result of appendicitis. And they sent her home again.

Still Alison and her husband had hoped it would be OK.

By the next morning, her fever wasn't responding to medication, so she returned to the ER a fourth time, where a doctor ordered an abdominal MRI to rule out appendicitis and a chest X-ray to rule out pneumonia. Then her ob-gyn arrived and performed a vaginal exam. The pain made her arch off the bed "like something from *The Exorcist*," she told me. She had refused pain medication, afraid it would harm the pregnancy. At one point, her suffering was so intense that her mother, who was standing nearby, slid down the wall and fainted.

Alison's doctor told her she needed a procedure to end the pregnancy. Her life could be in danger from the infection raging in her body. But then he stunned her and her parents by telling them that he had to wait for the hospital's ethics committee to approve the procedure. Directives for Catholic hospitals written by the bishops forbid abortion unless its "direct purpose" is "the cure of a proportionately serious pathological condition of a pregnant woman" that "cannot be safely postponed until the unborn child is viable."[2]

In other words, Catholic rules required that an ethics committee determine whether Alison was sick enough for the doctor to save her life.

"I remember being scared about that," Alison said. "You're telling me this is really serious and that my life is in danger, and we have to wait, and these people have to say it's OK for you to have this procedure you absolutely need."

These quandaries about how close to death a pregnant person must be before God permitted a doctor to save her would become a standard feature of the law in states like Texas, but that was still in the future, and Alison's family didn't know that. What they knew was that in 2013, when *Roe* was still the law of the land, in a blue state where the last time people voted for a Republican presidential candidate was Reagan thirty years earlier, a doctor was now contemplating sending Alison in an ambulance ninety miles south to Seattle. *Will I die on the way?* Alison wondered.

The ethics committee approved the procedure, her records show. At some point she was given misoprostol to soften her cervix in preparation for it. But before her doctor could begin, she miscarried into the toilet. She was so distraught she thought the white body floating in the water might be a hallucination.

"I didn't have to suffer like that," Alison told me through tears. "Everyone deserves adequate medical attention, and information, and choices."

It was 2019 when I published this story. And while I didn't know then what a miscarriage felt like, I already knew the most important thing I had found in my coverage of Catholic hospitals: that they were a harbinger. The final line of the article was a quote from Alison's mom, Steffany Raynes: "I don't want anybody to have to die because of a very narrow definition of protecting life."

Unbeknownst to many, the Catholic Church's rules govern care for one in six acute-care hospital beds across the United States. In Washington State, the number is even higher—40 percent of acute-care hospital beds are in a facility that follows Catholic rules.[3] In 2018, a study found that while one in six women nationwide name a Catholic hospital as their go-to place for reproductive health care, more than a third of these women aren't aware their hospital is Catholic.[4] Working for the news outlet *Rewire*, I documented how these organizations refused to provide contraception, even when the clinics they owned were the only option in town. I interviewed a woman in Indiana who had to ask a chaplain to leave five times in 2015 after he tried to pressure her into burying her miscarried fetus in a cemetery plot in accordance with Catholic beliefs. The woman, Kate Marshall, wanted to send the fetus for testing to determine the cause of her miscarriage. But a second chaplain accused her of sending the remains to "a medical slush pile." So, just before surgery to remove a very-wanted pregnancy, Marshall had been shaking with rage and crying.[5]

Now I understand, I wanted to tell her. *I would have hissed like a snake. I would have shattered like a glass on the floor.*

Not long after Marshall's ordeal, then-Indiana Governor Mike Pence had signed a bill requiring all miscarried or aborted fetal remains to be buried or cremated—yet another case of religious belief gaining the force of law.

While covering the Catholic hospital beat, I spoke to transgender patients who had been scheduled for much-needed surgeries only to have them canceled because the Catholic Church would only allow a uterus to be removed to treat a serious pathology; their gender-affirming procedure did not count.[6] I studied how, in my home state of Massachusetts, a Catholic health system was sold to a private equity firm named Cerberus Capital Management—the church doing business with a company named for a three-headed dog from hell that would run the business as a for-profit that nonetheless maintained the Catholic health-care restrictions.[7]

The truth was, covering this beat, I saw two phenomena colliding. One was the intrusion of religion into the health-care system, a trend that would only grow as the Supreme Court granted more power to religious corporations. The other was a disregard for the lives of women and transgender people—especially when those patients were Black.

In 2017, ProPublica and NPR investigated why the richest country in the world had a maternal mortality rate worse than every other wealthy country. They concluded that experts had spent years focusing on how to reduce infant mortality, while overlooking the people birthing those infants. As many as *half* of maternal deaths, they concluded, were *preventable*. Black women were three to four times more likely to die than white women.[8]

Once Trump was elected the first time, I began to see that the reporting I was doing on Catholic hospitals was a preview of the future.[9]

Soon, we were living in that future. After *Dobbs*, stories began emerging routinely from places like Texas and Louisiana and Alabama, where a health-care system that already minimized the suffering of women, especially women of color, was now much more regularly sending them home while they were miscarrying or telling them to wait for care to save their lives. The difference was that now, a lot more journalists were paying attention.

Soon, I was holding my breath, waiting for the next Rosie Jimenez.[10]

I didn't have to wait for long.

In September 2024, ProPublica reported that Amber Nicole Thurman had died after a hospital in suburban Atlanta delayed performing a dilation and curettage procedure to remove the tissue she had retained in her uterus after a medication abortion. She was twenty-eight and worked as a medical assistant and loved taking her six-year-old son to petting zoos and the beach. She wanted a procedural abortion in Georgia, but because of the state's six-week ban she had to travel four hours to North Carolina, where she missed her appointment because of standstill traffic. The clinic offered a medication abortion instead; the rare complication she suffered is easy to treat with a procedure, but Georgia doctors didn't perform that procedure because the state had made it a felony. Now her son was growing up without his mom.[11]

Days later, the outlet reported that another Georgia woman, Candi Miller, had been afraid to seek medical care because of the state's abortion ban after she experienced a similar complication. Her husband found her unresponsive in her bed with her three-year-old daughter lying next to her.[12]

Georgia's maternal mortality review committee had ruled these deaths "preventable." Weeks after ProPublica reported that fact, Georgia fired the entire committee, accusing members of disclosing confidential information.[13]

That wasn't all.

Three women had died in Texas, and ProPublica's reporting suggested their deaths, too, resulted from that state's antiabortion laws.

Porsha Ngumezi was thirty-five and left behind two sons, the youngest of whom had since begun chasing after any woman he saw on the street with long locks like his mother's, shouting: "That's Mommy."[14]

Josseli Barnica died just days after the Texas six-week ban with Jonathan Mitchell and Mark Lee Dickson's enforcement mechanism took effect, when doctors told her it would be a "crime" to treat her miscarriage.[15]

Nevaeh Crain, eighteen years old, died after being sent home from two emergency rooms in a case that felt eerily similar to Alison's.[16] I read this last story in my driveway, and when I got to the name of the hospital where she died I almost screamed. It was Christus, a Catholic health system I had investigated for its antiabortion policies in 2018.[17]

In the wake of this reporting, Democrats had seized on these deaths to show the lethal impact of Republican policies. Kamala Harris and Oprah met with Amber Nicole Thurman's family for an emotional interview ahead of the 2024 election.

But as someone who had been on the almost-dead-woman beat for years, I felt like everyone was missing the fact that these stories happened even before the bans. *Dobbs* was another layer of disregard for maternal life that had started long before Trump was elected. What's more, three of the women whose deaths ProPublica had covered were Black, and one was Latina, racial identities that had long faced discrimination in the medical system. I was afraid that, in our haste to show the impact of the bans, we had missed the bigger story.

So in the weeks after my miscarriage, I pored through articles and books about the history of pregnancy loss.

I read about Mylissa Farmer, who was living in southwest Missouri when she had a miscarriage while eighteen weeks pregnant in 2022. She went to the emergency room in Joplin, where she was turned away because Missouri had banned abortion after *Dobbs* and she was not sick enough to qualify for an exception to that ban. She traveled three hours to the University of Kansas Health System, where she was turned away because Kansas bans abortion at facilities run by the University of Kansas Hospital Authority.[18] Such bans are an iteration of the Hyde Amendment that was upheld by the Supreme Court's *Webster* decision in 1989—the one Faye Wattleton had decried as yet another attack on poor women.

The Kansas law predated the *Dobbs* decision by many years.[19] It was one of hundreds of antiabortion laws that I'd been reporting on as they chipped away at access in states across the country. Abortion was legal in Kansas. In fact, on the very day when Farmer went to the University of Kansas hospital, voters in the state were going to the polls to protect its legality. But Farmer's doctor told her it was too "risky" to induce labor to save her life because of the "heated" political environment. She was forced to drive several hours to Hope Clinic in Illinois. When she returned home, her ob-gyn diagnosed her with an infection.

Two eras of antiabortion policy had collided in Farmer's story—one that came after *Dobbs*, and one that existed long before.

Which is why, as I neared the end of my investigation, I began to feel like I was coming back to the beginning. That feeling only deepened when I read ProPublica's December report about a Coast Guard commander who suffered a miscarriage. The medical procedure she needed to treat it was denied by her military health insurance. After she hemorrhaged, she had to be carried by EMTs past her daughter's bedroom, wrapped in a tarp that reminded her of a body bag. She was finally treated after hemorrhaging for four hours.

"The statute barring the Defense Department from paying for most abortions goes back to 1985 and mirrors language in what's called the Hyde Amendment," ProPublica reported.

"Named for its author, Henry Hyde, a Republican representative from Illinois, Congress has attached the amendment to spending bills since the late 1970s to prohibit the use of federal funds on abortion."[20]

I thought of Bob Bauman, sitting in his home in Florida, listening to the wind chimes, forgotten by history, while his greatest accomplishment was still condemning women to suffer. I thought of Paul Haring dismissing the idea that his plan had caused Rosie's death. I thought of the bishops and their rules for hospitals and how their lobbyist had pressured Dan Flood to cave on the Hyde Amendment.

I read all these stories while my body healed, and in the evenings, I read Dorothy Roberts's book *Killing the Black Body*, about how coercion shaped Black women's reproduction. In the 1980s, Black women were drug-tested after miscarrying and arrested for suspected crack use. In the wake of *Dobbs*, the criminalization of pregnancy loss had only increased. The group Pregnancy Justice counted at least 412 prosecutions for pregnancy-related crimes in the first two years after Dobbs; all but 13 involved allegations of substance use during pregnancy.[21]

The space that to me felt so proprietary was always subject to public control, especially for women of color. The difference now was that *Dobbs* had made more people notice.

In the aftermath of my loss, these stories helped me find my way from grief to anger, and to a conclusion that was key to my investigation. For Black women who were criminalized, and Medicaid recipients and teens who couldn't get abortions, and for all the patients like Alison whose only hospital was Catholic, *Roe* had never lived up to its promise of a right to privacy. The death of *Roe* was a significant loss. But *Roe* itself had never been the perfect victim.

After my miscarriage, I crawled into that trusted haven of my adolescence and early motherhood—Agatha Christie mysteries. I would lie on the couch streaming film adaptations of Miss Marple, watching her solve unspeakable crimes over glasses of damson gin. I felt comforted as I watched her root out wickedness. And I realized why I found her so soothing.

Because in her version of the world, terrible crimes were as common as thatched roofs, and yet, certain as rain in England was the understanding that the killer would be caught and punished. Even better, they would confess. They would be sorry before they were carted away to justice.

In the real world of injustice I was investigating, the killers were seldom caught. Nor, when confronted, did they ever seem truly sorry.

CHAPTER 14

THE FIRST VICTIM

> Incidentally I have learnt a good deal—about
> the victim. And the victim, mademoiselle, is
> very often the clue to the mystery.
>
> —Hercule Poirot in *Murder in Mesopotamia* by Agatha Christie

IN AUGUST 1980, PAULINA CARDENAS TOOK THE STAGE AT THE DEMOcratic National Convention in New York City. The party's leaders had gathered to renominate the incumbent president, Jimmy Carter. Soon, the celebratory balloons that were supposed to rain down on the gathering would get stuck in the ceiling, a harbinger of just how little cause there would be for celebration come Election Day. Carter would lose by a spectacular margin. A Hollywood actor and former governor of California who just *loved* horses would win a staggering forty-four states, marking the fulfillment of Richard Viguerie's dream, the dawning of an era of conservativism, and the beginning of the loss of two decades of progress.

But Cardenas wasn't there to talk about Jimmy Carter.

She was there to talk about her friend Rosie Jimenez.

In a photo I found in Ellen Frankfort's old papers, Cardenas had dark hair, long lashes, and a wide smile. She was wearing a pin for another lost feminist hope: "ERA Yes."

If she was nervous as she stood there in front of the delegations from all fifty states, Paulina Cardenas managed to hide it.

"Rosie was one of twelve children in a family of migrant workers," she said, her voice steady.

"Like most Americans, she worked hard to better herself. She worked hard at many jobs. She went to a university on grants and a scholarship."

This tinny recording of Cardenas from the Pacifica Radio Archives was the last stop on my journey, one that Agatha Christie's detective Hercule Poirot believed was essential to solving any mystery: learning more about the victim.

"At twenty-seven she was only six months away from graduation, from being finally free of welfare," Cardenas said. "It meant being able to become a productive, taxpaying citizen, giving her five-year-old daughter a better future."[1]

There was that red herring again: "taxpaying citizen." Cardenas seemed to be trying to make an unwed woman of color who died from an abortion sympathetic to this privileged audience by describing her as an aspiring taxpayer. The pro-choice movement would emphasize Rosie's determination to better herself, too, always noting the undeposited scholarship check in her purse. But it was still not enough to change the policy that killed her.

"She was so very close to her dream," Cardenas said. "In desperation, with no money to go to a decent doctor as most of you delegates here could do, she found another poor woman who performed an illegal abortion."

The phrase "another poor woman" revealed the true culprit that Cardenas held responsible for Rosie's death. It was not the midwife, the only person who paid a price. It was poverty.

Indeed, in the years to come, reproductive justice activists would criticize the movement for pinning Rosie's death on Hyde alone.

"Abortion activists have placed the blame for Rosie's death on one policy in particular rather than the entire capitalist health care system, rife with policies and stigma fueled by racism, that keeps people from being able to receive the care they need," Renee Bracey Sherman and Regina Mahone wrote in their 2024 book, *Liberating Abortion*. "The fact is that money—or the lack of it—kept Rosie from receiving competent medical care—an issue that impacts communities today."[2]

Forty-four years earlier, Paulina Cardenas made essentially the same argument. She described how poor women were forced to use their food money to pay for abortions and how women and men of color were sterilized against their will.

"All of us, women and men, whatever the result, have been denied a basic human right: the right to decide whether and when to have children. A right which is denied the poor when government funding is withheld...

"My Rosie is dead; don't let yours die."

With that warning, she left the stage.

If only she had been heard.

Just weeks before Cardenas spoke at the convention, the Supreme Court had allowed the Hyde Amendment to stand. Galvanized by that decision, feminists convinced Convention delegates to adopt a proposal endorsing federal funding of abortion.[3]

So much would change in the decades to come, and yet, so little.

Forty-four years after Paulina Cardenas spoke about her friend Rosie, abortion took center stage again at the Democratic National Convention.

Josh and Amanda Zurawski stood onstage before a stark black background. Josh wore a navy-blue suit. Amanda was blond and petite, dressed in a white blazer and skirt with matching nails. The Zurawskis were white and married. They had wanted the baby Amanda carried. When Amanda began to miscarry, doctors in the state of Texas delayed her care for so long that she had to be intubated in the ICU with a life-threatening infection. Her family flew in to say goodbye.[4]

Texas banned abortion except in narrow circumstances, but in a detail most people would miss, the hospital where Amanda lay on the brink of death had already restricted abortion even before the law took effect. It was a Catholic hospital, like the one that had turned away Alison. In the years before *Dobbs*, the hospital might have sent Amanda to a different facility. Now that option, too, was gone.

"Every time I share our story, my heart breaks," Amanda Zurawski said. "For the baby girl we wanted desperately, for the doctors and nurses who couldn't help me deliver her safely. For Josh, who feared he'd lose me too.

"But I was lucky. I lived."

Kaitlyn Joshua, a Black woman who'd been turned away from two emergency rooms, stood nearby on the stage.

"Because of Louisiana's abortion ban, no one would confirm that I was miscarrying," she recalled. "I was in pain, bleeding so much my husband feared for my life."

Just months before Zurawski spoke at the Democratic National Convention, the Texas Supreme Court had reviewed the laws that had almost killed her. Twenty women had joined the suit after facing similar ordeals in Texas.[5] The court rejected their claims and refused to clarify the exceptions to the state's abortion bans.[6]

So much had changed and yet, so little.

I had investigated the unexpected suspects who contributed to the deaths of Rosie Jimenez and Becky Bell. I had talked to lawmakers whose names had been forgotten and to the architects of the nonprofit industrial complex and of modern conservatism. I'd talked to the Johnny Appleseed of the antiabortion movement, Mark Lee Dickson, and to Paul Haring, the true believer.

I had arrived at a deeper understanding of the killers of *Roe* and their motives. Some were motivated by sheer political opportunity and some by the desire to be remembered. Many believed that they were fighting the great civil rights struggle of their time. Some, like Will Goodman, Monica Migliorino Miller, and Mark Lee Dickson, were driven by a genuine, all-encompassing love for the unborn, a love often derived from a strong identification with the unwanted. They were motivated by a belief in their own specific understanding of God that loomed like a cross on a crane over the whole landscape. Whether they hated women or just wanted us to conform to their own sense of how we should behave, patriarchy had been like the Hamburglar, lurking around every corner in my investigation. But the motive that stood out to me most, the through line in so many of my conversations with the suspects, was an explanation simpler than I had ever imagined. It was a desire to please their God and to enter heaven. It was a stunningly straightforward explanation, but as Miss Marple knew, most crimes did turn out to be "so absurdly simple."

I had channeled Miss Marple to determine the motive. And now, I channeled her again as I tried to figure out why it mattered.

"I'm afraid that observing human nature for as long as I have done, one gets not to expect very much from it," Marple quipped in the novel *The Murder at the Vicarage*.[7] I felt the same way about my suspects, even the people on my side, like Bob Packwood. They weren't Good Guys or Bad Guys so much as members of a human race that is flawed and, above all, limited in its ability to understand people who are different from us.

At times, I'd transcended that limitation. In every conversation I'd had, no matter how difficult, there had been a moment of grace. On Election Day, I'd heard Mark Lee Dickson nudge a supporter and say of me: "She's with *The Nation*, but she's OK." He'd bought hot dogs for his volunteers and offered me, vegetarian that I am, a plastic clamshell container of corn chips drenched with fluorescent yellow cheese. Even Paul Haring, in his earnest attempt to save me from hell, had given me a glimpse of human goodness—that secular God my father believed in.

In these moments I felt I had scaled Arlie Russell Hochschild's "empathy wall" between red and blue America. Yet as I was finishing this book in June 2025, a man with a hit list of abortion providers opened fire on two state lawmakers and their spouses in Minnesota, killing two of them. I didn't have any illusion that scaling that wall would be enough to reconcile our differences or to stop what Richard Viguerie had called a spiritual civil war.

But I had seen the value of understanding your opponent. "If you don't understand them, you can't beat them," Frances Kissling had wisely said. Richard Viguerie agreed. He had studied the Left extensively only to discover that his liberal friends didn't seem all that interested in studying him back. Knowing your opponent is "one of the secrets to success in a military campaign," he told me.[8]

By listening, I had learned that my suspects weren't villains like the ones Miss Marple often encountered. They were human beings. And it was their humanity that gave me hope. Because if they were humans, their ideas could be defeated by other humans. Studying their playbook showed me they hadn't done anything special. They had worked hard, sometimes harder than our side and often in imitation of it. They were motivated by the sense that they were losing to the devil and by an enduring belief in heaven and the righteousness of their cause that allowed them to persevere, even when victories were limited.

But even though I understood their motives better now, I wasn't going to let them off the hook, like Hercule Poirot did at the end of *Murder on the Orient Express*. In Christie's novel, twelve people band together to commit a collective crime, each stabbing at the body until no one is sure who made the lethal cut. The death of *Roe* was just that kind of crime. Like the murder in Christie's novel, it had brought together people of all classes and backgrounds (most of them white) on a deadly mission. But in Christie's novel, the crime is justified, because the victim was himself a Bad Guy. My suspects doubtless saw their killing of *Roe* as similarly righteous. But there were far too many casualties for that to be the case. They had killed the right to autonomy for countless people. And in the process, they had contributed to the deaths of women whose names we knew, and more whose names we did not.

Their victim wasn't a villain like the one in *Murder on the Orient Express*. But *Roe* wasn't perfect, either. The Supreme Court ruling had never lived up to its promise, especially after the incremental cuts began. Rosie Jimenez and Becky Bell had died while *Roe* was still alive—and an untold number of people had been unable to raise the money or make the trip or secure the parental permission required to get abortions they needed.

So in the wake of *Roe*'s killing, I saw signs of hope. The abortion rights movement was finding new energy after *Dobbs*. The devil had won. And the movement's true believers, the ones committed to radical ideas that felt right if impossible, were giving me hope that Rosie's daughter, Monique, would get her wish.

Monique Jimenez keeps a scrapbook of pictures of her mother. In one photo, captured by CNN, her mother's face is turned to the side, her hair pulled back in a French twist as she feeds her infant daughter a bottle, a serene look on her face.[9] In another, Rosie smiles, dark hair encircling her heart-shaped face, as she accepts her GED certificate. Monique has told reporters that she has only fleeting memories of Rosie—like one of her mother cooking ground beef and vegetable soup, a recipe Monique still makes to remember her. Her aunts used to tell her stories about how her mother loved the beach and dressing up with wigs. Monique remembers just one detail from the funeral. As she watched her mother's coffin get lowered into the dirt, she asked: "Where is my mommy going?"[10]

Growing up, eating tortillas smeared with jelly at her grandparents' restaurant, Monique knew nothing about how her mother died. It was only when she was nineteen that her aunt told her the truth, handing her a book with her mother's face on the cover, by Ellen Frankfort and Frances Kissling.

Monique studied at the college her mother attended, and she became a special education teacher, like her mother wanted to become. When she got married, she chose her mother's birthday as the date: August 5.

"It meant a lot to me to do it on that day," she told *The Texas Observer*. "I always feel like when someone passes away, people forget about them. I don't want it to be like that."

Today, Monique lives in a state where abortion is banned, and yet, because of medication abortion, and the boldness of providers who circulate it through the mail from blue states and activists who send it surreptitiously, it's more available and affordable than ever. Thanks to a burgeoning network of telehealth services and informal community support networks, today Rosie could have ordered medication abortion online for five dollars. (As of this writing, the Trump administration is considering whether to restrict the mailing of abortion pills.)

Today, Monique lives in a state where infant mortality has surged and where maternal health is among the worst in the country, and where sheriffs reported a spate of people leaving newborns in dumpsters in 2024.[11]

But Monique also lives in a state where the movement's true believers are campaigning for a long shot bill to overturn the state's bans on Medicaid and private insurance coverage of abortion. They're not alone. A new energy swept states and municipalities after the murder of *Roe*. In the first three months after the decision, a record number of seventeen states and at least twenty-four municipalities passed legislation or issued policies to protect and expand abortion access, including four states and at least eleven localities that addressed financial barriers to abortion.[12] Since *Dobbs*, Rhode Island, Colorado, Nevada, and Delaware have all passed provisions to fund abortion under Medicaid. On parental consent, the ground has begun to shift, too; after Massachusetts became the first state to pass legislation removing parental consent for sixteen- and seventeen-year-olds, Illinois repealed its parental notification law in 2021.[13]

These incremental cuts to the Hyde Amendment are the closest Rosie Jimenez will come to justice. There will be no confession from the killers, no jail time for anyone but another poor woman. But true to her daughter's wish, Rosie has not been forgotten.

As I finished this book, I was pregnant with my second child, and inclined to believe in new beginnings. The devil might be in the White House, but I could see the reinforcements coming off the train, the true believers with their bold ideas making their way to the front line.

It was true that even after killing *Roe*, abortion opponents kept cutting away at abortion rights. Trump and Republicans in Congress passed a provision in the budget bill to eliminate Medicaid funding to Planned Parenthood in 2025. Yet at the same time, in Washington, DC, in every congressional session since 2015, lawmakers have introduced a bill to repeal the Hyde Amendment, a bill that stands no chance of passage. It's a shot in the dark, a light shining out from a burger bar in the middle of hell, but that is how the abortion rights movement will win. It's how the antiabortion movement won.

And in every legislative session since 2019, at the Texas state capitol, a group of Democratic lawmakers has introduced a bill that would restore full coverage of abortion.

The impetus for the law came from abortion funds in Texas, the groups that have paid for abortion because the state and federal governments will not. The latest version of their bill would require coverage of sterilization and contraception, too. The bill has never gone far, Zaena Zamora, executive director of the South Texas abortion fund Frontera Fund, acknowledged. But they keep introducing it, she said, "because this is what people want."[14]

So each session, they introduce the bill they know won't pass, and they call it Rosie's Law.

ACKNOWLEDGMENTS

I ALWAYS FEARED THAT HAVING CHILDREN WOULD HURT MY CAREER, BUT IT turned out that becoming a mom, at the time and with the partner I chose, was what made me feel like I could write a book. After I pushed a baby into being in a pandemic, I knew I could do hard things. My darling Tully, you made me braver and my world bigger and more beautiful. Daniel, thank you for your patience and support and for chasing after Tully while I wrote. When we got married you promised to support my writing. This book is a testament to the strength of your promise. Finally, little Robin June, thank you for keeping your mommy company by sleeping on my chest as I put the finishing touches on this book.

I want to thank my father, who showed me that being a writer was fun, my sister, who knows better than most people how to do hard things, and my mother, who gave me my favorite definition of *feminist* when I asked if she considered herself one and she replied, "I don't like to take any shit, if that's what you mean." Yes, that's what I meant.

I'm grateful to the team at Legacy Lit, including my visionary editor, Krishan Trotman, who pushed me to write in the first person and embrace the murder mystery theme. The book you envisioned was much more fun to write than the one I pitched. Thanks to my agent, Katherine Flynn, and the team at Calligraph for expertly guiding this newbie author.

The accomplished young journalists Inci Sayki, Ivonne Ortiz, and Sofia Ahmed did an extraordinary job fact-checking the book. Inci also did incredibly diligent research, uncovering and parsing hard-to-find documents. All errors in the book are mine alone.

I'm grateful to the scholars and writers who read and corrected drafts or excerpts: Renee Bracey Sherman, Mary Ziegler, Gillian Frank, Tracy Weitz,

Acknowledgments

Prudence Flowers, Anne Rumberger, Kevin Levin, Carol Mason, and, most of all, Bill Littlefield.

Sean Kelly, Nicola Beisel, Lauren Rankin, and Cindy Mallette generously shared their research. Wesley David Miller Jr. shared Ellen Frankfort's papers.

Rebecca Traister was a supportive mentor. Annie Banducci was a discerning early reader.

Heron Greenesmith was a true friend after my miscarriage.

Martyna Starosta was my writing buddy.

Laura Gottesdiener was my book doula.

Charina Nadura and Ariel Boone were my Britneys.

Lily Shield and Kelly Nichols were my pro-choice coconspirators.

Professor Tracy Breton taught me to always look for the divorce files.

Amy Goodman and the team at Democracy Now! taught me to speak truth to power.

Emily Douglas is my beloved editor at *The Nation*.

Our social justice supper club was a sweet refuge.

Sofia Resnick offered me a lovely second home in DC. She and other fellow abortion journalists, including Susan Rinkunas, Garnet Henderson, Julianne McShane, Kelcie Moseley-Morris, Nina Martin, and Rebecca Grant, were a source of wisdom and inspiration.

My group chat with Renee Bracey Sherman and Gretchen Sisson, each authors of paradigm-shifting books on abortion rights, was a lifeline; thank you for the epic joint voice memo that prompted me to change the title.

My ComstockCon writing club offered accountability and solidarity.

My therapist, Rebecca Freedman, helped me realize I could outrun the tiger, although I usually didn't need to.

I want to thank all the English teachers who look after the misfit future writers, especially Mr. Koup, Mr. Flaggert, Ms. Mallory, Mr. Lundberg, and Ms. Arnett. Your words of encouragement stayed with me.

Finally, I want to thank all the activists working to advance reproductive freedom. It may feel like the killers have won, but because of you, I know that we will.

NOTES

Introduction

1. Pew Research Center, "Majority of Public Disapproves of Supreme Court's Decision to Overturn Roe v. Wade," July 6, 2022, https://www.pewresearch.org/politics/2022/07/06/majority-of-public-disapproves-of-supreme-courts-decision-to-overturn-roe-v-wade/.

2. Chelsea Conaboy, "Motherhood Brings the Most Dramatic Brain Changes of a Woman's Life," *Boston Globe*, July 17, 2018, https://www.bostonglobe.com/magazine/2018/07/17/pregnant-women-care-ignores-one-most-profound-changes-new-mom-faces/.

3. Tyler Rowley, "Remembering Joseph Manning (1931–2023) for His Staunch Support of the Unborn," *Rhode Island Catholic*, August 10, 2023, https://www.thericatholic.com/stories/remembering-joseph-manning-1931-2023-for-his-staunch-support-of-the-unborn,13867.

4. For an account of Alliance Defending Freedom's pivotal role in the legal case that overturned *Roe*, see Elizabeth Dias and Lisa Lerer, *The Fall of Roe: The Rise of a New America* (Flatiron Books, 2024).

Chapter 1

1. Sean Q. Kelly and Scott A. Frisch, "The 'Hyde Amendment' and the Modern Appropriations Process," paper delivered at Congress and History Conference, Library of Congress, Washington, DC, June 1, 2017, https://scholarworks.calstate.edu/concern/presentations/rr1725028.

2. Paul Haring, author interview, Annandale, December 15, 2023.

3. "Whose Choice? How the Hyde Amendment Harms Poor Women," Center for Reproductive Rights, 2010, https://www.reproductiverights.org/sites/default/files/documents/Hyde_Report_FINAL_nospreads.pdf.

4. Mark Aldridge, *Marple: Expert on Wickedness* (HarperCollins, 2024).

5. Rhonda Copelon and Sylvia A. Law, "'Nearly Allied to Her Right to Be'—Medicaid Funding for Abortion: The Story of *Harris v. McRae*" in *Women and the Law Stories*, E. Schneider and S. Wildman (eds) (Foundation Press, 2011), 207.

6. Gillian Frank, "The Colour of the Unborn: Antiabortion and Anti-Bussing Politics in Michigan, United States, 1967–1973," *Gender & History* 26, no. 2 (2014): 351–78, doi:10.1111/1468-0424.12073.

7. The Supreme Court cases were *Beal v. Doe* and *Maher v. Roe*. For more, see Copelon and Law, "Nearly Allied to Her Right to Be."

8. Cynthia Soohoo, "Hyde-Care for All: The Expansion of Abortion-Funding Restrictions

Notes

Under Health Care Reform," 15 CUNY L. Rev. 391 (2012), available at 10.31641/clr150217; Megan K. Donovan, "In Real Life: Federal Restrictions on Abortion Coverage and the Women They Impact," *Guttmacher Policy Review* 20 (2017), https://www.guttmacher.org/gpr/2017/01/real-life-federal-restrictions-abortion-coverage-and-women-they-impact.

9. Rosalind Pollack Petchesky, *Abortion and Women's Choice: The State, Sexuality, and Reproductive Freedom*, 2nd ed. (Verso Books, 2024), 249–50.

10. Analysis conducted by the Guttmacher Institute for the author, August 4, 2025, citing the following studies: Guttmacher Institute, "US States Have Enacted 1,381 Abortion Restrictions Since Roe v. Wade Was Decided in 1973," June 21, 2022, https://www.guttmacher.org/infographic/2022/us-states-have-enacted-1381-abortion-restrictions-roe-v-wade-was-decided-1973; Isabel Guarnieri and Kimya Forouzan, Guttmacher Institute, "State Policy Trends 2023: In the First Full Year Since Roe Fell, a Tumultuous Year for Abortion and Other Reproductive Health Care," December 2023, https://www.guttmacher.org/2023/12/state-policy-trends-2023-first-full-year-roe-fell-tumultuous-year-abortion-and-other; Kimya Forouzan, Isabel Guarnieri, Mollie Fairbanks, and Talia Curhan, Guttmacher Institute, "State Policy Trends 2024: Antiabortion Policymakers Redouble Attacks on Bodily Autonomy," December 2024, https://www.guttmacher.org/2024/12/state-policy-trends-2024-antiabortion-policymakers-redouble-attacks-bodily-autonomy; Guttmacher Institute, State Legislation Tracker, as of June 15, 2025, https://www.guttmacher.org/state-legislation-tracker.

11. Congressional Record Bound Version—House, June 13, 1978, 17264, https://www.congress.gov/95/crecb/1978/06/13/GPO-CRECB-1978-pt13-5-1.

12. Camille Walsh, "'Taxpayer Dollars': The Origins of Austerity's Racist Catchphrase," *Mother Jones*, April 5, 2021, https://www.motherjones.com/politics/2021/04/taxpayer-dollars-the-origins-of-austeritys-racist-catchphrase/.

13. National Women's Law Center with help from the Autistic Women & Nonbinary Network, "Forced Sterilization of Disabled People in the United States," 2021, https://nwlc.org/wp-content/uploads/2022/01/%C6%92.NWLC_SterilizationReport_2021; "Sterilizing the Sick, Poor to Cut Welfare Costs: North Carolina's History of Eugenics," ABC News, aired July 17, 2011, https://abcnews.go.com/Health/WomensHealth/sterilizing-sick-poor-cut-welfare-costs-north-carolinas/story?id=14093458.

14. Harriet B. Presser, "The Role of Sterilization in Controlling Puerto Rican Fertility," *Population Studies* 23, no. 3 (November 1969), https://www.jstor.org/stable/2172875.

15. Dorothy Roberts, *Killing the Black Body: Race, Reproduction, and the Meaning of Liberty*, 2nd ed. (Vintage Books, 2017), 90.

16. Linda Villarosa, "The Long Shadow of Eugenics in America," *New York Times*, June 8, 2022, https://www.nytimes.com/2022/06/08/magazine/eugenics-movement-america.html.

17. Roberts, "Killing the Black Body," 92; original source: "Sterilization Charges Grow," *Washington Post*, July 24, 1973, A12.

18. "Interactive Map: US Abortion Policies and Access After Roe," Guttmacher Institute, policies current as of August 19, 2025, https://states.guttmacher.org/policies/?protections=state-medicaid-funds-cover-abortion.

Notes

19. "Critical Role of Abortion Funds Post-Roe," National Network of Abortion Funds, January 18, 2024, https://abortionfunds.org/abortion-funds-post-roe/.

20. Lorie Konish, "63% of Workers Unable to Pay a $500 Emergency Expense, Survey Finds: How Employers May Help Change That," CNBC, aired August 31, 2023, https://www.cnbc.com/2023/08/31/63percent-of-workers-are-unable-to-pay-a-500-emergency-expense-survey.html.

21. R. Schroeder, I. Munoz, S. Kaller, N. Berglas, C. Stewart, and U. D. Upadhyay, *Trends in Abortion Care in the United States*, 2017–2021, Advancing New Standards in Reproductive Health (ANSIRH) (University of California, 2022), 28.

22. Paul Haring, author interview, Annandale, September 14, 2023.

23. HB 92, 59th R.S., "Relating to providing that no suit for divorce shall be heard, or divorce granted, before the expiration of 180 days after the suit is filed if there are children under 18 years of age born of the marriage sought to be dissolved or adopted by the parties to the suit," 1965, Legislative Reference Library of Texas, https://lrl.texas.gov/legis/billsearch/billdetails.cfm?billFileID=140872&from=advancedsearch.

24. Jane Hurst, *The History of Abortion in the Catholic Church: The Untold Story* (Catholics for a Free Choice, 1989).

25. Frances Kissling, "How the Vatican Almost Embraced Birth Control," *Mother Jones*, May/June 2010, https://www.motherjones.com/politics/2010/04/catholic-church-vatican-bishops-birth-control/.

26. Pope Paul VI, *Humanae Vitae*, 1968, https://www.papalencyclicals.net/paul06/p6humana.htm.

27. U.S. District Court, Western District of Texas, SA 71 CA 11, Paul B. Haring vs. Commander, Willford Hall United States Air Force Base Medical Center Lackland Air Force Base et al. (filed January 15, 1971).

28. "Judge Rejects Suit to Halt Abortions by the Air Force," *New York Times*, January 21, 1971, https://www.nytimes.com/1971/01/21/archives/judge-rejects-suit-to-halt-abortions-by-the-air-force.html.

29. Mary Ziegler, *Personhood: The New Civil War over Reproduction* (Yale University Press, 2025), 54.

30. Mary Ziegler, *Personhood*, 58.

31. Susan Roberts, "Surprised by All These Abortion Bans? Meet Americans United for Life—the Most Significant Antiabortion Group You've Never Heard Of," *Washington Post*, May 31, 2019, https://www.washingtonpost.com/politics/2019/05/31/surprised-by-all-these-abortion-bans-meet-americans-united-life-most-significant-pro-life-group-youve-never-heard/.

32. Paul Byrne Haring, Plaintiff, v. W. Michael Blumenthal, Defendant, Civ. A. No. 78-0085, United States District Court, District of Columbia (April 10, 1979).

33. Sean Kelly, author interview, February 7, 2023.

34. Ballotpedia: Paul Haring, https://ballotpedia.org/Paul_Haring, accessed August 22, 2025.

35. Elizabeth Dias and Lisa Lerer, *The Fall of Roe: The Rise of a New America* (Flatiron Books, 2024).

Notes

36. Felicity Barringer, "The 1992 Campaign: Campaign Issues; Clinton and Gore Shifted on Abortion," *New York Times*, July 20, 1992, https://www.nytimes.com/1992/07/20/us/the-1992-campaign-campaign-issues-clinton-and-gore-shifted-on-abortion.html.

37. (Former) Rep. Elizabeth Holtzman, author interview, New York, December 7, 2023.

38. David Talbot, "This Hypocrite Broke Up My Family," *Salon*, September 17, 1998, https://www.salon.com/1998/09/17/cov_16newsb/.

39. Congressional Record Bound Version—House, June 25, 1975, 20863.

40. Kelly and Frisch, "The 'Hyde Amendment.'"

41. Charles E. Rice, *The Vanishing Right to Live: An Appeal for a Renewed Reverence for Life* (Doubleday, 1969), 2.

42. Henry Hyde, *For Every Idle Silence* (Servant Publications, 1985), 17.

43. Kelly and Frisch, "The 'Hyde Amendment.'"

44. Congressional Record—House, June 17, 1977, 19700.

45. Stanley K. Henshaw, Theodore J. Joyce, Amanda Dennis, Lawrence B. Finer, and Kelly Blanchard, *Restrictions on Medicaid Funding for Abortions: A Literature Review*, Guttmacher Institute, June 2009, https://www.guttmacher.org/report/restrictions-medicaid-funding-abortions-literature-review/.

46. For more analysis on this rhetoric in *The Gospel of Life*, see Carol Mason, *Killing for Life: The Apocalyptic Narrative of Pro-Life Politics* (Cornell University Press, 2002), 170.

47. John Paul II, *The Gospel of Life: Evangelium Vitae* (Pauline Books & Media, 1995), 98–99.

48. "Paul Haring's Proposal," September 16, 1974 (courtesy of Sean Kelly).

49. Arlie Russell Hochschild, *Strangers in Their Own Land: Anger and Mourning on the American Right* (New Press, 2016), 233–34.

50. Bernard Nathanson, *Aborting America: A Doctor's Personal Report on the Agonizing Issue of Abortion* (Life Cycle Books, 1979), 20–21.

51. Nathanson, *Aborting America*, 156.

52. Bernard Nathanson, "Sounding Board: Deeper into Abortion," *New England Journal of Medicine* 291, no. 22 (November 28, 1974), https://www.nejm.org/doi/10.1056/NEJM197411282912213?url_ver=Z39.88-2003&rfr_id=ori:rid:crossref.org&rfr_dat=cr_pub%20%200pubmed.

53. Alan Cooperman, "Most U.S. Parents Pass Along Their Religion and Politics to Their Children," Pew Research Center, May 10, 2023, https://www.pewresearch.org/short-reads/2023/05/10/most-us-parents-pass-along-their-religion-and-politics-to-their-children/.

54. "One-in-Five U.S. Adults Were Raised in Interfaith Homes," Pew Research Center, October 26, 2016, https://www.pewresearch.org/religion/2016/10/26/one-in-five-u-s-adults-were-raised-in-interfaith-homes/.

55. Alan Cooperman, author interview, January 16, 2025.

56. Gianna Emanuela Molla, 2023 March for Life, accessed on YouTube, https://www.youtube.com/watch?v=mPs94jEzb9g.

57. Allan and Veronica Caballero, *St. Gianna Beretta Molla* (Theotokos Kids, 2022).

Notes

58. Ellen Frankfort and Frances Kissling, *Rosie: The Investigation of a Wrongful Death* (Dial Press, 1979), 1–2.

59. "Party Affiliation: 57th Legislature," Legislative Reference Library of Texas, https://lrl.texas.gov/legeleaders/members/partyListSession.cfm?leg=57.

60. Jennifer Holland, *Tiny You: A Western History of the Antiabortion Movement* (University of California Press, 2020), 4.

61. Holland, *Tiny You*, 2.

62. Holland, *Tiny You*, 210.

63. For more on civil rights supporters in the early antiabortion movement, see Mary Ziegler, *Personhood: The New Civil War over Reproduction* (Yale University Press, 2025), 69–70.

64. Paul Haring, author interview, January 24, 2025.

65. Paul Haring, author interview, March 6, 2024.

66. Hyde, *For Every Idle Silence*, 21.

Chapter 2

1. Bob Bauman, author phone interview, December 8, 2022.

2. James Kirchick, *Secret City: The Hidden History of Gay Washington* (Henry Holt, 2022).

3. Robert Bauman, *The Gentleman from Maryland: The Conscience of a Gay Conservative* (Arbor House, 1986).

4. "Robert Bauman," *Making Gay History* podcast, season 11, https://makinggayhistory.org/podcast/robert-bauman/.

5. Bob Bauman, email to author, December 1, 2022.

6. "Helms Sings a Song of 'Dixie'; Moseley-Braun Looks Away," Associated Press, August 6, 1993, https://www.latimes.com/archives/la-xpm-1993-08-06-mn-20952-story.html.

7. "Former Sen. Jesse Helms Dies at 86," CBS News, July 4, 2008, https://www.cbsnews.com/news/former-sen-jesse-helms-dies-at-86.

8. Jesse Helms, *When Free Men Shall Stand: A Sobering Look at the Supertaxing, Superspending Superbureaucracy in Washington* (Zondervan, 1976), 103–5.

9. Bryan Hardin Thrift, *Conservative Bias: How Jesse Helms Pioneered the Rise of Right-Wing Media and Realigned the Republican Party* (University Press of Florida, 2014).

10. Ernest B. Furgurson, *Hard Right: The Rise of Jesse Helms* (W. W. Norton, 1986).

11. Steven Sinding, author interview, February 6, 2024; for more on Ravenholt, see Michelle Goldberg, *The Means of Reproduction: Sex, Power, and the Future of the World* (Penguin Press, 2009), chap. 2.

12. Congressional Record Bound Version—House, December 4, 1973, 39317, https://www.congress.gov/93/crecb/1973/12/04/GPO-CRECB-1973-pt30-5-1.pdf.

13. *The Global Gag Rule and the Helms Amendment: Dual Policies, Deadly Impact*, Guttmacher Institute, May 2021, https://www.guttmacher.org/fact-sheet/ggr-helms-amendment.

14. Ellen Gaddy, "It's Time to End My Grandfather's Harmful Legacy—the Helms Amendment," *Politico*, July 28, 2022, https://www.politico.com/news/magazine/2022/07/28/biden-repeal-helms-amendment-on-abortion-00048533.

Notes

15. Ellen Gaddy, author interview, October 3, 2023.
16. Ellen Gaddy, email to author, February 2, 2024.
17. William F. Buckley Jr., *Up from Liberalism* (First Honor Book Edition, 1965), 202-3.
18. Richard Viguerie, author interview, Manassas, March 6, 2024.
19. Congressional Record Bound Version—Senate, November 30, 1973, 38961.
20. "Capital 'Scope," *Syracuse Herald-Journal*, February 24, 1974, page 12, accessed via https://www.newspapers.com/image/1086329940/.
21. "Paul Haring's Proposal," September 16, 1974 (courtesy of Sean Kelly).
22. Paul Haring, author phone interview, March 6, 2024.
23. Randy Engel, author phone interview, October 3, 2023.
24. Congressional Record Bound Version—House, June 27, 1974, 21687-21694.
25. Congressional Record Bound Version, 31455, September 17, 1974; Statement of the Conference Committee quoted in the Congressional Record Bound Version—9802, April 10, 1975 (originally cited in Sean Kelly and Scott Frisch, "The 'Hyde Amendment' and the Modern Appropriations Process," June 2019).
26. (Former) Rep. Elizabeth Holtzman, author interview, December 16, 2022.
27. Kirchick, *Secret City*, 471.
28. Richard L. Madden, "A New Gadfly Keeps an Eye on the House," *New York Times*, April 5, 1976, page 66.
29. Bob Bauman, author interview, December 8, 2022.
30. Margaret Goodman, author interview, January 19, 2024.
31. "Speech to the Maryland Right to Life Banquet October 29, 1977," Box 133, Folder 16, 1976, Henry Hyde Papers, University Archives, Loyola University, Chicago (originally cited in Kelly and Frisch, "The 'Hyde Amendment' and the Modern Appropriations Process").
32. Bauman, *Gentleman from Maryland*, 113.
33. Bauman, *Gentleman from Maryland*, 121–22.
34. Bauman, *Gentleman from Maryland*, 124.
35. Bauman, *Gentleman from Maryland*, 121.
36. Kirchick, *Secret City*, 471.
37. Bauman, *Gentleman from Maryland*, 156–57.
38. Bauman, *Gentleman from Maryland*, 209.
39. Agatha Christie, *The Thirteen Problems* (Signet, 2000), 3.

Chapter 3

1. Florence Graves and Charles Shepard, "Packwood Accused of Sexual Advances," *Washington Post*, November 21, 1992.
2. S. Rep. 104–37, Calendar No. 183, Resolution for Disciplinary Action (1995), https://www.congress.gov/104/crpt/srpt137/CRPT-104srpt137.
3. Congressional Record Bound Version—Senate, June 28, 1976, 20882.
4. Adam Clymer, "Henry J. Hyde, a Power in the House of Representatives, Dies at 83," *New York Times*, November 30, 2007, https://www.nytimes.com/2007/11/30/washington/30hyde.html.

Notes

5. Sara Matthiesen, *Reproduction Reconceived: Family Making and the Limits of Choice After Roe v. Wade* (University of California Press, 2021).

6. Daniel K. Williams, *Defenders of the Unborn: The Pro-Life Movement Before Roe v. Wade* (Oxford University Press, 2016), 100.

7. Gloria Feldt, author Zoom interview, May 29, 2025.

8. Williams, *Defenders of the Unborn*, 220.

9. Bernard Weinraub, "Abortion Curbs Endrssed, 10–7, by Senate Panel," *New York Times*, March 11, 1982, https://www.nytimes.com/1982/03/11/us/abortion-curbs-endorsed-10-7-by-senate-panel.html.

10. Mary Ziegler, *After Roe: The Lost History of the Abortion Debate* (Harvard University Press, 2015), 126.

11. Colman McCarthy, "Jackson's Reversal on Abortion," *Washington Post*, May 20, 1988, https://www.washingtonpost.com/archive/opinions/1988/05/21/jacksons-reversal-on-abortion/.

12. Karen Mulhauser, email to author, November 23, 2023.

13. Ziegler, *After Roe*, 203–6.

14. Congressional Record Bound Version—Senate, August 25, 1976, 27676.

15. Rick Perlstein, *Nixonland: The Rise of a President and the Fracturing of America* (Scribner, 2008), 652.

16. Elizabeth Dias and Lisa Lerer, *The Fall of Roe: The Rise of a New America* (Flatiron Books, 2024), 29–30.

17. Bob Packwood, author interview, Lake Oswego, August 14, 2024.

18. Mark Kirchmeier, *Packwood: The Public and Private Life from Acclaim to Outrage* (HarperCollins, 1995), 63.

19. Kirchmeier, *Packwood*, 79.

20. Congressional Record Bound Version—Senate, February 24, 1970, 4538.

21. Congressional Record Bound Version—Senate, April 23, 1970, 12672.

22. Dorothy Roberts, *Killing the Black Body: Race, Reproduction, and the Meaning of Liberty*, 2nd ed. (Vintage Books, 2017), 89.

23. Congressional Record Bound Version—House, June 24, 1976, 20411.

24. Carol Werner, author interview, Washington, DC, March 4, 2024.

25. Memo re: Labor-HEW Appropriations Conference Committee (H.R. 14232), July 30, 1976, Box 238, Folder 9, National Abortion Rights Action League archives, Schlesinger Library, Harvard University.

26. Memo re: Labor-HEW Appropriations Conference Committee (H.R. 14232), July 23, 1976, Box 238, Folder 9, National Abortion Rights Action League archives, Schlesinger Library, Harvard University.

27. Memo re: House Vote on Hyde Amendment to Labor-HEW Appropriations Bill, August 11, 1976, Box 238, Folder 10, National Abortion Rights Action League archives, Schlesinger Library, Harvard University.

28. Memo re: Hyde Amendment, Box 73, F Memos, July 1976, Edward William Brooke Papers, Library of Congress (courtesy of Nicola Beisel).

29. Mark Gallagher, phone interview with Sean Kelly and Scott Frisch, May 2017, shared with author.

Notes

30. Memo re: HEW Conference Report Abortion Language, September 17, 1976, Box 236, Folder 8, National Abortion Rights Action League archives, Schlesinger Library, Harvard University.

31. Congressional Record—House, August 10, 1976, 26782, cited in Kelly and Frisch.

32. Congressional Record Bound Version—Senate, September 17, 1976, 30997; Congressional Record Bound Version—House, September 16, 1976, 30901.

33. Barbara Boxer, *The Art of Tough* (Grand Central, 2017), referenced at https://www.npr.org/2017/11/27/566096392/when-bob-packwood-was-nearly-expelled-from-the-senate-for-sexual-misconduct.

34. Michael Jordan Smith, "Bob Packwood's Redemption Story," *Politico*, February 25, 2014, https://www.politico.com/magazine/story/2014/02/bob-packwood-lobbying-politics-103966/. See also Stephen Engelberg, "Packwood Diaries: A Rare Look at Washington's Tangled Web," *New York Times*, September 10, 1995, sec. 1, p. 1, https://www.nytimes.com/1995/09/10/us/chronicle-abuse-packwood-papers-special-report-packwood-diaries-rare-look.html.

35. Bob Packwood, diary entry for Monday, June 28, 1976, 10:00 a.m. (courtesy of Elaine Franklin).

36. Bob Packwood, diary entry for Wednesday, June 29, 1977, 8:00 a.m. (courtesy of Elaine Franklin).

37. Kirchmeier, *Packwood*, 16, 27.

38. Smith, "Bob Packwood's Redemption Story."

39. Bob Packwood, diary entry for Monday, February 23, 1970 (courtesy of Elaine Franklin).

40. Bob Packwood, diary entry for Wednesday, August 25, 1976 (courtesy of Elaine Franklin).

41. Kirchmeier, *Packwood*, 225.

42. Office of Gloria Steinem, email to author, February 4, 2025.

43. Gena Hutton and Mary Heffernan, author interview, Eugene, Oregon, August 15, 2024.

44. Rotary Club Speech, January 4, 1994, Albany, Oregon, https://www.c-span.org/program/public-affairs-event/oregon-senatorial-speech/42174.

45. "More Packwood Allegations Revealed," Associated Press, December 6, 1992, https://www.latimes.com/archives/la-xpm-1992-12-06-mn-3381-story.html.

Chapter 4

1. Charles Duncan, news segment on the arrest of Maria Pineda, WFAA-TV, Dallas, filmed on June 9, 1978, archival footage provided to author by WFAA.

2. Alexa Garcia-Ditta, "Reckoning with Rosie," *Texas Observer*, November 3, 2015, https://www.texasobserver.org/rosie-jimenez-abortion-medicaid/.

3. Ellen Frankfort and Frances Kissling, *Rosie: The Investigation of a Wrongful Death* (Dial Press, 1979), 153–59.

4. Frankfort and Kissling, *Rosie*, 27.

5. Frankfort and Kissling, *Rosie*, 3–4.

Notes

6. "Abortion," *MacNeil/Lehrer Report*, November 8, 1977, https://americanarchive.org/catalog/cpb-aacip-507-tq5r786j1v?proxy_start_time=380.10869.

7. Ann Marie Kimball, author interviews, January 22 and 23, 2025.

8. Bill Peterson, "Doubts Arise About Abortion Martyr," *Washington Post*, November 27, 1977, https://www.washingtonpost.com/archive/politics/1977/11/28/doubts-arise-about-abortion-martyr/c5221023-5a6a-4510-85a7-58e07dd41778/.

9. Frankfort and Kissling, *Rosie*, 6.

10. Garcia-Ditta, "Reckoning with Rosie."

11. McAllen, Texas Police Department, police report, jacket number 6199, June 9, 1978.

12. Laura Foreman, "President Defends Court's Action Curbing Federal Aid for Abortion," *New York Times*, July 13, 1977, https://www.nytimes.com/1977/07/13/archives/president-defends-courts-action-curbing-federal-aid-for-abortion.html.

13. Peter Nicholas and James Oliphant, "Obama Signs Order Affirming Ban on Federal Funds for Abortion," *Los Angeles Times*, March 25, 2010, https://www.latimes.com/archives/la-xpm-2010-mar-25-la-na-obama-healthcare25-2010mar25-story.html.

14. Frankfort and Kissling, *Rosie*, 158.

15. Frankfort and Kissling, *Rosie*, 153.

16. Frances Kissling, email to author, September 22, 2023.

17. Jennifer Dunning, "Books: 'Rosie,' a Death After an Illegal Abortion," *New York Times*, October 12, 1979, https://www.nytimes.com/1979/10/12/archives/books-rosie-a-death-after-an-illegal-abortion.html.

18. "Ellen Frankfort, 50, Is Dead; Author on Feminist Issues," *New York Times*, May 25, 1987, https://www.nytimes.com/1987/05/25/obituaries/ellen-frankfort-50-is-dead-author-on-feminist-issues.html.

19. "Pro-Choice Activists Celebrate January 22, Commemorate 1973 High Court Decision," *NARAL Newsletter* 11, no. 1 (January–February 1979).

20. Frankfort and Kissling, *Rosie*, 138.

21. Karen Mulhauser, author interviews, Washington, DC, December 14 and 15, 2023.

22. "Nation: The Fanatical Abortion Fight," *Time*, July 9, 1979, https://content.time.com/time/subscriber/article/0,33009,920454-2,00.html.

23. "Gallup Poll Finds Little Change in Views on Abortion," *New York Times*, April 22, 1979, https://www.nytimes.com/1979/04/22/archives/gallup-poll-finds-little-change-in-views-on-abortion-catholics-in.html.

24. Bill Peterson, "American Public, by Wide Majority, Supports Legalized Abortion," *Washington Post*, June 7, 1981, referenced in Mary Ziegler, *Roe: The History of a National Obsession* (Yale University Press, 2023), 25.

25. Roger Craver, author interview, Martha's Vineyard, January 26, 2024.

26. Memorandum to National Abortion Rights Action League from Craver, Mathews, Smith and Company, Subject: End of the Year Report, December 5, 1978, box 38, folder 2, National Abortion Rights Action League archives, Schlesinger Library, Harvard University.

Notes

27. Ann Crittenden, "Pro-Abortion Group Sets a Major Political Drive," *New York Times*, June 14, 1982, https://www.nytimes.com/1982/06/14/style/pro-abortion-group-sets-a-major-political-drive.html.

28. NARAL Cold Appeal, final copy, December 13, 1977, box 38, folder 1, National Abortion Rights Action League archives, Schlesinger Library, Harvard University.

29. Memorandum to the National Abortion Rights Action League from Craver, Mathews, Smith, and Company, July 1, 1977, Memorandum of Proposal and Agreement, box 38, folder 1, National Abortion Rights Action League archives, Schlesinger Library, Harvard University.

30. NARAL draft fund appeals, box 38, folder 1, National Abortion Rights Action League archives, Schlesinger Library, Harvard University.

31. NARAL-PAC Membership Appeal, final draft, September 20, 1978, box 38, folder 1, National Abortion Rights Action League archives, Schlesinger Library, Harvard University.

32. Frances Kissling, author interviews, Mexico City and Cuernavaca, October 13–16, 2023.

33. Maria Antonieta Alcalde Castro, author interview, Mexico City, October 13, 2023.

34. Ellen Goodman, "Abortion Rally's Message to the Wobbly Middle," *Boston Globe*, April 11, 1989, p. 19.

35. Robert M. Smith, Memorandum to National Abortion Rights Action League, "Review of Where We Stand," September 1, 1978, box 38, folder 1, National Abortion Rights Action League archives, Schlesinger Library, Harvard University.

Chapter 5

1. Faye Wattleton, *Life on the Line* (Random House, 1996), 191–92.

2. Thomas Frank, *Listen, Liberal: Or, What Ever Happened to the Party of the People?* (Metropolitan Books, 2016), 246.

3. Jonathan Franklin and Eve Zuckoff, "After Migrants Arrived in Martha's Vineyard, a Community Gathered to Welcome Them," NPR, September 16, 2022, https://www.npr.org/2022/09/16/1123369533/migrants-marthas-vineyard-community-help.

4. Jess Bidgood and Julie Bosman, "On Martha's Vineyard, a Frosty Summer for Alan Dershowitz," *New York Times*, July 3, 2018, https://www.nytimes.com/2018/07/03/us/marthas-vineyard-trump.html; Eunki Seonwoo, "Good Pierogi Doesn't Back Down to Dershowitz," *MV Times*, August 6, 2025, https://www.mvtimes.com/2025/08/06/good-pierogi-doesnt-back-dershowitz/.

5. James Ridgeway, "The Men Who Stuff Your Mailbox," *The Times* (Shreveport, Louisiana), June 20, 1982, accessed at https://www.newspapers.com/image/220158245/.

6. Roger Craver, author interview, Martha's Vineyard, January 26, 2024.

7. Richard A. Viguerie, *Go Big: The Marketing "Secrets" of Richard A. Viguerie* (American Target Advertising, 2022), 6.

8. NARAL Cold Appeal, final copy, December 13, 1977, box 38, folder 1, National Abortion Rights Action League archives, Schlesinger Library, Harvard University.

9. Roger Craver, Mathews, Smith et al., Memorandum to The National Abortion Rights

Notes

Action League, July 1, 1977, Memorandum of Proposal and Agreement, Box 38, Folder 1, National Abortion Rights Action League archives, Schlesinger Library, Harvard University.

10. Robert M. Smith, Memorandum to National Abortion Rights Action League, "Review of Where We Stand," September 1, 1978, Box 38, Folder 1, National Abortion Rights Action League archives, Schlesinger Library, Harvard University.

11. Memorandum to The National Abortion Rights Action League from Craver, Mathews, Smith, and Company, July 11, 1980, Subject: Authorization to Order Lists, Box 38, Folder 6, National Abortion Rights Action League archives, Schlesinger Library, Harvard University.

12. INCITE! Women of Color Against Violence, *The Revolution Will Not Be Funded: Beyond the Non-Profit Industrial Complex* (Duke University Press, 2007).

13. Megan Ming Frances, "The Price of Civil Rights: Black Lives, White Funding, and Movement Capture," *Law & Society Review* 53, no. 1 (March 2019), https://www.jstor.org/stable/i40217668.

14. Terry O'Neill, author interview, May 1, 2025.

15. Richard Burke, "The Thomas Confirmation; Women Accusing Democrats of Betrayal," *New York Times*, October 17, 1991, https://www.nytimes.com/1991/10/17/us/the-thomas-confirmation-women-accusing-democrats-of-betrayal.html.

16. Judy Klemesrud, "Planned Parenthood's New Head Takes a Fighting Stand," *New York Times*, February 3, 1978, https://timesmachine.nytimes.com/timesmachine/1978/02/03/110914700.html?pageNumber=14.

17. Robyn Rosen and Jessica Furgerson, "Planned Parenthood Before and After Roe: Historical Lessons for the Current Fight," *Sage Journals* 24, no. 1, https://journals.sagepub.com/doi/full/10.1177/15327086231217220.

18. Wattleton, *Life on the Line*, 191.

19. Faye Wattleton, author interview, July 24, 2025.

20. Wattleton, *Life on the Line*, 188.

21. Wattleton, *Life on the Line*, 35, 41.

22. Faye Wattleton, author interview, New York, May 29, 2024.

23. Wattleton, *Life on the Line*, 208–11.

24. Lois Romano, "The Reliable Source," *Washington Post*, July 17, 1992, https://www.washingtonpost.com/archive/lifestyle/1992/07/17/the-reliable-source/b00ce903-ad1e-4f1c-9687-7ae524ac85bf/.

25. William J. Fleming, letter, PPFA III, Box 123, Faye Wattleton's Correspondence, 1989–1991, Folder: FW letters by B Snow Jan–Aug 1990, Planned Parenthood Federation of America Archives, Smith College.

26. Faye Wattleton, author interview, July 24, 2025.

27. Rosalind Petchesky, author interview, April 11, 2024.

28. Rhonda Copelon and Sylvia A. Law, "'Nearly Allied to Her Right to Be'—Medicaid Funding for Abortion: The Story of *Harris v. McRae*," *Women and the Law Stories*, chap. 6, https://www.law.nyu.edu/sites/default/files/ECM_PRO_075040.

29. "Minutes: January 14, 1981," Box 32, Folder 5—Cobwebbing—pro-choice leadership meetings, 1980–81, National Abortion Rights Action League archives, Schlesinger Library, Harvard University.

Notes

30. "About Faye Wattleton," July 1979, PPFA III SSC MS 00371b, Box 14, Folder 1, "Faye Wattleton," Planned Parenthood Federation of America Archives, Smith College.

31. "Backgrounder: Faye Wattleton, President, Planned Parenthood Federation of America," January 1981, PPFA III SSC MS 00371b, Box 14, Folder 1, "Faye Wattleton," Planned Parenthood Federation of America Archives, Smith College.

32. Gloria Feldt, author Zoom interview, May 29, 2025.

33. Marianne Szegedy-Maszak, "Calm, Cool and Beleaguered," *New York Times Magazine*, August 6, 1989, https://www.nytimes.com/1989/08/06/magazine/calm-cool-and-beleaguered.html.

34. James Risen and Judy L. Thomas, *Wrath of Angels: The American Abortion War* (Basic Books, 1998), 115.

35. "Minutes: February 16, 1981," Box 32, Folder 5—Cobwebbing—pro-choice leadership meetings, 1980–81, National Abortion Rights Action League archives, Schlesinger Library, Harvard University.

36. Karen Mulhauser, author interviews, Washington, DC, December 14–15, 2023.

37. For more on Mulhauser's story, see Mary Ziegler, *Roe: The History of a National Obsession* (Yale University Press, 2023).

38. Amy Littlefield, "Where the Pro-Choice Movement Went Wrong," *New York Times*, December 1, 2021, https://www.nytimes.com/2021/12/01/opinion/abortion-planned-parenthood-naral-roe-v-wade.html.

39. "Testimony of Karen Mulhauser," Senate Labor-HEW Appropriations Subcommittee on Medicaid Funding of Abortion, March 28, 1979, Box 254, Folder 4, "Testimony Before Congress 1979," National Abortion Rights Action League archives, Schlesinger Library, Harvard University, accessed online at: https://veteranfeministsofamerica.org/wp-content/uploads/2018/11/1979-rape-testimony.

40. For more on this strategy, see William Saletan, *Bearing Right: How Conservatives Won the Abortion War* (University of California Press, 2003).

41. Walter Isaacson, "The Battle over Abortion," *Time*, April 6, 1981, https://time.com/archive/6697308/the-battle-over-abortion/.

Chapter 6

1. Alexandra Jane DiBranco, "Strategic Organizing, Dangerous Rhetoric, and Philanthropic Decision-Making in the U.S. New Right," Yale Graduate School of Arts and Sciences Dissertations, Fall 2022, https://elischolar.library.yale.edu/cgi/viewcontent.cgi?article=1847&context=gsas_dissertations.

2. Agatha Christie, *The Big Four* (New York: Dell, 1965), 42.

3. For more on the Council for National Policy and Hillsdale College, see Anne Nelson, *Shadow Network: Media, Money, and the Secret Hub of the Radical Right* (Bloomsbury Publishing, 2019).

4. Richard Viguerie, author interview, Manassas, March 6, 2024.

5. Richard A. Viguerie v. Elaine O. Viguerie, In Chancery No. 63825, Circuit Court of Fairfax County, VA, 1980.

6. Richard A. Viguerie v. Elaine O. Viguerie, In Chancery No. 3460, Circuit Court of Rappahannock County, VA, Hearing, February 2, 1989.

Notes

7. Richard Viguerie, author phone interviews, August 15 and 18, 2025.

8. Lloyd Grove, "The Graying of Richard Viguerie," *Washington Post*, June 28, 1989, https://www.washingtonpost.com/archive/lifestyle/1989/06/29/the-graying-of-richard-viguerie/1756753f-5b37-4600-8da3-000f206fb1fa/.

9. Randall Balmer, *Bad Faith: Race and the Rise of the Religious Right* (Eerdmans, 2021), 44.

10. Balmer, *Bad Faith*, xii.

11. Max Blumenthal, "Agent of Intolerance," *Nation*, May 16, 2007, https://www.thenation.com/article/archive/agent-intolerance/.

12. Balmer, *Bad Faith*, 80.

13. Richard A. Viguerie, *Go Big: The Marketing "Secrets" of Richard A. Viguerie* (Manassas: American Target Advertising, 2022), 16.

14. Daniel Williams, *Defenders of the Unborn: The Pro-Life Movement Before Roe v. Wade* (Oxford University Press, 2016), 254–55.

15. Lydia Saad, "Broader Support for Abortion Rights Continues Post-Dobbs," Gallup, June 14, 2023, https://news.gallup.com/poll/506759/broader-support-abortion-rights-continues-post-dobbs.aspx.

Chapter 7

1. Randall Balmer, *Bad Faith: Race and the Rise of the Religious Right* (Eerdmans, 2021), 69.

2. Balmer, *Bad Faith*, 70.

3. Ronald Smothers, "Election Results Troubling Blacks," *New York Times*, November 9, 1984, https://www.nytimes.com/1984/11/09/us/election-results-troubling-blacks.html.

4. Heritage Foundation, "Mandate for Leadership: The Conservative Promise," Project 2025 Presidential Transition Project, 2023, https://static.heritage.org/project2025/2025_MandateForLeadership_FULL.

5. Prudence Flowers, *The Right-to-Life Movement, the Reagan Administration, and the Politics of Abortion* (Palgrave MacMillan, 2019), 26–27.

6. D. K. Williams, "The GOP's Abortion Strategy: Why Pro-Choice Republicans Became Pro-Life in the 1970s," *Journal of Policy History* 23, no. 4 (2011): 513–39.

7. Cardinal Joseph Bernardin, "Consistent Ethic of Life" (Sheed and Ward, 1988), https://archive.org/details/consistentethic0000unse.

8. Flowers, *Right-to-Life Movement*, 72; original citation: Donald Critchlow, "Mobilizing Women: The 'Social Issues,'" in *The Reagan Presidency: Pragmatic Conservatism and Its Legacies* (University of Kansas, 2003), 309.

9. Ronald Reagan, *Abortion and the Conscience of a Nation* (Thomas Nelson, 1984), 63.

10. William Saletan, *Bearing Right: How Conservatives Won the Abortion War* (University of California Press, 2003).

11. Angela Davis, *Women, Race, and Class* (Random House, 1981).

12. Kristin Kobes Du Mez, *Jesus and John Wayne: How White Evangelicals Corrupted a Faith and Fractured a Nation* (Liveright, 2020).

13. Peter Smith, "White Evangelical Voters Show Steadfast Support for Donald Trump's Presidency," Associated Press, November 7, 2024, https://apnews.com/article/white-evangelical-voters-support-donald-trump-president-dbfd2b4fe5b2ea27968876f19ee20c84.

Notes

14. James Risen and Judy Thomas, *Wrath of Angels: The American Abortion War* (Basic Books, 1998), 130.

15. "Preliminary Plan Outline for Mobilizing Pro-Life Forces for 1984 Reagan Campaign," letter from David N. O'Steen, Director, Committee for a Pro-Life Congress to Lyn Nofziger and Ralph Whitworth, February 8, 1984.

16. Risen and Thomas, *Wrath of Angels*, 107.

17. Ronald Reagan, *Reagan Diaries* (HarperCollins, 2007), 214.

18. Kristin Luker, *Abortion and the Politics of Motherhood* (University of California Press, 1984), 218, 251, 219.

19. Risen and Thomas, *Wrath of Angels*, 107–8.

20. Luker, *Abortion and the Politics of Motherhood*, 223.

21. "Report on Pro-Life Literature Drop for Paul S. Trible, U.S. Senate Race in Virginia 1982," Marjorie Higgins, Consultant for Committee for a Pro-Life Congress.

22. Flowers, *Right-to-Life Movement*, 137.

23. Ivette Gomez, Karen Diep, Brittni Frederiksen, Usha Ranji, and Alina Salganicoff, "Abortion Experiences, Knowledge, and Attitudes Among Women in the U.S.: Findings from the 2024 KFF Women's Health Survey," https://www.kff.org/womens-health-policy/issue-brief/abortion-experiences-knowledge-attitudes-among-u-s-women-2024-womens-health-survey/.

24. "Public Opinion on Abortion," Pew Research Center, June 12, 2025, https://www.pewresearch.org/religion/fact-sheet/public-opinion-on-abortion/.

25. Patti Davis, "How My Father, Ronald Reagan, Grappled with Abortion," *New York Times*, May 22, 2022, https://www.nytimes.com/2022/05/22/opinion/ronald-reagan-patti-davis-abortion.html.

26. Patti Davis, *Dear Mom and Dad* (Liveright, 2024), 40.

Chapter 8

1. Addie Bell, author phone interview, September 6, 2024.

2. Testimony of Addison Bell, Indiana State Legislature, August 2, 2022, posted by ACLU on X: https://x.com/ACLUIndiana/status/1554922006268846088.

3. Nelson Price, "A Daughter Lost," *Indianapolis News*, January 22, 1990, https://www.newspapers.com/image/312965458/?match=1&terms=%22becky%20bell%22%20AND%20%22indianapolis%22.

4. Speech by Maine state Rep. Gideon, Legislative Record, House of Representatives, State of Maine, June 17, 2015, H920, https://www.maine.gov/legis/lawlib/lldl/abortion/elegrec_2015-06-17_hd_ph0914-0921.pdf.

5. Heidi Moseson et al., "Abortion-Related Laws and Concurrent Patterns in Abortion Incidence in Indiana, 2010–2019," *American Journal of Public Health* 113, no. 4 (April 2023): 429-37, https://pmc.ncbi.nlm.nih.gov/articles/PMC10003501/.

6. Veronica Stracqualursi, Laura Ly, and Kiely Westhoff, "Indiana Becomes First State Post-Roe to pass law banning most abortions," CNN, August 6, 2022, https://www.cnn.com/2022/08/05/politics/indiana-state-house-abortion-bill/index.html.

7. Indiana State Rep. Carey Hamilton, author interview, August 12, 2024.

8. John T. Curran, "Reflections of Abortion Testimonies at the Indiana Statehouse,"

Notes

Corpus Christi for Unity and Peace Blog, August 11, 2022, https://www.corpuschristi forunityandpeace.org/reflections-of-abortion-testimonies-at-the-indiana-statehouse/.

9. Indiana General Assembly Senate Bill 404, now Public Law 173, https://iga.in.gov /legislative/2017/bills/senate/404/details.

10. Testimony of Karen and Bill Bell, Indiana Senate Judiciary Committee, February 22, 2017, https://iga.in.gov/session/2017/video/committee_judiciary_4200.

11. Judy Mann, "Illegal Abortion's Deadly Price," *Washington Post*, August 3, 1990, https://www.washingtonpost.com/archive/local/1990/08/03/illegal-abortions -deadly-price/bd016dad-2c53-4b3d-9b99-274b054c0c9b/; Mary Lou Greenberg, "Another American Tragedy, The Death of Becky Bell, Interview with Bill and Karen Bell," *On the Issues Magazine*, January 20, 1990, https://ontheissuesmagazine.com/abortion /another-american-tragedy-the-death-of-becky-bell-interview-with-bill-and-karen-bell/.

12. Cody McDevitt, "A Note on the Minnesota Assassination," *Repro Rights NOW* newsletter, June 15, 2025. Interview conducted by McDevitt for the forthcoming book, *Given No Choice: A History of Abortion Rights*.

13. Shoshanna Ehrlich, author phone interview, September 25, 2024. For more, see Shoshanna Ehrlich, *Who Decides? The Abortion Rights of Teens* (Praeger, 2006).

14. Lizzie Presser, "She Wanted an Abortion: A Judge Said She Wasn't Mature Enough to Decide," ProPublica, November 29, 2022, https://www.propublica.org/article /how-states-limit-teen-access-to-abortion.

15. "Victory: Federal Court Grants Preliminary Injunction Blocking Abortion Restrictions," ACLU of Indiana, June 29, 2017, https://www.aclu-in.org/en/press-releases /victory-federal-court-grants-preliminary-injunction-blocking-abortion-restrictions.

16. James R. Butcher, *No Regrets* (WestBow Press, 2022), 1–3.

17. Butcher, *No Regrets*, 8.

18. Butcher, *No Regrets*, 21.

19. Butcher, *No Regrets*, 54.

20. James R. Butcher, author phone interview, January 23, 2025.

21. "Abortion," *MacNeil/Lehrer Report*, November 8, 1977, https://american archive.org/catalog/cpb-aacip-507-tq5r786j1v?proxy_start_time=380.10769.

22. Butcher, *No Regrets*, 31.

23. James R. Butcher, author phone interview, January 24, 2025.

Chapter 9

1. Footage of the Summer of Mercy, KMUW, August 9, 1991, accessed on YouTube: https://www.youtube.com/watch?v=NjbJb7Tal1M&t=338s.

2. James Risen and Judy L. Thomas, *Wrath of Angels: The American Abortion War* (Basic Books, 1998), 318.

3. Risen and Thomas, *Wrath of Angels*, 323–24.

4. Risen and Thomas, *Wrath of Angels*, 220.

5. "Anti-Choice Violence and Intimidation," Reproductive Freedom for All, November 1, 2016, https://reproductivefreedomforall.org/wp-content/uploads /2016/12/1.-Anti-Choice-Violence-and-Intimidation.

6. Randall Terry, author interview, Washington, DC, October 4, 2024.

Notes

7. Carol Mason, *Killing for Life: The Apocalyptic Narrative of Pro-Life Politics* (Cornell University Press, 2002), 21.

8. Jessica Winter, "The Link Between the Capitol Riot and Antiabortion Extremism," *New Yorker*, March 11, 2021, https://www.newyorker.com/news/daily-comment/the-link-between-the-capitol-riot-and-antiabortion-extremism.

9. Mary Mapes, interview on CNN, January 28, 2010, accessed on YouTube: https://www.youtube.com/watch?v=B6iA9qdNAzo.

10. For more analysis of *Whatever Happened to the Human Race?*, see Carol Mason, *Killing for Life*, 115–18.

11. Susan Faludi, *Backlash: The Undeclared War Against American Women* (Crown, 1991), 407–12.

12. Risen and Thomas, *Wrath of Angels*, 54, 64–67.

13. Risen and Thomas, *Wrath of Angels*, 63, 296.

14. Julianne Wiley, email to author, February 14, 2025.

15. Risen and Thomas, *Wrath of Angels*, 189–90.

16. Risen and Thomas, *Wrath of Angels*, 102–3.

17. Risen and Thomas, *Wrath of Angels*, 202, 212, 187.

18. Linda Greenhouse, "New Poll Finds Wide Support for Abortion Rights," *New York Times*, January 21, 1988, https://www.nytimes.com/1988/01/21/us/new-poll-finds-wide-support-for-abortion-rights.html.

19. Theodore Schleifer and Kenneth P. Vogel, "In Election's Final Days, Dark Money and 'Gray Money' Fund Hidden Agendas," *New York Times*, October 30, 2024, https://www.nytimes.com/2024/10/30/us/politics/dark-money-presidential-campaign.html.

20. Risen and Thomas, *Wrath of Angels*, 307.

21. Amy Littlefield, "The Paradoxes Facing the Christian Right in the 2024 Election," *Nation*, October 9, 2024, https://www.thenation.com/article/politics/pray-vote-stand-abortion-trump-tony-perkins/.

22. Faludi, *Backlash*, 407.

23. Faludi, *Backlash*, 402.

24. Risen and Thomas, *Wrath of Angels*, 220.

25. Lauren Rankin, author interview, February 21, 2025.

Chapter 10

1. Risen and Thomas, *Wrath of Angels*, 323, 334.

2. "Rescue at Washington Abortion Clinic!" Facebook video recorded by Jonathan Darnel, October 22, 2020, https://www.facebook.com/watch/live/?v=420631786000084.

3. U.S. v. Handy, U.S. District Court for the District of Columbia, August 1, 2023, https://www.documentcloud.org/documents/23901546-us-v-handy-trial-brief-8123-jezebel/.

4. Amanda Robb, "Inside an Abortion Clinic Invasion," *Ms.*, January 18, 2024, https://msmagazine.com/2024/01/18/anti-abortion-surgi-clinic-washington-dc-trump-biden-face-act/.

5. Monica Migliorino Miller, author interview, Ann Arbor, February 20, 2023. For more on Monica Migliorino Miller, see Karissa Haugeberg, *Women Against Abortion: Inside*

Notes

the Largest Moral Reform Movement of the Twentieth Century (University of Illinois Press, 2017).

6. Monica Migliorino Miller, *Abandoned: The Untold Story of the Abortion Wars* (Saint Benedict Press, 2012), 280–81.

7. Miller, *Abandoned*, 282–83.

8. Gallup, "Abortion Trends by Party Identification," accessed August 13, 2025, https://news.gallup.com/poll/246278/abortion-trends-party.aspx.

9. Thomas Hilu, "Pro-Life Democrats Feel Shut Out of Party Influence," *Dispatch*, August 21, 2024, https://thedispatch.com/article/pro-life-democrats-feel-shut-out-of-party-influence/.

10. Rick Perlstein, *Nixonland: The Rise of a President and the Fracturing of America* (Scribner, 2008), 652.

11. Sean Salai, "Remembering Nixon's Catholic Coup: An Interview with Pat Buchanan," *America—The Jesuit Review*, August 5, 2014, https://www.americamagazine.org/all-things/2014/08/05/remembering-nixons-catholic-coup-interview-pat-buchanan/.

12. Ziad Munson, *The Making of Pro-Life Activists: How Social Movement Mobilization Works* (University of Chicago Press, 2002).

13. Miller, *Abandoned*, 11–15.

14. Miller, *Abandoned*, 22.

15. Miller, *Abandoned*, 43–44.

16. Miller, *Abandoned*, 3–6, 131–32.

17. Miller, *Abandoned*, 172–74.

18. Miller, *Abandoned*, 251–52.

19. Monica Miller, email to author, August 13, 2025.

20. Risen and Thomas, *Wrath of Angels*, 117.

21. Red Rose Rescue Code of Conduct, accessed August 22, 2025, https://www.redroserescue.com/about.

22. American Freedom Law Center, "About," accessed August 13, 2025, https://www.americanfreedomlawcenter.org/about/.

23. Robert Muise, author interview, March 14, 2023.

24. Nancy Kaffer, "Opinion: This Abortion Provider's Mission Was Inspired by Her Illegal Abortion at 16," Michigan Public Radio, July 4, 2022, https://www.michiganpublic.org/2022-07-04/opinion-this-abortion-providers-mission-was-inspired-by-her-illegal-abortion-at-16.

25. Renee Chelian, author interview, Southfield, February 21, 2023.

26. Monica Migliorino Miller, author interview, Southfield, February 21, 2023.

27. Lara Chelian, author interview, Southfield, February 21, 2023.

28. State of Michigan 46th Judicial District Court (Oakland County), People of the City of Southfield v. Monica Marie Miller et al., Motion Sentencing before the Honorable Cynthia M. Arvant, Thursday, March 30, 2023.

29. Monica Migliorino Miller, author interview, April 13, 2023.

30. Jonah McKeown and Joe Bukuras, "As Pavone Misconduct Allegations Mount, Amarillo Diocese Maintains Silence," Catholic News Agency, February 8, 2023,

Notes

https://www.catholicnewsagency.com/news/253593/pavone-misconduct-allegations-mount-amarillo-diocese-maintains-silence.

31. "Vatican Defrocks an Antiabortion Priest Who Once Placed an Aborted Fetus on an Altar," Associated Press, December 18, 2022, https://www.npr.org/2022/12/18/1143935979/vatican-defrocks-an-antiabortion-priest-who-once-placed-an-aborted-fetus-on-an-.

32. Herb Geraghty, email to author, October 25, 2023.

33. Frank Pavone, Facebook post, December 19, 2022, https://www.facebook.com/fatherfrankpavone/posts/maybe-the-reason-so-many-cannot-say-a-man-is-a-man-or-a-woman-is-a-woman-is-that/700015091574010/.

34. Herb Geraghty and Frank Pavone, author interview, Pittsburgh, June 23, 2023.

35. Will Goodman, author interview, Southfield, February 22, 2023.

36. Will Goodman, author phone interview, June 4, 2025.

37. Will Goodman, author interview, Southfield, February 22, 2023.

38. Will Goodman, message to author, September 12, 2023.

39. Will Goodman, message to author, September 20, 2023.

40. "Seven Defendants Sentenced for Federal Conspiracy Against Rights and Freedom of Access to Clinic Entrances (FACE) Act Convictions Related to 2020 DC Clinic Invasion and Blockade," Department of Justice press release, May 15, 2024, https://www.justice.gov/archives/opa/pr/seven-defendants-sentenced-federal-conspiracy-against-rights-and-freedom-access-clinic.

41. Will Goodman, author phone interview, May 22, 2024.

42. Will Goodman, author phone interview, June 4, 2025.

43. Will Goodman, author phone interview, May 22, 2024.

Chapter 11

1. Nancy Keenan, author phone interview, May 2, 2025.

2. "Obama's Health Care Speech to Congress," prepared text, *New York Times*, September 9, 2009, https://www.nytimes.com/2009/09/10/us/politics/10obama.text.html.

3. "Barack Obama Addresses Planned Parenthood," July 7, 2007, https://www.youtube.com/watch?v=uUl99id2SvM.

4. David Alexander, "Obama Says Abortion Rights Law Not a Top Priority," Reuters, April 29, 2009, https://www.reuters.com/article/markets/us/obama-says-abortion-rights-law-not-a-top-priority-idUSN29466420/.

5. Molly Ball, "How Nancy Pelosi Saved the Affordable Care Act," *Time*, May 6, 2020, https://time.com/5832330/nancy-pelosi-obamacare/.

6. "Executive Order 13535—Patient Protection and Affordable Care Act's Consistency with Longstanding Restrictions on the Use of Federal Funds for Abortion," White House press release, March 24, 2010, https://obamawhitehouse.archives.gov/the-press-office/executive-order-patient-protection-and-affordable-care-acts-consistency-with-longst.

7. Heather Boonstra and Elizabeth Nash, "A Surge of State Abortion Restrictions Puts Providers—and the Women They Serve—in the Crosshairs," *Guttmacher Policy Review* 17, no. 1 (2014), https://www.guttmacher.org/gpr/2014/03/surge-state-abortion-restrictions-puts-providers-and-women-they-serve-crosshairs.

Notes

8. In total, of the 1,230 state provisions introduced in 2011, 627 restricted abortion access, and an additional 134 restricted non-abortion reproductive health information or services; these included bills to promote abstinence-only sex education, curtail family planning funding and minors' access to non-abortion services, and provisions to criminalize substance use in pregnancy. Analysis conducted for author by Elizabeth Nash.

9. Sujatha Jesudason, author Zoom interview, June 9, 2025.

10. Meaghan Winter, *All Politics Is Local: Why Progressives Must Fight for the States* (Bold Type Books, 2019).

11. Donna Crane, author Zoom interview, May 25, 2025.

12. Laurie Rubiner, author Zoom interview, May 20, 2025.

13. Gloria Feldt, author Zoom interview, May 29, 2025.

14. Terry O'Neill, author Zoom interview, May 1, 2025.

15. Eleanor Smeal, author interview, Arlington, March 6, 2024.

16. For more on James Bopp and Citizens United, see Mary Ziegler, *Dollars for Life: The Antiabortion Movement and the Fall of the Republican Establishment* (Yale University Press, 2022).

17. David Cohen, author Zoom interview, May 29, 2025. See also David Cohen, "Chaos and the United States Supreme Court," *LEX Magazine* 4, October 15, 2021, https://issuu.com/drexelkline/docs/lex4_full_magazine_r6.

18. Lawrence Baum and Neal Devins, "Federalist Court: How the Federalist Society Became the De Facto Selector of Republican Supreme Court Justices," *Slate*, January 31, 2017, https://slate.com/news-and-politics/2017/01/how-the-federalist-society-became-the-de-facto-selector-of-republican-supreme-court-justices.html.

19. Amy Littlefield, "Where the Pro-Choice Movement Went Wrong," *New York Times*, December 1, 2021, https://www.nytimes.com/2021/12/01/opinion/abortion-planned-parenthood-naral-roe-v-wade.html.

20. "An Interview with Carol Moseley Braun by the US Senate Historical Office," April 15, 1999, https://www.senate.gov/about/resources/pdf/moseley-braun-carol-full-transcript-with-index.pdf.

21. Carol Moseley Braun, author phone interview, May 13, 2025.

22. Alix Strauss, "Key Moments Since 1992, 'The Year of the Woman,'" *New York Times*, April 2, 2017, https://www.nytimes.com/interactive/2017/04/02/us/02timeline-listy.html.

23. Clarence Page, "Freedom of Choice May Fall Victim to Divided Forces," *Chicago Tribune*, August 11, 1993, https://www.chicagotribune.com/1993/08/11/freedom-of-choice-may-fall-victim-to-divided-forces/.

24. Karen Hosler, "House Votes to Keep Abortion Ban, Attempt to Repeal 'Hyde Amendment' Fails by 255–178 Vote After Bitter Debate," *Baltimore Sun*, July 1, 1993, https://www.baltimoresun.com/1993/07/01/house-votes-to-keep-abortion-ban-attempt-to-repeal-hyde-amendment-fails-by-255-178-vote-after-bitter-debate/.

25. Congressional Record Bound Version—House, June 30, 1993, 14890.

26. Congressional Record Bound Version—House, June 30, 1993, 14893.

Notes

27. Page, "Freedom of Choice."

28. Elizabeth Ross, "Freedom of Choice Act Splits Activists in Pro-Choice Movement," *Christian Science Monitor*, April 9, 1993, https://www.csmonitor.com/1993/0409/09022.html.

29. "Freedom of Choice Act in Peril," *New York Times*, July 17, 1993, https://www.nytimes.com/1993/07/17/opinion/freedom-of-choice-act-in-peril.html.

30. Kate Michelman, "Standing Together the Key," Special to the *Washington Post*, July 20, 1993, https://www.newspapers.com/image/346756977/?match=1&terms=%22Freedom%20of%20Choice%20Act%22%20AND%20%22hyde%20amendment%22.

31. William Saletan, *Bearing Right: How Conservatives Won the Abortion War* (University of California Press, 2003).

32. Saletan, *Bearing Right*, 229.

33. Page, "All or Nothing on Abortion."

34. David Nir, "Only 12 of the 64 Democrats Who Voted for the Stupak Amendment Are Still in the House," Daily Kos, January 26, 2015, https://www.dailykos.com/stories/2015/1/26/1360314/-Only-12-of-the-64-Democrats-who-voted-for-the-Stupak-Amendment-are-still-in-the-House.

35. Julie Hirschfield Davis, "Abortion Rights Groups Struggle to Rebound," Associated Press, November 15, 2009, https://www.theledger.com/story/news/2009/11/15/abortion-rights-groups-struggle-to-rebound/26224319007/.

36. Cecile Richards with Lauren Peterson, *Make Trouble: Standing Up, Speaking Out, and Finding the Courage to Lead* (Touchstone, 2018), 193–94.

37. Clare Coleman, author phone interview, May 12, 2025.

38. Jessica Arons, "From Pro-Choice to Pro-Coverage," *Democracy Journal* 36 (Spring 2015), https://democracyjournal.org/magazine/36/from-pro-choice-to-pro-coverage/; "Interactive: How State Policies Shape Access to Abortion Coverage," KFF, January 8, 2025, https://www.kff.org/womens-health-policy/interactive-how-state-policies-shape-access-to-abortion-coverage/.

39. Sharon Lerner, "Nowhere to Hyde," *Nation*, April 1, 2010, https://www.thenation.com/article/archive/nowhere-hyde/.

40. Dr. Toni M. Bond, author phone interview, August 18, 2025.

41. "Convening on Expanding Low Income Women's Access to Abortion: May 14 & 15, 2010, Post Convening Summary Report" (courtesy of Stephanie Poggi).

42. Megan Peterson, author phone interview, July 23, 2025.

43. Destiny Lopez, author phone interview, May 21, 2025.

44. Kierra Johnson, author video interview, May 14, 2025.

45. Ravina Daphtary, author video interview, May 30, 2025.

46. Stephanie Poggi, "The End of Abortion Funding Restrictions?" *Nation*, September 30, 2013, https://www.thenation.com/article/archive/end-abortion-funding-restrictions/.

47. Jodi Jacobson, "Playing Offense: Advocates Seek Legislation to Protect, Advance Reproductive Rights," Rewire, November 13, 2013, https://rewirenewsgroup.com/2013/11/13/playing-offense-advocates-seek-legislation-to-protect-advance-reproductive-rights/.

48. Jessi Leigh Swenson, author video interview, May 21, 2025.

49. Kimberly Inez McGuire, author video interview, May 27, 2025.

50. Allison Cowett, author phone interview, July 10, 2025.

Notes

51. Memo to: CAARE/FSG Leadership, From: Jessi Leigh Swenson, "RE: Hill Outreach Plan Feedback and Clarification," 2014 (courtesy of Jessi Leigh Swenson).

52. "All* Above All Announces the Be Bold Road Trip," press release, August 4, 2014, https://www.prnewswire.com/news-releases/all-above-all-announces-the-be-bold-road-trip-269825021.html.

53. Lydia Stuckey, author interview, June 6, 2025.

54. Molly Redden, "Clinton Leads Way on Abortion Rights as Democrats Seek End to Decades-Old Rule," *Guardian*, July 26, 2016, https://www.theguardian.com/us-news/2016/jul/26/abortion-rights-clinton-hyde-amendment-federal-funds.

55. Katie Glueck, "Joe Biden Denounces Hyde Amendment, Reversing His Position," *New York Times*, June 6, 2019, https://www.nytimes.com/2019/06/06/us/politics/joe-biden-hyde-amendment.html.

56. Nourbese Flint, author video interview, July 30, 2025.

Chapter 12

1. Cassandra Jaramillo and Kavitha Surana, "A Woman Died After Being Told It Would Be a 'Crime' to Intervene in Her Miscarriage at a Texas Hospital," ProPublica, October 30, 2024, https://www.propublica.org/article/josseli-barnica-death-miscarriage-texas-abortion-ban.

2. Megan Stringer and Sareen Habeshian, "Where Texans Traveled for Abortions After Roe Fell," *Axios*, June 24, 2024, https://www.axios.com/local/san-antonio/2024/06/24/where-texans-travel-abortion-roe-overturned.

3. "Interstate Travel for Abortion: Patients Traveling out of Texas," Monthly Abortion Provision Study, Guttmacher Institute, accessed August 22, 2025, https://www.guttmacher.org/monthly-abortion-provision-study.

4. Isaac Maddow-Zimet and Candace Gibson, "Despite Bans, Number of Abortions in the United States Increased in 2023," Guttmacher Institute Policy Analysis, March 2024, https://www.guttmacher.org/2024/03/despite-bans-number-abortions-united-states-increased-2023; and "#WeCount report, April 2022 to December 2024," Society for Family Planning, accessed August 14, 2025, https://societyfp.org/research/wecount/wecount-december-2024-data/.

5. Mark Lee Dickson, author phone interview, April 18, 2023.

6. Amy Littlefield, "The Poison Pill in the Mifepristone Lawsuit That Could Trigger a National Abortion Ban," *Nation*, April 26, 2023, https://www.thenation.com/article/society/comstock-act-jonathan-mitchell/.

7. Glenn Canfield Obituary, February 1, 2006, https://www.legacy.com/us/obituaries/legacyremembers/glenn-canfield-obituary?id=27070010.

8. Mark L. Dickson, "A Pardon for the Most Lustful Minded Sinner," image captured by the Internet Archive, December 1, 2003, https://web.archive.org/web/20031201015427/http://www.sovereignlove.o-f.com/lustminded.html.

9. Savannah Bronson, author phone interview, December 13, 2024.

10. Mimi Swartz, "Who's Bankrolling These Prominent Abortion-Rights Opponents?," *Texas Monthly*, June 14, 2024, https://www.texasmonthly.com/news-politics/whos-bankrolling-these-prominent-abortion-rights-opponents/.

Notes

11. Mark Lee Dickson, author phone interview, August 19, 2025.
12. Mark Lee Dickson, author phone interview, May 10, 2024.
13. Video footage of Mark Lee Dickson, filmed in 2018 (courtesy of Debbie Hollis).
14. Amy Littlefield et al., "A Strike at the Heart of Roe," *Reveal*, February 12, 2022, https://revealnews.org/podcast/a-strike-at-the-heart-of-roe/.
15. Drucilla Tigner, author interview, December 16, 2024.
16. Amy Littlefield, "Where the Pro-Choice Movement Went Wrong."
17. Allie Morris, "Meet Sen. Bryan Hughes, the Texas Republican Leading the Party's Hard Turn to the Right," *Dallas Morning News*, October 15, 2021, https://www.dallasnews.com/news/politics/2021/10/15/meet-sen-bryan-hughes-the-texas-republican-leading-the-partys-hard-turn-to-the-right/.
18. "White Oak, Texas Ghost Sightings," GhostsOfAmerica.Com, 2011, https://www.ghostsofamerica.com/7/Texas_White_Oak_ghost_sightings4.html#google_vignette.
19. Amy Sohn, *The Man Who Hated Women: Sex, Censorship & Civil Liberties in the Gilded Age* (Farrar, Straus and Giroux, 2021), 9–10.
20. Amy Littlefield, "'The Message They've Received Is That You Don't Deserve to Be Cared For': Life on the Abortion Borderland," *Nation*, June 23, 2023, https://www.thenation.com/article/society/abortion-clinics-dobbs-texas/.
21. Amy Littlefield, "The Poison Pill in the Mifepristone Lawsuit That Could Trigger a National Abortion Ban."
22. Supreme Court of New Mexico Administrative Office of the Courts, "NM Supreme Court Rules That Local Governments Cannot Restrict Abortion Services," press release, January 9, 2025, https://nmcourts.gov/wp-content/uploads/2025/01/NM-Supreme-Court-rules-that-local-governments-cannot-restrict-abortion-services-Jan.-9-2025.pdf.
23. "An Ordinance Outlawing Abortion, Declaring Amarillo a Sanctuary City for the Unborn, Making Various Provisions and Findings, Providing for Severability, and Establishing an Effective Date," December 29, 2023, accessed at https://www.myhighplains.com/wp-content/uploads/sites/87/2024/09/amarillo-scftu-ordinance-12-29-2023.docx-1.pdf.
24. Hassan Ali Kanu, "Anti-Abortion Activists Pushed Amarillo to Help Save the Mifepristone Case," *American Prospect*, September 6, 2024, https://prospect.org/justice/2024-09-06-anti-abortion-activists-amarillo-mifepristone-case/.
25. Tom Scherlen, author interview, December 5, 2024.
26. Mark Lee Dickson, email to author, August 24, 2025.
27. Don Tipps, author interview, December 4, 2024.
28. Mark Lee Dickson, email to author, August 25, 2025.
29. Mark Lee Dickson, "Re: Sanctuary City for the Unborn Ordinance," email to Lynn Beard, June 24, 2023, City of Abilene, obtained through public records request.
30. Agatha Christie, "The Thumb Mark of St. Peter," *Thirteen Problems* (Signet, 2000), 70.
31. Adam Stockford, author interview, December 10, 2024.
32. Mark Lee Dickson and Adam Stockford messages, Hillsdale, Michigan, 2021 (courtesy of Democracy Forward).

Notes

33. Ben McNabb message exchange with J. J. Oznick, Eastland, Texas, June 2021 (courtesy of Democracy Forward).

34. Minutes of the City of Eastland City Commission Regular Meeting, June 21, 2021. (courtesy of Democracy Forward).

35. Ben McNabb, text messages to author, December 5 and 11, 2024.

36. Rachel Monroe, "The Conservative Strategy to Ban Abortion Nationwide," *New Yorker*, October 30, 2024, https://www.newyorker.com/news/letter-from-the-southwest/the-conservative-strategy-to-ban-abortion-nationwide.

37. Dickson supporter, author interview, Amarillo, November 5, 2024.

38. Harper Metcalf, author interview, Amarillo, November 5, 2024.

39. Deanda v. Becerra, No. 23-10159 (5th Cir. 2024), https://law.justia.com/cases/federal/appellate-courts/ca5/23-10159/23-10159-2024-03-12.html.

40. Alex Deanda, author interview, Amarillo, November 5, 2024.

41. Mark Lee Dickson, author interview, Washington, DC, October 5, 2024.

42. Mark Lee Dickson, author interview, Amarillo, November 5, 2024.

43. "What Is AAPLOG's Position on 'Abortion to Save the Life of the Mother'?" AAPLOG, June 9, 2009, https://aaplog.org/what-is-aaplogs-position-on-abortion-to-save-the-life-of-the-mother-2/.

44. Lizzie Presser, Andrea Suozzo, Sophie Chou, and Kavitha Surana, "Texas Banned Abortion: Then Sepsis Rates Soared," ProPublica, February 20, 2025, https://www.propublica.org/article/texas-abortion-ban-sepsis-maternal-mortality-analysis.

45. Dexie Organ, author interview, Amarillo, November 5, 2024. Organ material and additional reporting from Amarillo originally published in *Nation*: Amy Littlefield, "What We Learn from the Texas Town That Voted for Abortion and for Trump," *Nation*, November 14, 2024, https://www.thenation.com/article/politics/amarillo-texas-abortion-election/

46. Jackie Payne, author video interview, June 5, 2025.

47. Cathy Welch and Mark Lee Dickson, author interviews, Amarillo, November 5, 2024.

48. Amy Littlefield, "The Toughest Fight to Win Back Abortion Rights Is On in Florida," *Nation*, August 26, 2024, https://www.thenation.com/article/society/florida-abortion-amendment-4-dobbs/

49. Sanctuary Cities for the Unborn, https://sanctuarycitiesfortheunborn.com, accessed August 22, 2025.

Chapter 13

1. Amy Littlefield, "A Miscarrying Woman Nearly Died After a Catholic Hospital Sent Her Home Three Times," *Rewire News Group*, September 25, 2019, https://rewirenewsgroup.com/2019/09/25/miscarriage-catholic-hospital/.

2. "Ethical and Religious Directives for Catholic Health Care Services," 6th ed., United States Conference of Catholic Bishops, https://www.usccb.org/resources/ethical-religious-directives-catholic-health-service-sixth-edition-2016-06_0.pdf.

Notes

3. Tess Solomon, Lois Uttley, Patty HasBrouck, and Yoolim Jung. "Bigger and Bigger: The Growth of Catholic Health Systems," Community Catalyst, 2020, https://www.communitycatalyst.org/wp-content/uploads/2022/11/2020-Cath-Hosp-Report-2020-31.pdf.

4. Jocelyn Wascher, Luciana Hebert, Lori Freedman, and Debra Stulberg, "Do Women Know Whether Their Hospital Is Catholic? Results from a National Survey," *Contraception*, 2018, www.contraceptionjournal.org/article/S0010-7824(18)30193-8/abstract.

5. Amy Littlefield, "Catholic Hospital Pressured Women to Bury Their Fetuses—Then Pence Made It Law," *Rewire News Group*, November 2, 2017, https://rewirenewsgroup.com/2017/11/02/catholic-hospital-pressured-women-bury-fetuses-pence-made-law/.

6. Amy Littlefield, "Catholic Hospital Denies Transgender Man a Hysterectomy on Religious Grounds," *Rewire News Group*, August 31, 2016, https://rewirenewsgroup.com/2016/08/31/catholic-hospital-denies-transgender-man-hysterectomy-on-religious-grounds/; and Amy Littlefield, "Trans Man Denied Surgery at Catholic Hospital Lives in Constant Fear," *Rewire News Group*, January 10, 2017, https://rewirenewsgroup.com/2017/01/10/trans-man-denied-surgery-catholic-hospital-lives-constant-fear/.

7. Lois Uttley and Christine Khaikin, "Growth of Catholic Hospitals and Health Systems: 2016 Update on the Miscarriage of Medicine Report," MergerWatch, 2016, https://static1.1.sqspcdn.com/static/f/816571/27061007/1465224862580/MW_Update-2016-MiscarrOfMedicine-report.

8. Nina Martin, ProPublica and Renee Montagne, NPR News, "Lost Mothers," 2017, https://www.propublica.org/series/lost-mothers.

9. Amy Littlefield, "Catholic Hospitals Offer a Preview of Life Without 'Roe': And Bishops Just Tightened the Rules," *Rewire News Group*, June 29, 2018, https://rewirenewsgroup.com/2018/06/29/catholic-hospitals-offer-preview-life-without-roe-bishops-just-tightened-rules/.

10. Amy Littlefield, "'She Had a Heartbeat Too': Waiting for One Dead Woman," *Nation*, March 14, 2023, https://www.thenation.com/article/society/texas-abortion-lawsuit/.

11. Kavitha Surana, "Abortion Bans Have Delayed Emergency Medical Care: In Georgia, Experts Say This Mother's Death Was Preventable," ProPublica, September 16, 2024, https://www.propublica.org/article/georgia-abortion-ban-amber-thurman-death.

12. Kavitha Surana, "Afraid to Seek Care Amid Georgia's Abortion Ban, She Stayed at Home and Died," ProPublica, September 18, 2024, https://www.propublica.org/article/candi-miller-abortion-ban-death-georgia.

13. Amy Yurkanin, "Georgia Dismissed All Members of Maternal Mortality Committee After ProPublica Obtained Internal Details of Two Deaths," ProPublica, November 21, 2014, https://www.propublica.org/article/georgia-dismisses-maternal-mortality-committee-amber-thurman-candi-miller.

14. Lizzie Presser and Kavitha Surana, "A Third Woman Died Under Texas' Abortion Ban. Doctors Are Avoiding D&Cs and Reaching for Riskier Miscarriage Treatments," ProPublica, November 25, 2024, https://www.propublica.org/article/porsha-ngumezi-miscarriage-death-texas-abortion-ban.

Notes

15. Cassandra Jaramillo, "A Woman Died After Being Told It Would be a 'Crime' to Intervene in Her Miscarriage at a Texas Hospital," ProPublica, October 30, 2024, https://www.propublica.org/article/josseli-barnica-death-miscarriage-texas-abortion-ban.

16. Lizzie Presser and Kavitha Surana, "A Pregnant Teenager Died After Trying to Get Care in Three Visits to Texas Emergency Rooms," ProPublica, November 1, 2024, https://www.propublica.org/article/nevaeh-crain-death-texas-abortion-ban-emtala.

17. Amy Littlefield and Laura Gottesdiener, "Meet Christus, the US Catholic Health Chain Restricting Access to Reproductive Care in Mexico," *Rewire News Group*, November 27, 2018, https://rewirenewsgroup.com/2018/11/27/meet-christus-the-us-catholic-health-chain-restricting-access-to-reproductive-care-in-mexico/.

18. Anna Spoerre, "Missouri Woman Sues University of Kansas Hospital That Denied Her an Emergency Abortion," *Missouri Independent*, July 31, 2024, https://missouriindependent.com/2024/07/31/missouri-woman-sues-university-of-kansas-hospital-emergency-abortion/.

19. Amy Littlefield, "'Not Dead Enough': Public Hospitals Deny Life-Saving Abortion Care to People in Need," *Rewire News Group*, March 7, 2019, https://rewirenewsgroup.com/2019/03/07/not-dead-enough-public-hospitals-deny-life-saving-abortion-care-to-people-in-need/.

20. Erin Edwards and Robin Fields, "A Coast Guard Commander Miscarried. She Nearly Died After Being Denied Care," ProPublica, December 13, 2024, https://www.propublica.org/article/elizabeth-nakagawa-miscarriage-military-tricare-abortion-policy.

21. Pregnancy Justice, "Pregnancy as a Crime: An Interim Update on the First Two Years After Dobbs," September 25, 2025, https://www.pregnancyjusticeus.org/resources/pregnancy-as-a-crime-an-interim-update-on-the-first-two-years-after-dobbs/.

Chapter 14

1. "Women Speak at the Democratic National Convention," Pacifica Radio Archives, August 1980, https://archive.org/details/pacifica_radio_archives-AZ0487.

2. Renee Bracey Sherman and Regina Mahone, *Liberating Abortion: Claiming Our History, Sharing Our Stories, and Building the Reproductive Future We Deserve* (Amistad, 2024), 143.

3. Leslie Bennetts, "Rights and Abortion Planks Are Achieved by Feminists; Compromise Rejected Seeking to Avoid a Fight," *New York Times*, August 13, 1980, https://www.nytimes.com/1980/08/13/archives/rights-and-abortion-planks-are-achieved-by-feminists-compromise.html.

4. "Women Share Stories of Being Denied Emergency Abortions at Democratic National Convention," NBC News, August 19, 2024, https://www.youtube.com/watch?v=u_eKg7W3R1s.

5. Zurawski v. State of Texas, Center for Reproductive Rights, filed March 6, 2023, https://reproductiverights.org/case/zurawski-v-texas-abortion-emergency-exceptions/zurawski-v-texas/.

6. Supreme Court of Texas, No. 23-0629, State of Texas et. al v. Amanda Zurawski

et al., Opinion delivered May 31, 2024, https://reproductiverights.org/wp-content/uploads/2024/05/Zurawski-v-Texas-SCOTX-Opinion.

7. Agatha Christie, *The Murder at the Vicarage* (William Morrow, 1930), 18.

8. Richard Viguerie, author phone interview, August 15, 2025.

9. Nicole Chavez, "Texas Woman Died After an Unsafe Abortion Years Ago: Her Daughter Fears Same Thing May Happen Again," CNN, October 11, 2021, https://www.cnn.com/2021/10/11/us/texas-abortion-rosie-jimenez/index.html.

10. Alexa Garcia-Ditta, "Reckoning with Rosie," *Texas Observer*, November 3, 2015, https://www.texasobserver.org/rosie-jimenez-abortion-medicaid/.

11. Molly Hennessy-Fiske, "'Baby in a Dumpster': A Spate of Abandoned Newborns Unsettles Texas," *Washington Post*, December 28, 2024, https://www.washingtonpost.com/nation/2024/12/28/abandoned-baby-texas-abortion-ban/.

12. "Meeting the Moment Post-Dobbs: A Review of Proactive Abortion Policies Passed in States & Localities, June 24–October 1, 2022," National Institute for Reproductive Health, November 30, 2022, https://nirhealth.org/resources/meeting-the-moment-post-dobbs/.

13. "Groundbreaking Massachusetts Abortion Law Repeals Parental Consent for Older Teens," Carrie N. Baker, *Ms.*, December 29, 2020, https://msmagazine.com/2020/12/29/massachusetts-abortion-law-roe-act/; and "Illinois Expands Access to Abortion Care, Ends Enforcement of Parental Notice Law," ACLU of Illinois, June 1, 2022, https://www.aclu-il.org/en/press-releases/illinois-expands-access-abortion-care-ends-enforcement-parental-notice-law.

14. Zaena Zamora, author phone interview, August 18, 2025.